HELLBOY AND THE BUREAU FOR PARANORMAL RESEARCH AND DEFENSE

1954

Created by MIKE MIGNOLA

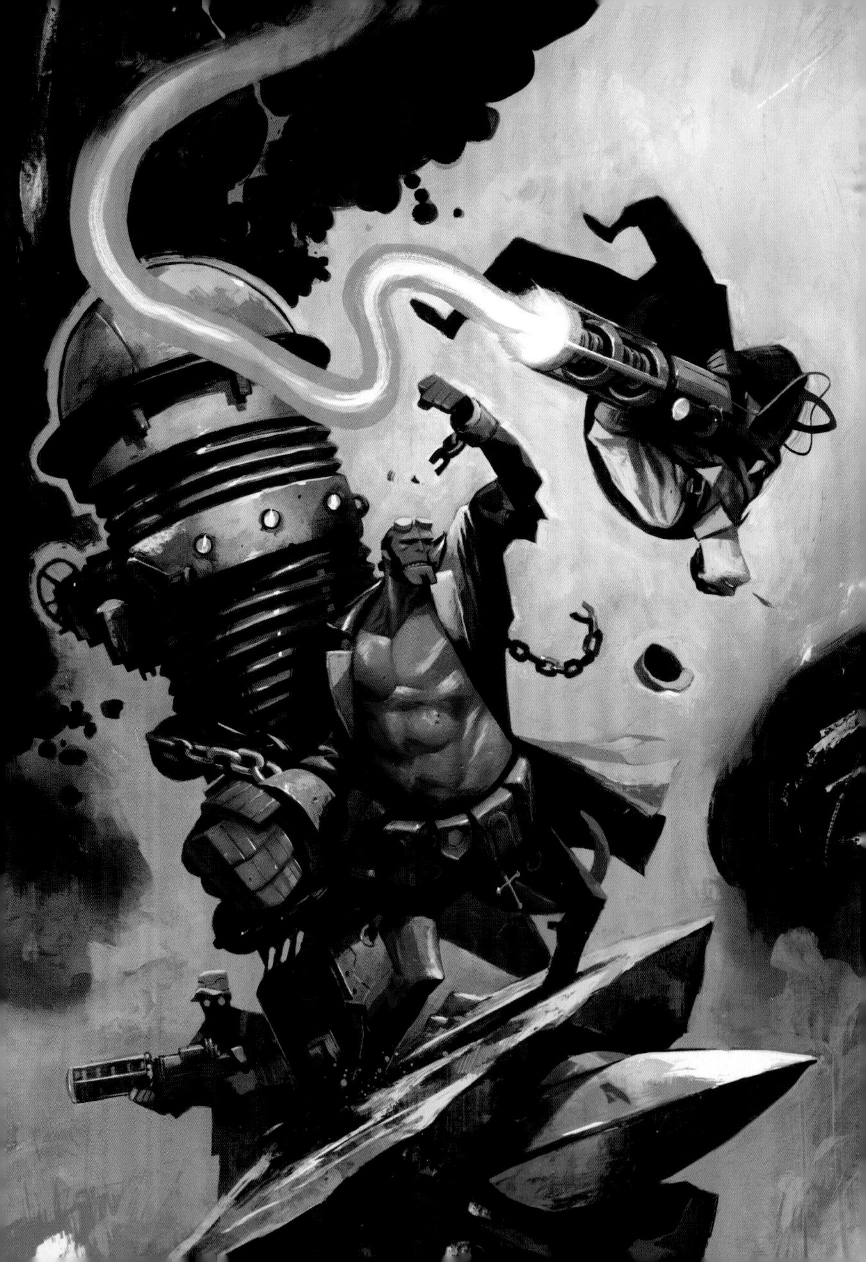

MIKE MIGNOLA'S

HELLBOY

AND THE B.P.R.D. 1954

BLACK SUN

✠

Story by MIKE MIGNOLA
& CHRIS ROBERSON

Art by STEPHEN GREEN

THE UNREASONING BEAST

✠

Story by MIKE MIGNOLA
& CHRIS ROBERSON

Art by PATRIC REYNOLDS

GHOST MOON

✠

Story by MIKE MIGNOLA
& CHRIS ROBERSON

Art by BRIAN CHURILLA

THE MIRROR

✠

Story by MIKE MIGNOLA

Art by RICHARD CORBEN

Colors by DAVE STEWART

Letters by CLEM ROBINS

Cover art by MIKE MIGNOLA & DAVE STEWART

Chapter break art by MIKE HUDDLESTON

Publisher MIKE RICHARDSON ✠ *Editor* SCOTT ALLIE
Assistant Editor KATII O'BRIEN ✠ *Collection Designer* JUSTIN COUCH
Digital Art Technician CHRISTINA McKENZIE

DARK HORSE BOOKS

Published by Dark Horse Books, a division of Dark Horse Comics, Inc.
10956 SE Main Street, Milwaukie, OR 97222

DarkHorse.com
International Licensing (503) 905-2377 ✠ Comic Shop Locator Service: comicshoplocator.com

First edition: January 2018 ✠ ISBN 978-1-50670-207-0

1 3 5 7 9 10 8 6 4 2
Printed in China

This book collects Hellboy and the B.P.R.D.: 1954—Black Sun #1-#2, Hellboy and the B.P.R.D.: 1954—The Unreasoning Beast,
Hellboy and the B.P.R.D.: 1954—Ghost Moon #1–#2, and "Hellboy: The Mirror" *from Free Comic Book Day 2015.*

Library of Congress Cataloging-in-Publication Data

Names: Mignola, Michael, author. | Roberson, Chris, artist. | Green, Stephen
(Comic book artist), artist. | Reynolds, Patric, artist. | Churilla, Brian. |
Corben, Richard. | Stewart, Dave, colourist, artist. | Robins, Clem, 1955-
letterer. | Huddleston, Mike, artist.
Title: Hellboy and the B.P.R.D., 1954.
Other titles: B.P.R.D. 1954
Description: First edition. | Milwuakie, OR : Dark Horse Books, 2018. |
"Colors by Dave Stewart ; letters by Clem Robins ; cover art by Mike
Mignola with Dave Stewart ; chapter break art by Mike Huddleston." | "This
book collects Hellboy and the B.P.R.D.: 1954-Black Sun #1-#2, Hellboy and
the B.P.R.D.: 1954-The Unreasoning Beast, Hellboy and the B.P.R.D.:
1954-Ghost Moon #1-#2, and "Hellboy: The Mirror" from Free Comic Book Day
2015."
Identifiers: LCCN 2017033705 | ISBN 9781506702070 (paperback)
Subjects: LCSH: Comic books, strips, etc. | BISAC: COMICS & GRAPHIC NOVELS /
Horror.
Classification: LCC PN6727.M53 H375 2018 | DDC 741.5/973--dc23
LC record available at https://lccn.loc.gov/2017033705

BLACK SUN

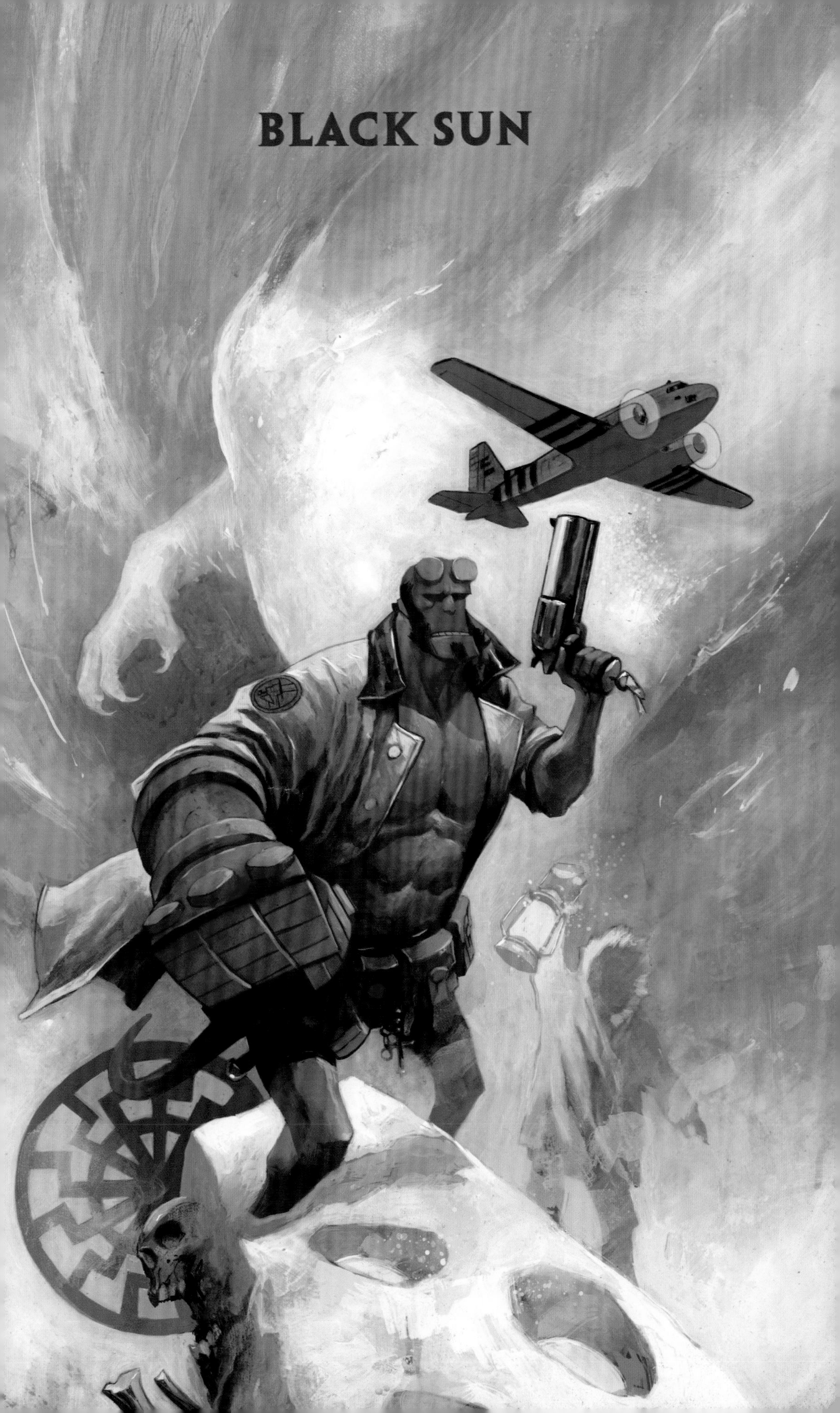

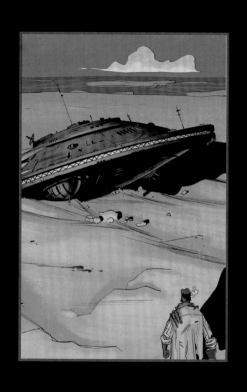

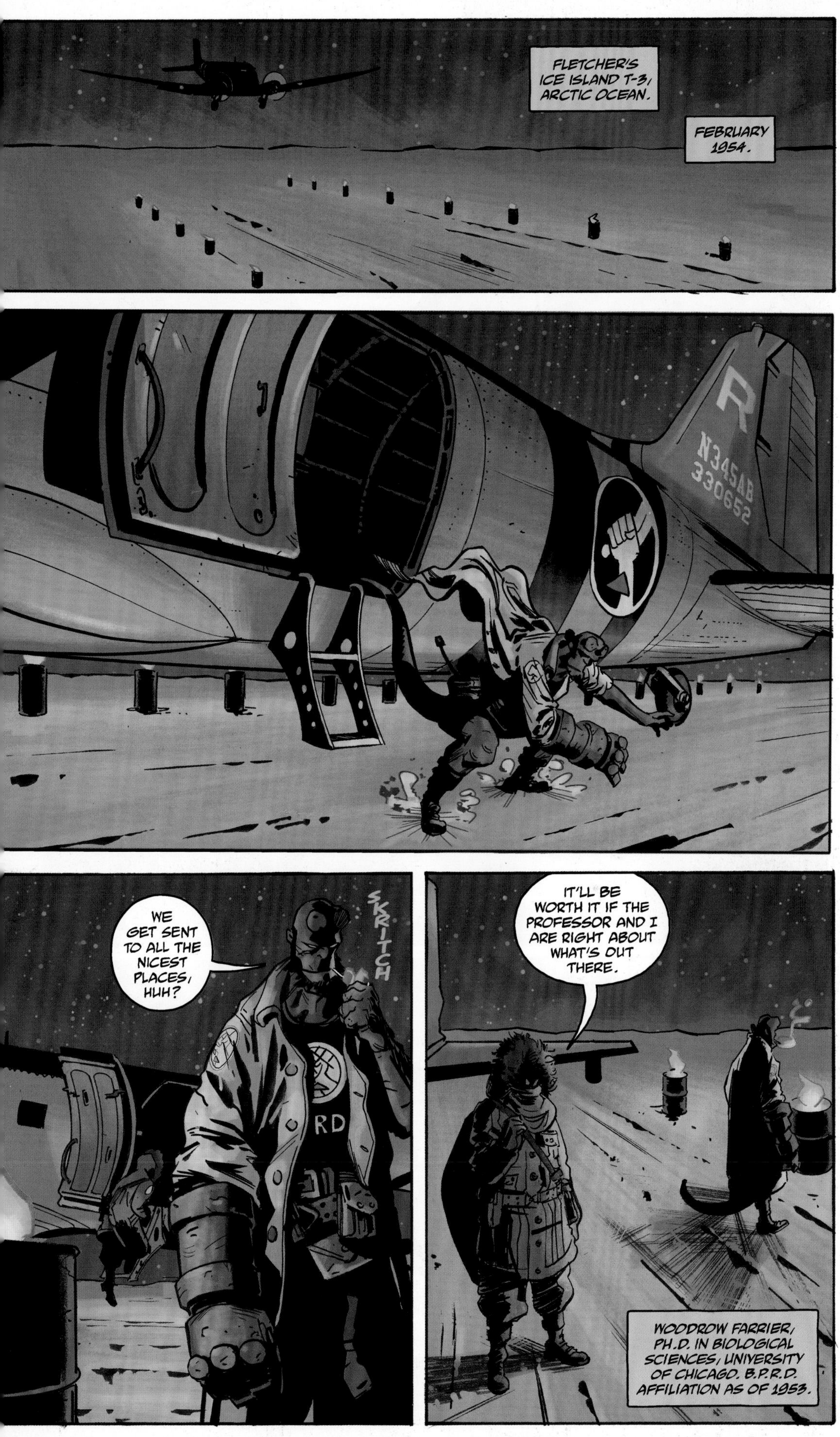
FLETCHER'S ICE ISLAND T-3, ARCTIC OCEAN.
FEBRUARY 1954.
R
N345AB
330652
WE GET SENT TO ALL THE NICEST PLACES, HUH?
SKRITCH
RD
IT'LL BE WORTH IT IF THE PROFESSOR AND I ARE RIGHT ABOUT WHAT'S OUT THERE.
WOODROW FARRIER, PH.D. IN BIOLOGICAL SCIENCES, UNIVERSITY OF CHICAGO. B.P.R.D. AFFILIATION AS OF 1953.

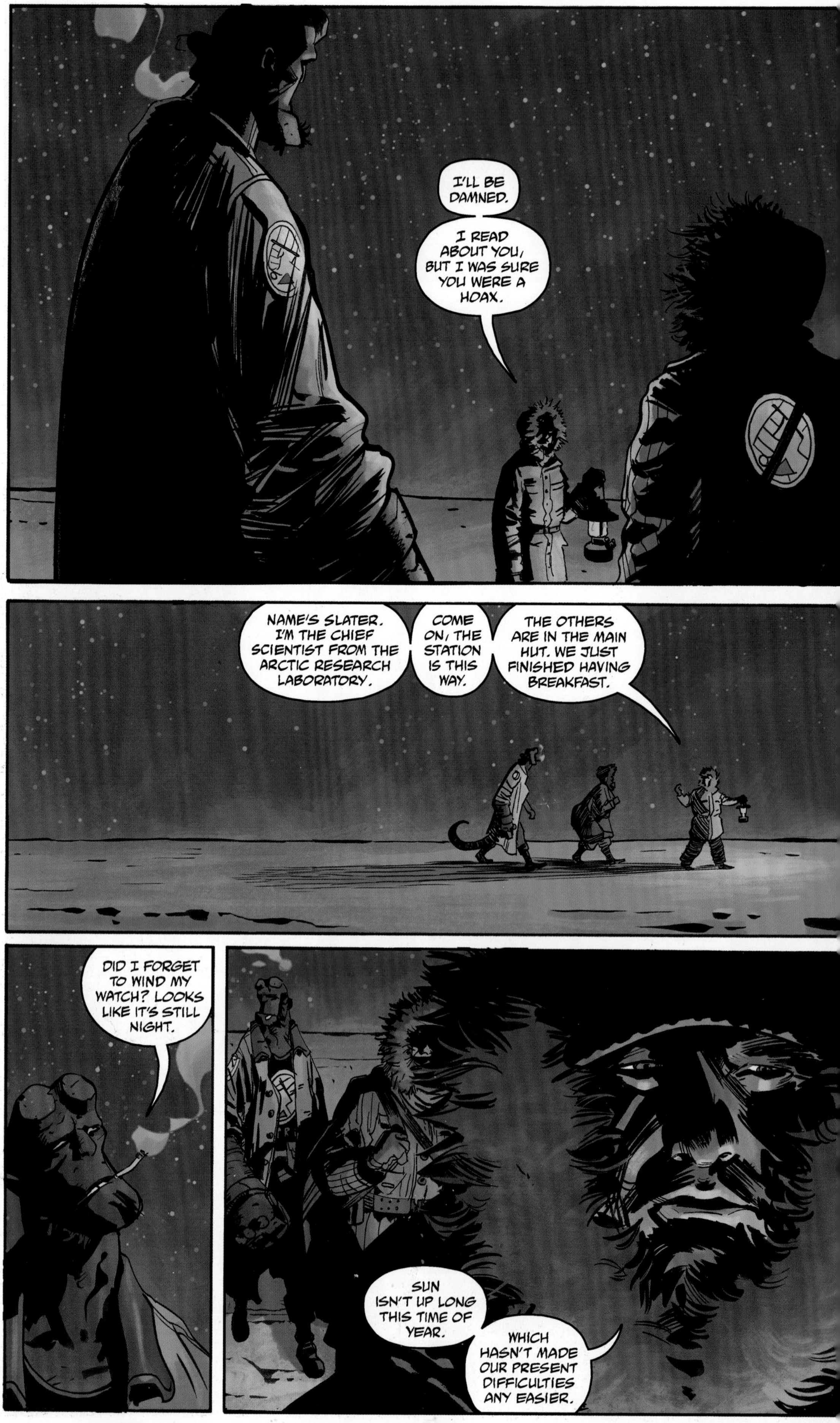
I'LL BE DAMNED.
I READ ABOUT YOU, BUT I WAS SURE YOU WERE A HOAX.
NAME'S SLATER. I'M THE CHIEF SCIENTIST FROM THE ARCTIC RESEARCH LABORATORY.
COME ON, THE STATION IS THIS WAY.
THE OTHERS ARE IN THE MAIN HUT. WE JUST FINISHED HAVING BREAKFAST.
DID I FORGET TO WIND MY WATCH? LOOKS LIKE IT'S STILL NIGHT.
SUN ISN'T UP LONG THIS TIME OF YEAR.
WHICH HASN'T MADE OUR PRESENT DIFFICULTIES ANY EASIER.

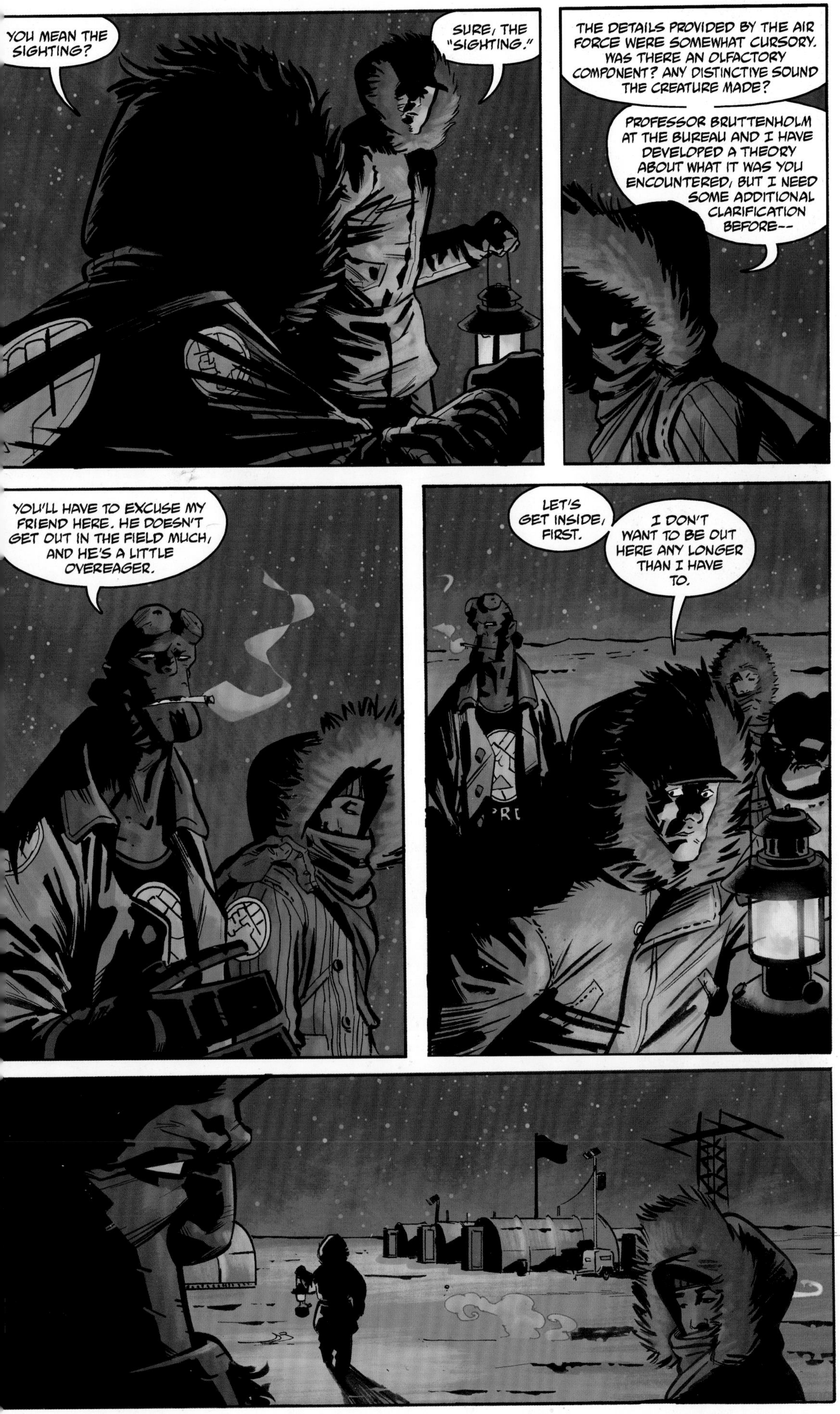

YOU MEAN THE SIGHTING?
SURE, THE "SIGHTING."
THE DETAILS PROVIDED BY THE AIR FORCE WERE SOMEWHAT CURSORY. WAS THERE AN OLFACTORY COMPONENT? ANY DISTINCTIVE SOUND THE CREATURE MADE?
PROFESSOR BRUTTENHOLM AT THE BUREAU AND I HAVE DEVELOPED A THEORY ABOUT WHAT IT WAS YOU ENCOUNTERED, BUT I NEED SOME ADDITIONAL CLARIFICATION BEFORE--
YOU'LL HAVE TO EXCUSE MY FRIEND HERE. HE DOESN'T GET OUT IN THE FIELD MUCH, AND HE'S A LITTLE OVEREAGER.
LET'S GET INSIDE, FIRST.
I DON'T WANT TO BE OUT HERE ANY LONGER THAN I HAVE TO.

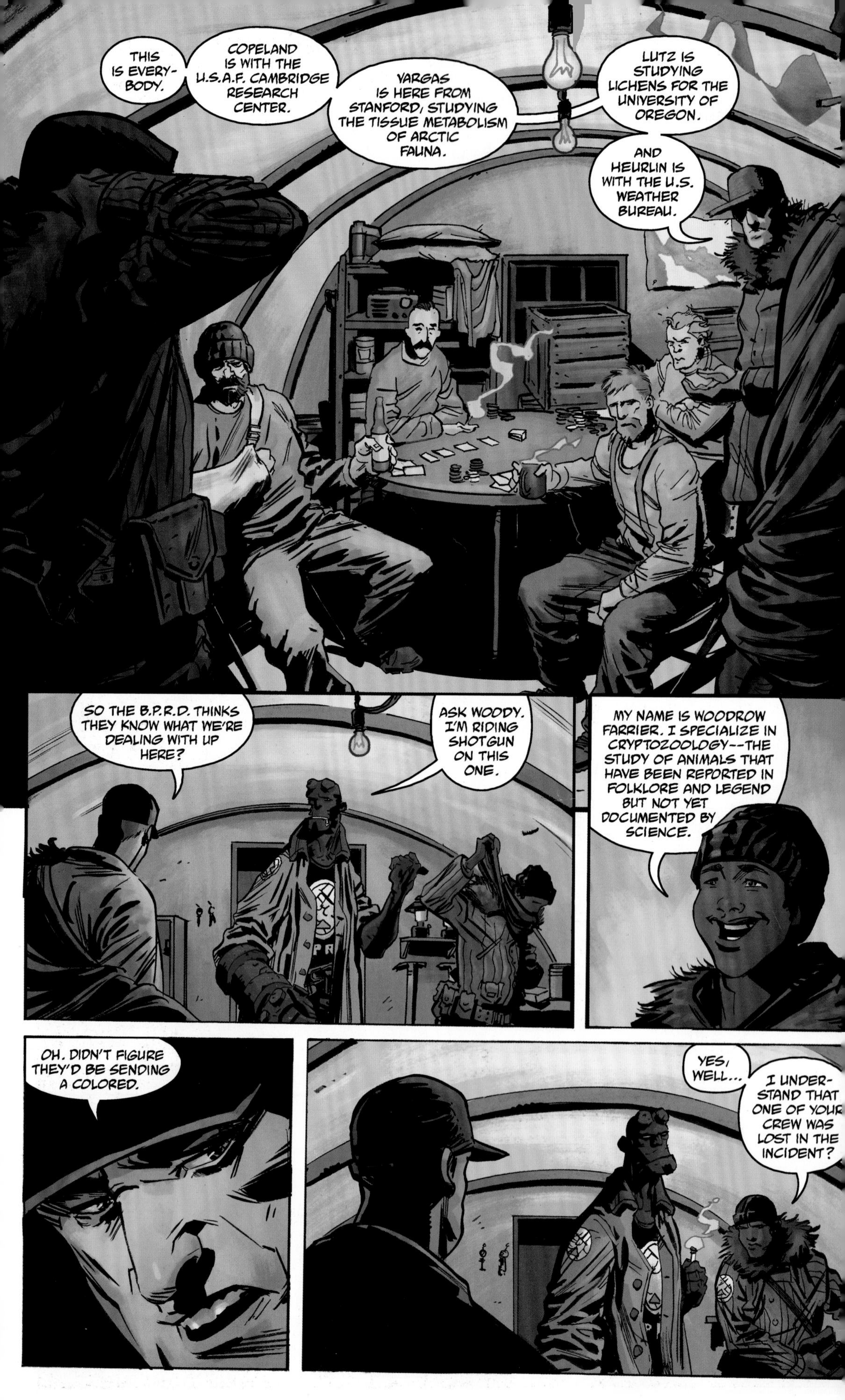
THIS IS EVERY-BODY.
COPELAND IS WITH THE U.S.A.F. CAMBRIDGE RESEARCH CENTER.
VARGAS IS HERE FROM STANFORD, STUDYING THE TISSUE METABOLISM OF ARCTIC FAUNA.
LUTZ IS STUDYING LICHENS FOR THE UNIVERSITY OF OREGON.
AND HEURLIN IS WITH THE U.S. WEATHER BUREAU.
SO THE B.P.R.D. THINKS THEY KNOW WHAT WE'RE DEALING WITH UP HERE?
ASK WOODY. I'M RIDING SHOTGUN ON THIS ONE.
MY NAME IS WOODROW FARRIER. I SPECIALIZE IN CRYPTOZOOLOGY--THE STUDY OF ANIMALS THAT HAVE BEEN REPORTED IN FOLKLORE AND LEGEND BUT NOT YET DOCUMENTED BY SCIENCE.
OH. DIDN'T FIGURE THEY'D BE SENDING A COLORED.
YES, WELL...
I UNDER-STAND THAT ONE OF YOUR CREW WAS LOST IN THE INCIDENT?

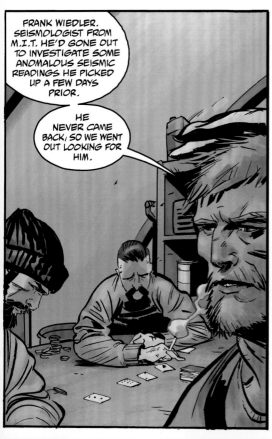

FRANK WIEDLER, SEISMOLOGIST FROM M.I.T. HE'D GONE OUT TO INVESTIGATE SOME ANOMALOUS SEISMIC READINGS HE PICKED UP A FEW DAYS PRIOR.

HE NEVER CAME BACK, SO WE WENT OUT LOOKING FOR HIM.

"WE FOUND HIM.

"WHAT WAS LEFT OF HIM, ANYWAY. HE'D BEEN PRETTY BADLY TORN UP.

"WE WERE BRINGING HIS BODY BACK TO THE STATION WHEN IT HAPPENED.

"THE NIGHT WAS FULL DARK BY THEN, AND WE DIDN'T SEE IT COMING. ONE MINUTE THERE WAS NOTHING, AND THE NEXT...

"IT WAS A GOOD THING I HAD A FLARE GUN ON ME.

"I DON'T THINK IT DID MUCH MORE THAN ANNOY THAT THING, BUT IT GAVE US TIME TO GET AWAY."

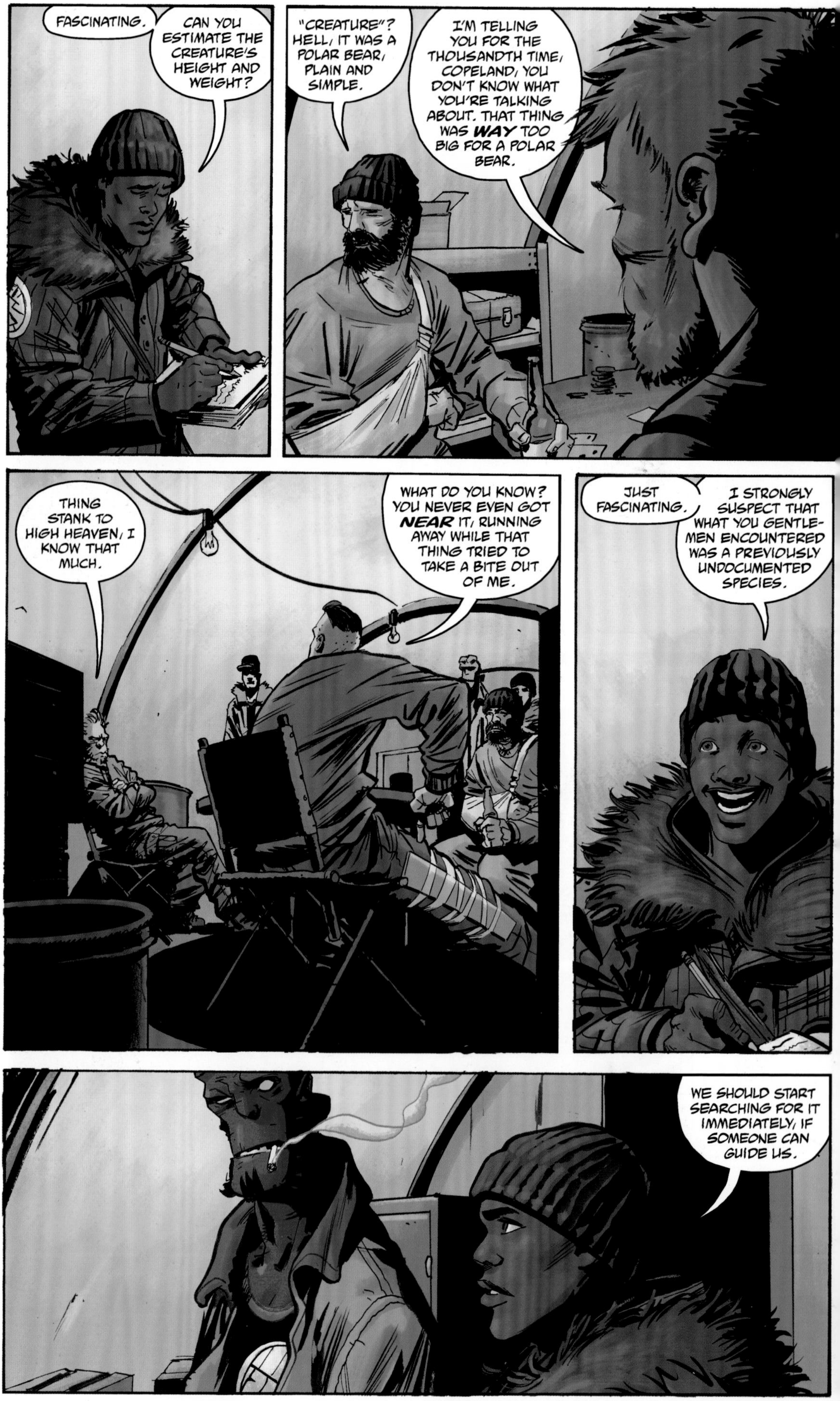
FASCINATING.
CAN YOU ESTIMATE THE CREATURE'S HEIGHT AND WEIGHT?
"CREATURE"? HELL, IT WAS A POLAR BEAR, PLAIN AND SIMPLE.
I'M TELLING YOU FOR THE THOUSANDTH TIME, COPELAND, YOU DON'T KNOW WHAT YOU'RE TALKING ABOUT. THAT THING WAS WAY TOO BIG FOR A POLAR BEAR.
THING STANK TO HIGH HEAVEN, I KNOW THAT MUCH.
WHAT DO YOU KNOW? YOU NEVER EVEN GOT NEAR IT, RUNNING AWAY WHILE THAT THING TRIED TO TAKE A BITE OUT OF ME.
JUST FASCINATING.
I STRONGLY SUSPECT THAT WHAT YOU GENTLEMEN ENCOUNTERED WAS A PREVIOUSLY UNDOCUMENTED SPECIES.
WE SHOULD START SEARCHING FOR IT IMMEDIATELY, IF SOMEONE CAN GUIDE US.

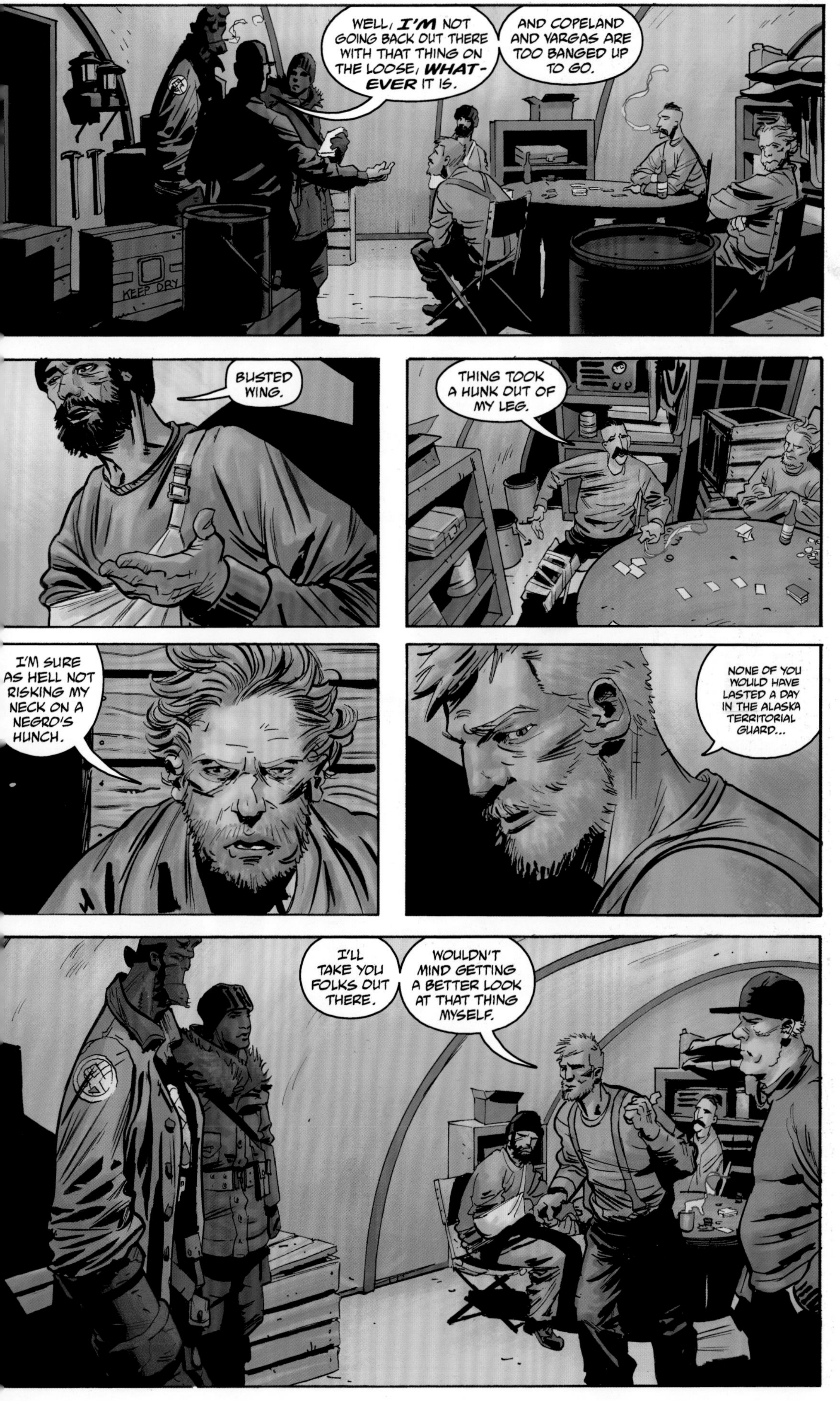
WELL, I'M NOT GOING BACK OUT THERE WITH THAT THING ON THE LOOSE, WHAT-EVER IT IS.
AND COPELAND AND VARGAS ARE TOO BANGED UP TO GO.
KEEP DRY
BUSTED WING.
THING TOOK A HUNK OUT OF MY LEG.
I'M SURE AS HELL NOT RISKING MY NECK ON A NEGRO'S HUNCH.
NONE OF YOU WOULD HAVE LASTED A DAY IN THE ALASKA TERRITORIAL GUARD...
I'LL TAKE YOU FOLKS OUT THERE.
WOULDN'T MIND GETTING A BETTER LOOK AT THAT THING MYSELF.

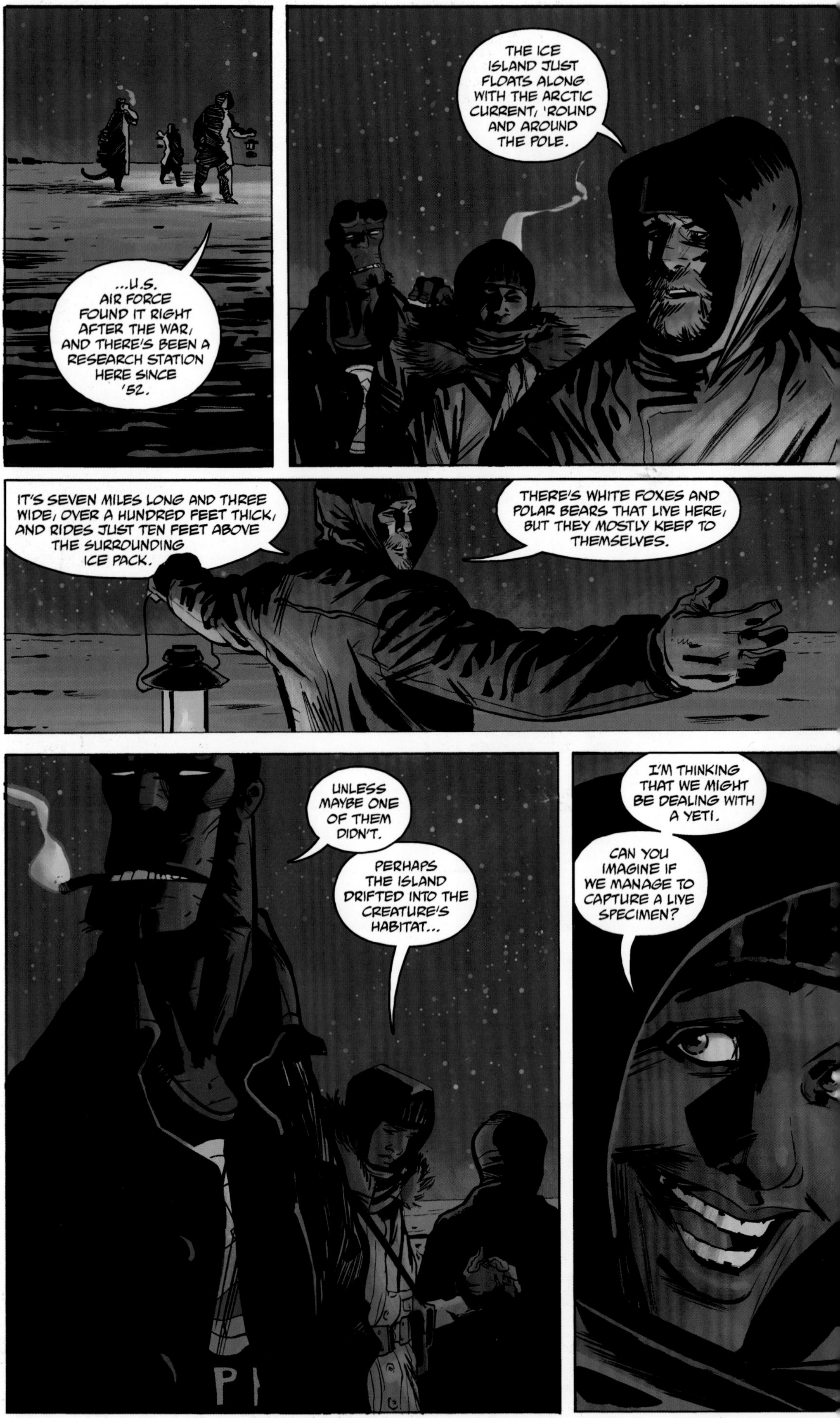

...U.S. AIR FORCE FOUND IT RIGHT AFTER THE WAR, AND THERE'S BEEN A RESEARCH STATION HERE SINCE '52.
THE ICE ISLAND JUST FLOATS ALONG WITH THE ARCTIC CURRENT, 'ROUND AND AROUND THE POLE.
IT'S SEVEN MILES LONG AND THREE WIDE, OVER A HUNDRED FEET THICK, AND RIDES JUST TEN FEET ABOVE THE SURROUNDING ICE PACK.
THERE'S WHITE FOXES AND POLAR BEARS THAT LIVE HERE, BUT THEY MOSTLY KEEP TO THEMSELVES.
UNLESS MAYBE ONE OF THEM DIDN'T.
PERHAPS THE ISLAND DRIFTED INTO THE CREATURE'S HABITAT...
I'M THINKING THAT WE MIGHT BE DEALING WITH A YETI.
CAN YOU IMAGINE IF WE MANAGE TO CAPTURE A LIVE SPECIMEN?

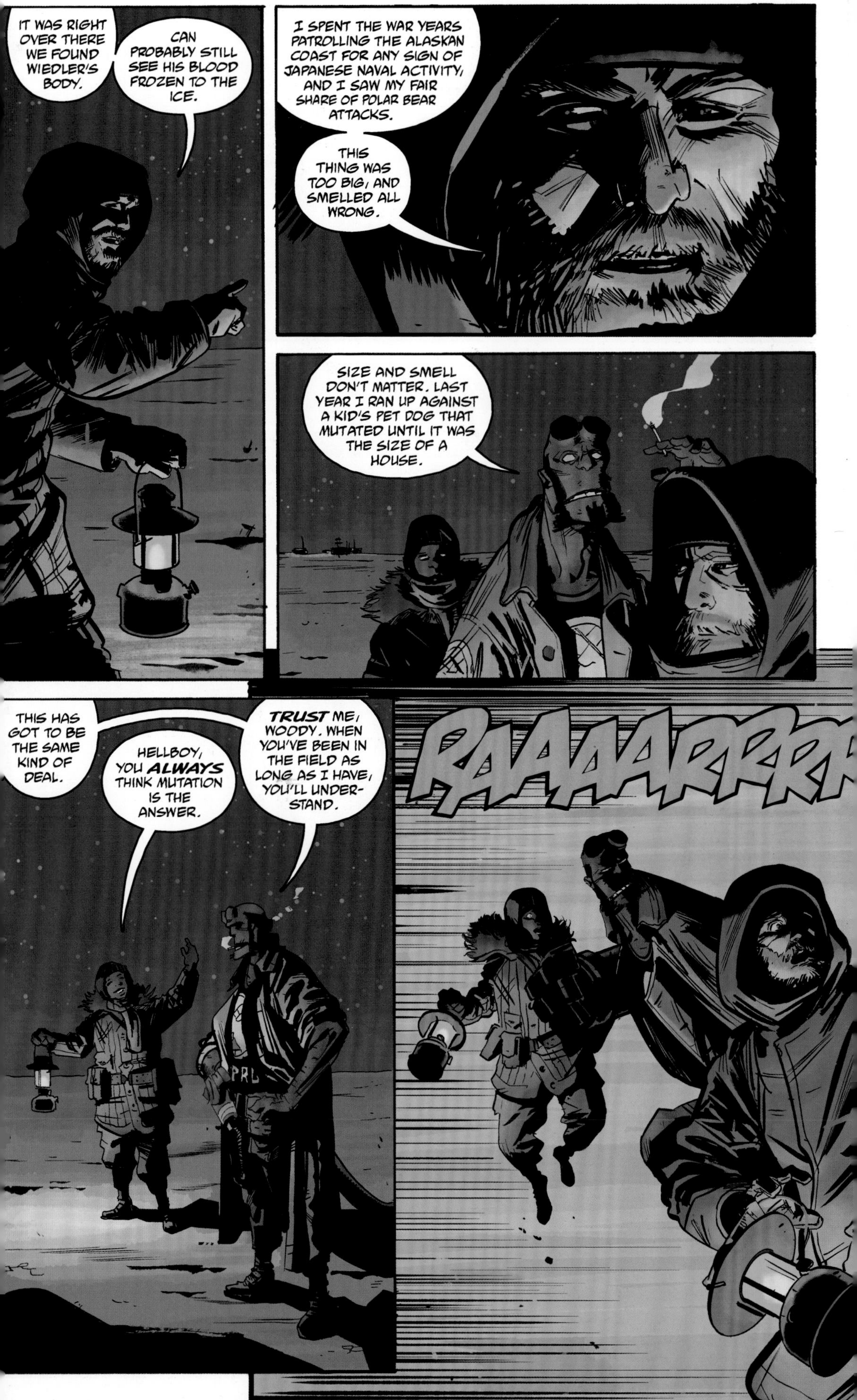
IT WAS RIGHT OVER THERE WE FOUND WIEDLER'S BODY.
CAN PROBABLY STILL SEE HIS BLOOD FROZEN TO THE ICE.
I SPENT THE WAR YEARS PATROLLING THE ALASKAN COAST FOR ANY SIGN OF JAPANESE NAVAL ACTIVITY, AND I SAW MY FAIR SHARE OF POLAR BEAR ATTACKS.
THIS THING WAS TOO BIG, AND SMELLED ALL WRONG.
SIZE AND SMELL DON'T MATTER. LAST YEAR I RAN UP AGAINST A KID'S PET DOG THAT MUTATED UNTIL IT WAS THE SIZE OF A HOUSE.
THIS HAS GOT TO BE THE SAME KIND OF DEAL.
HELLBOY, YOU **ALWAYS** THINK MUTATION IS THE ANSWER.
TRUST ME, WOODY. WHEN YOU'VE BEEN IN THE FIELD AS LONG AS I HAVE, YOU'LL UNDERSTAND.
RAAAARRRR

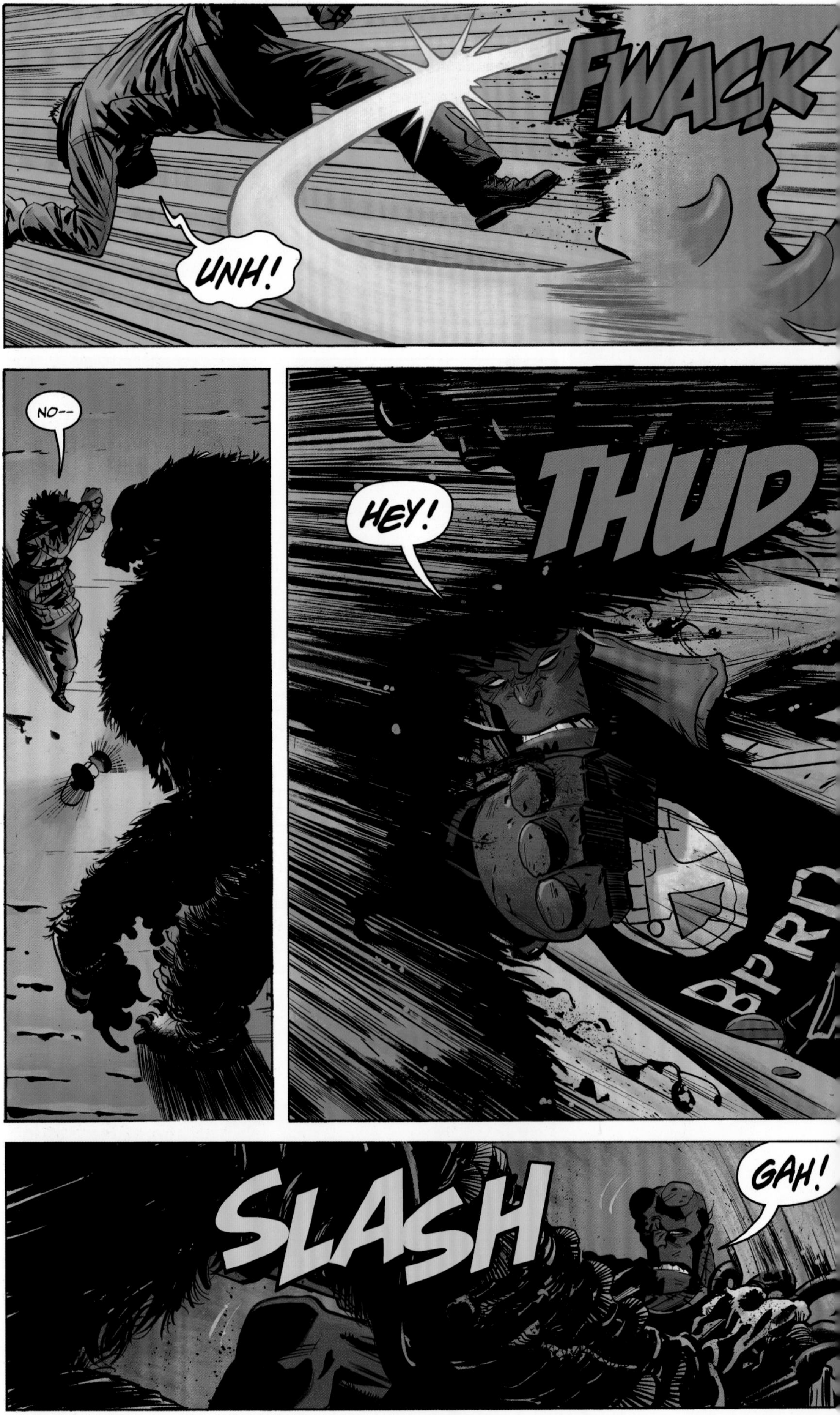
FWACK
UNH!
NO--
HEY!
THUD
SLASH
GAH!

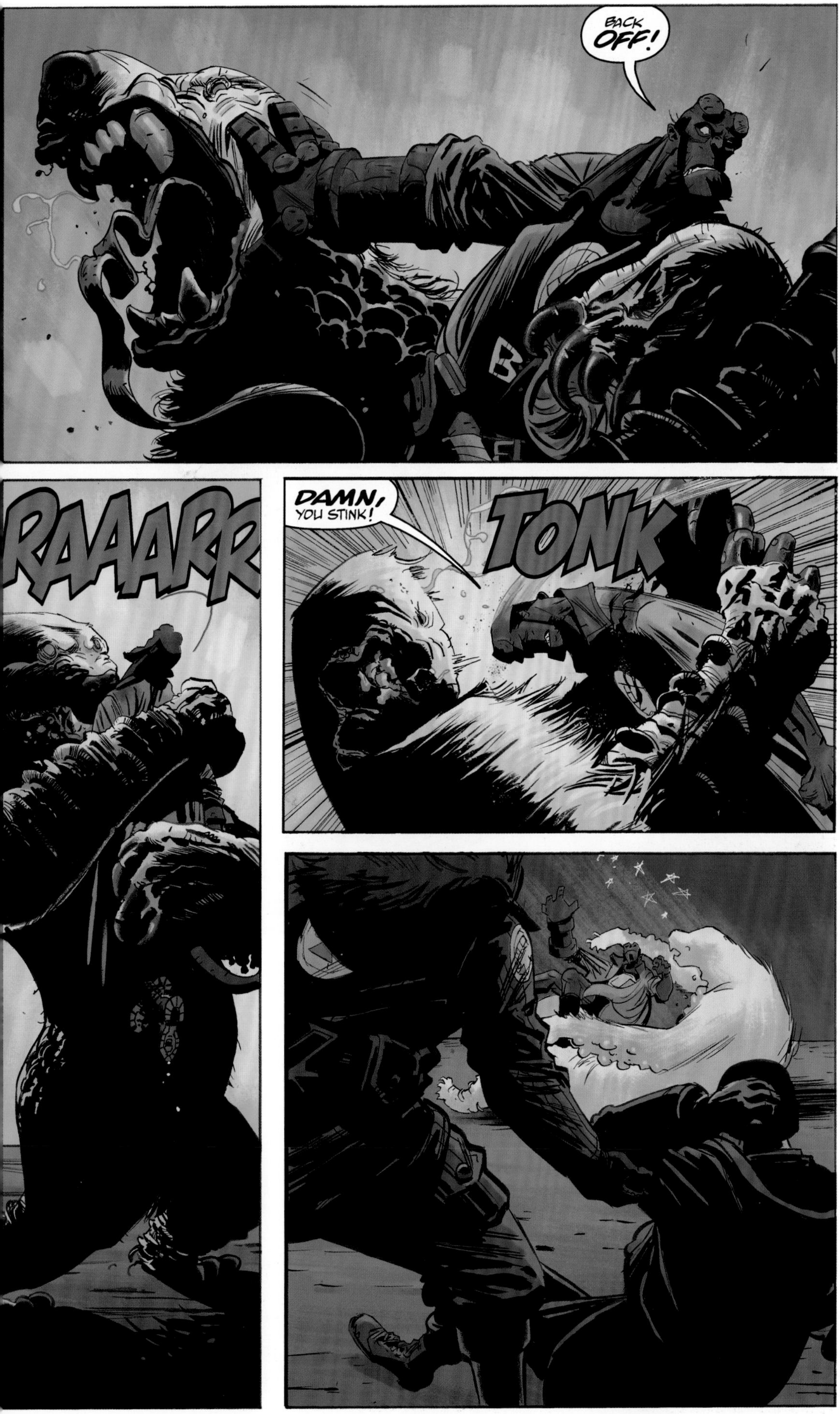
BACK OFF!
RAAARR
DAMN, YOU STINK!
TONK

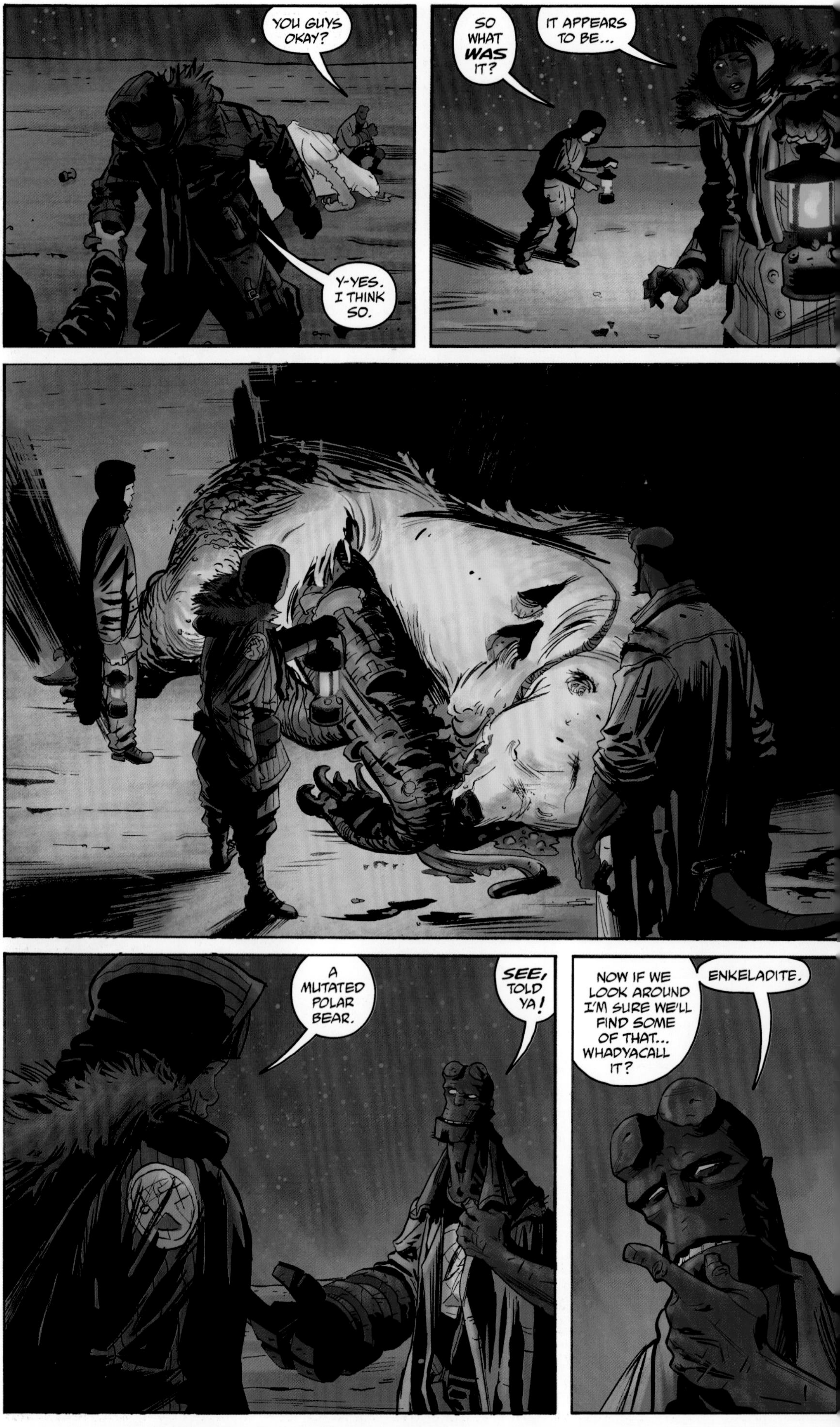
YOU GUYS OKAY?
Y-YES. I THINK SO.
SO WHAT WAS IT?
IT APPEARS TO BE...
A MUTATED POLAR BEAR.
SEE, TOLD YA!
NOW IF WE LOOK AROUND I'M SURE WE'LL FIND SOME OF THAT... WHADYACALL IT?
ENKELADITE.

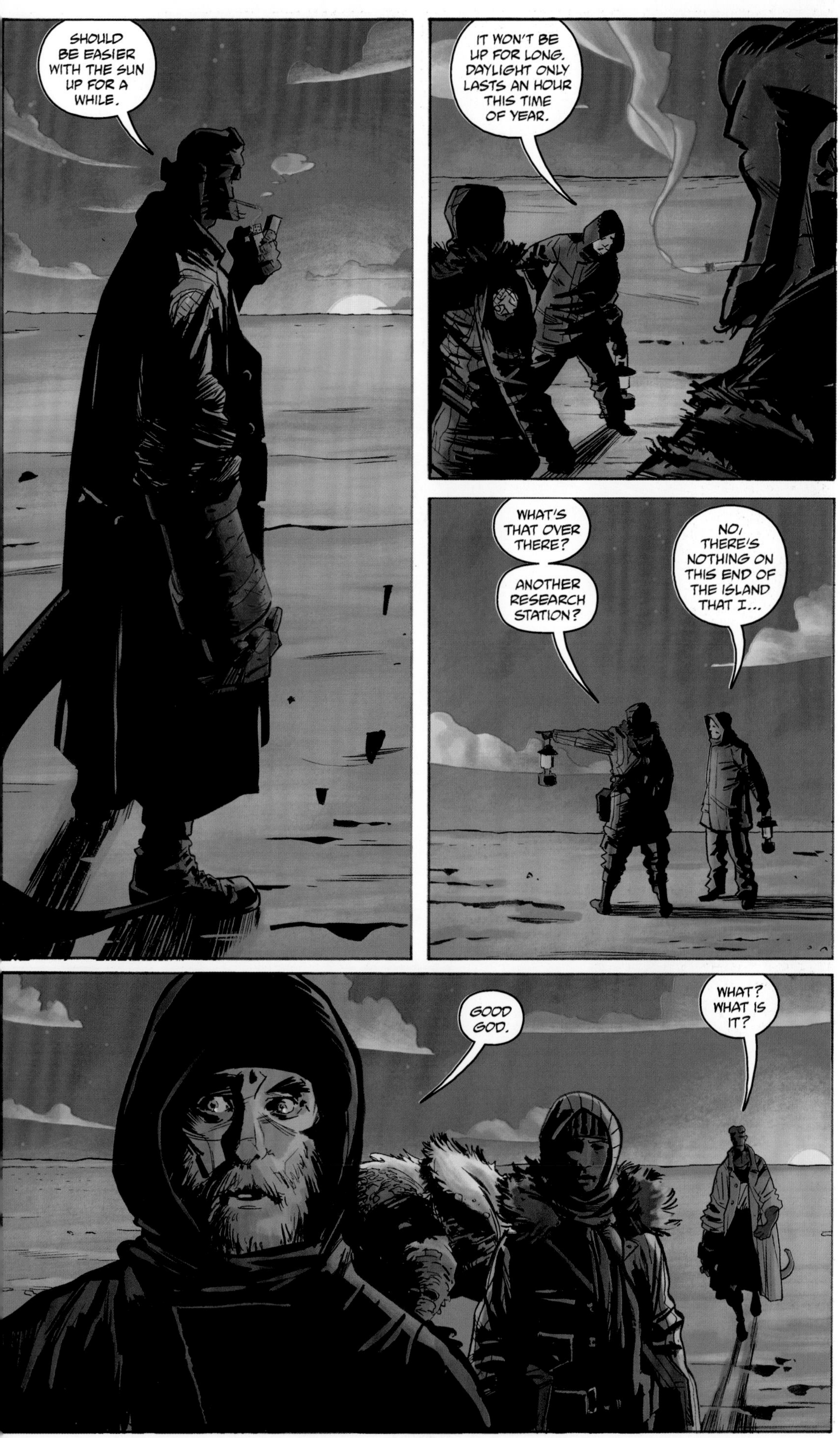
SHOULD BE EASIER WITH THE SUN UP FOR A WHILE.
IT WON'T BE UP FOR LONG. DAYLIGHT ONLY LASTS AN HOUR THIS TIME OF YEAR.
WHAT'S THAT OVER THERE?
ANOTHER RESEARCH STATION?
NO, THERE'S NOTHING ON THIS END OF THE ISLAND THAT I...
GOOD GOD.
WHAT? WHAT IS IT?

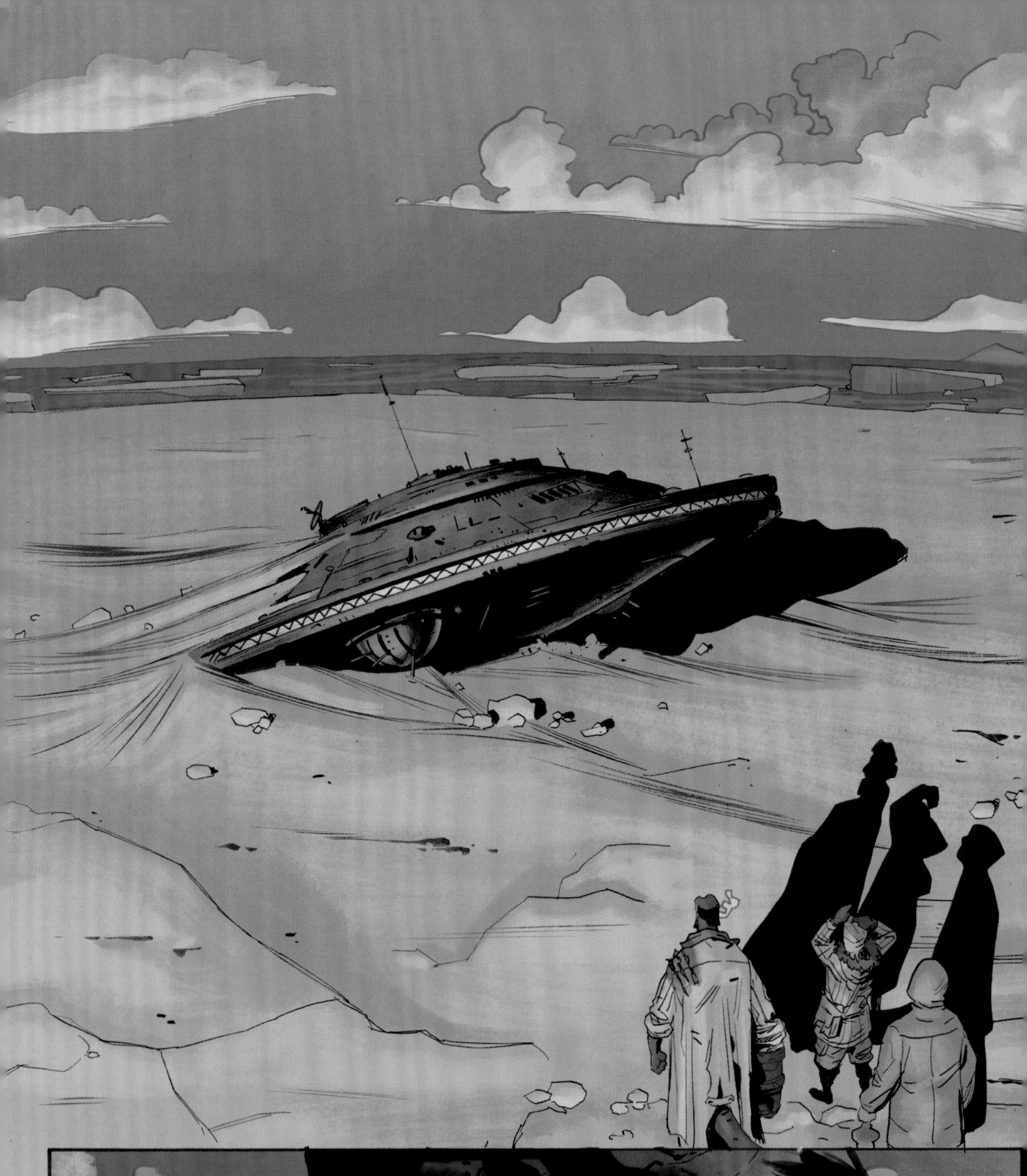
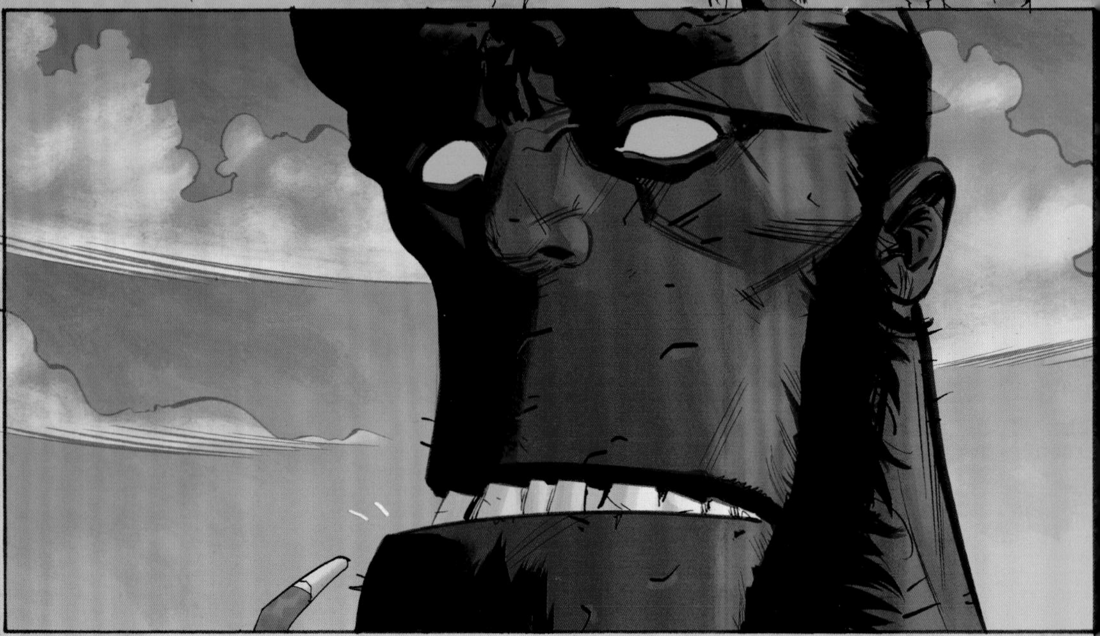

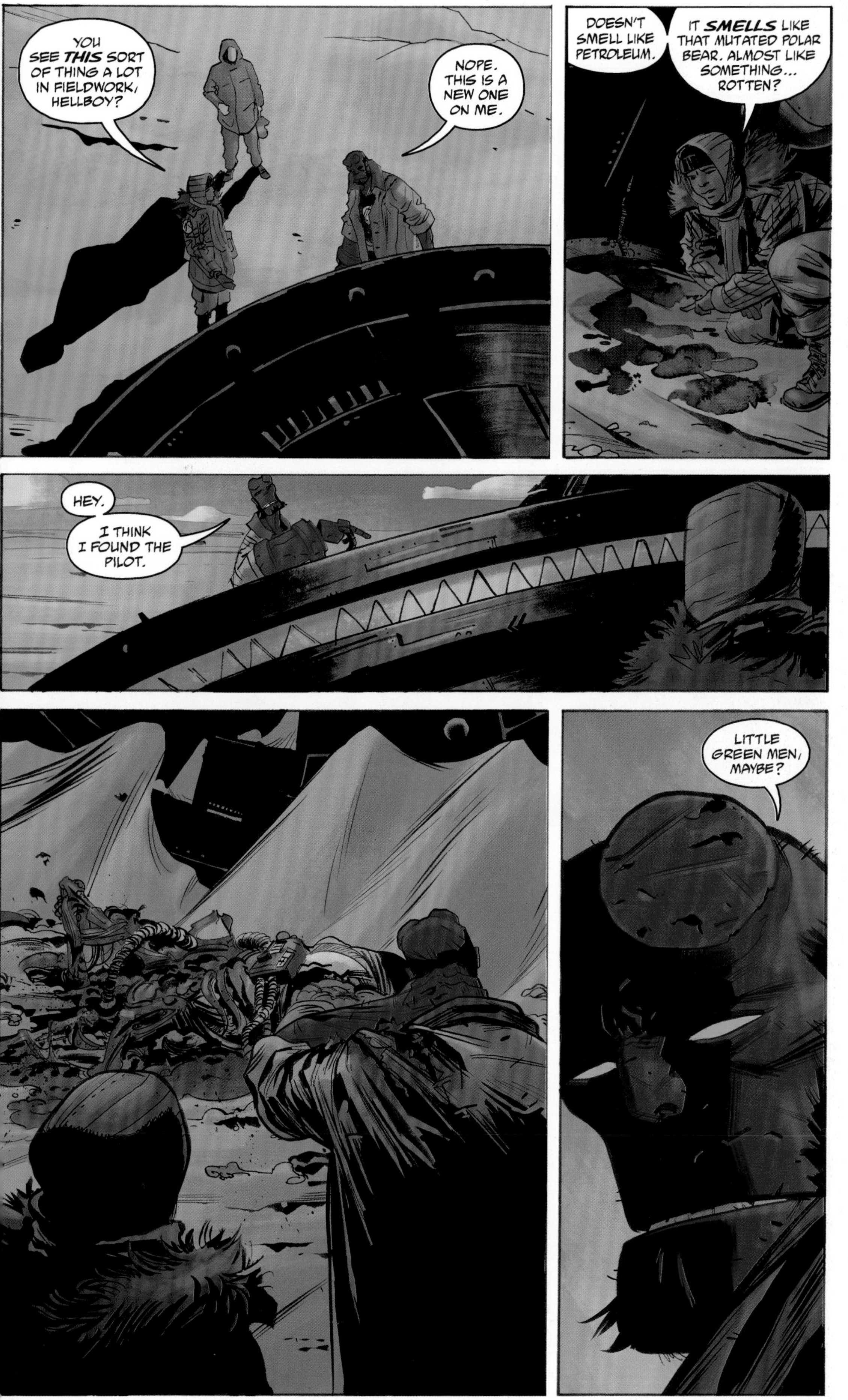
YOU SEE **THIS** SORT OF THING A LOT IN FIELDWORK, HELLBOY?
NOPE. THIS IS A NEW ONE ON ME.
DOESN'T SMELL LIKE PETROLEUM.
IT **SMELLS** LIKE THAT MUTATED POLAR BEAR. ALMOST LIKE SOMETHING... ROTTEN?
HEY.
I THINK I FOUND THE PILOT.
LITTLE GREEN MEN, MAYBE?

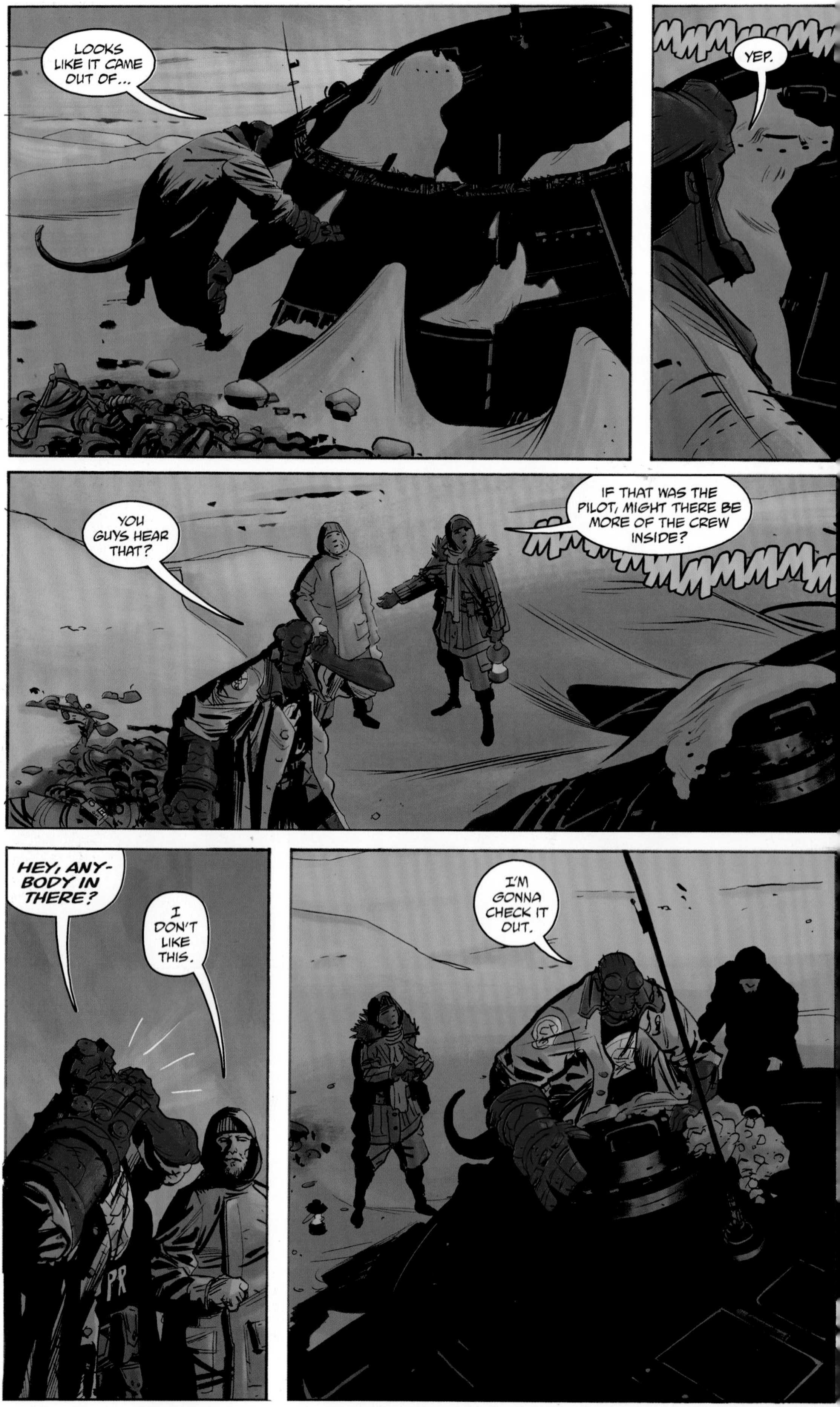
LOOKS LIKE IT CAME OUT OF...
YEP.
YOU GUYS HEAR THAT?
IF THAT WAS THE PILOT, MIGHT THERE BE MORE OF THE CREW INSIDE?
HEY, ANY-BODY IN THERE?
I DON'T LIKE THIS.
I'M GONNA CHECK IT OUT.

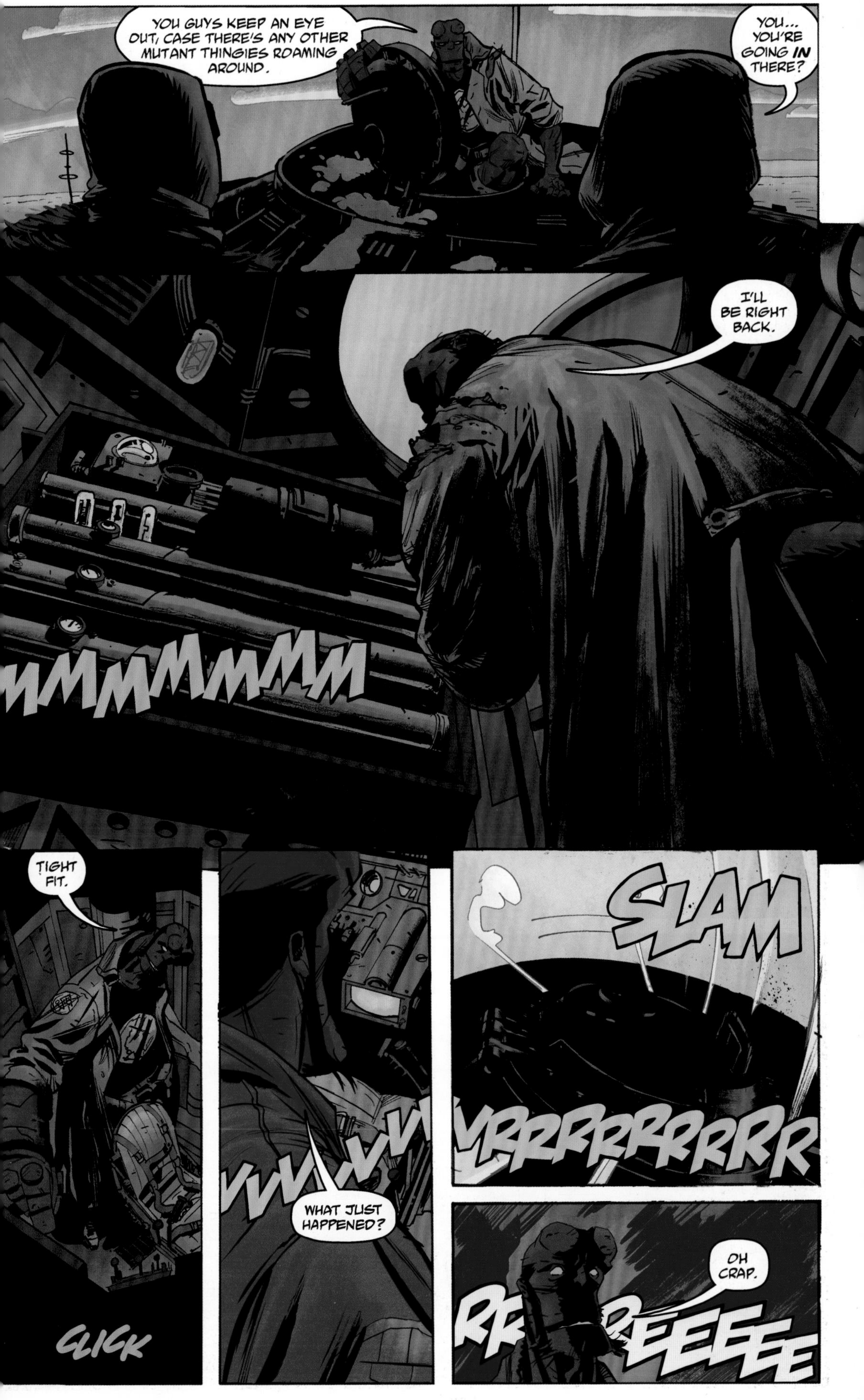
YOU GUYS KEEP AN EYE OUT, CASE THERE'S ANY OTHER MUTANT THINGIES ROAMING AROUND.
YOU... YOU'RE GOING IN THERE?
I'LL BE RIGHT BACK.
MMMMMMMM
TIGHT FIT.
CLICK
VVVVVVVRRRRRRRRRR
WHAT JUST HAPPENED?
SLAM
OH CRAP.
RRRREEEEEE

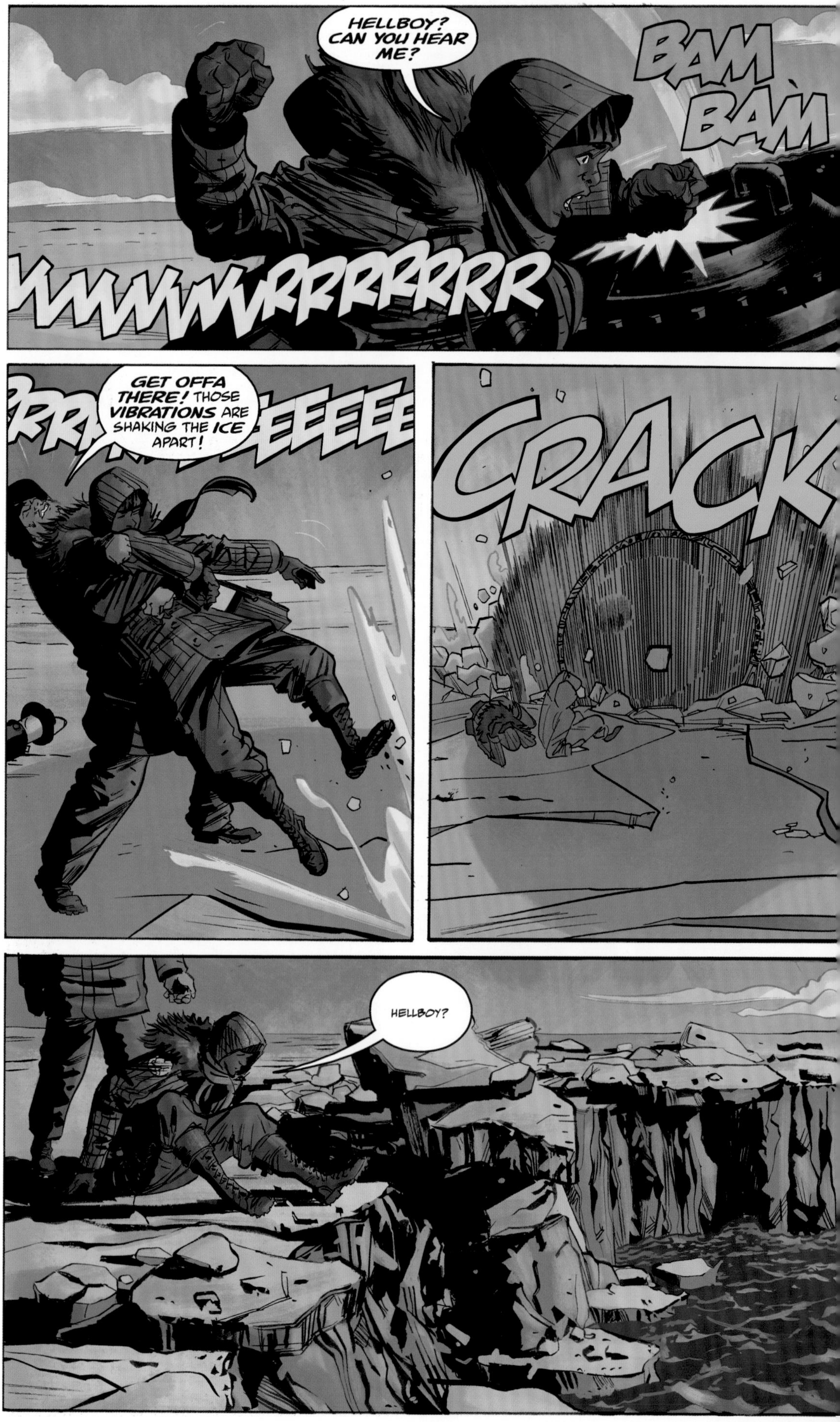
HELLBOY? CAN YOU HEAR ME?
BAM BAM
WWWWWRRRRRRRR
GET OFFA THERE! THOSE VIBRATIONS ARE SHAKING THE ICE APART!
CRACK
HELLBOY?

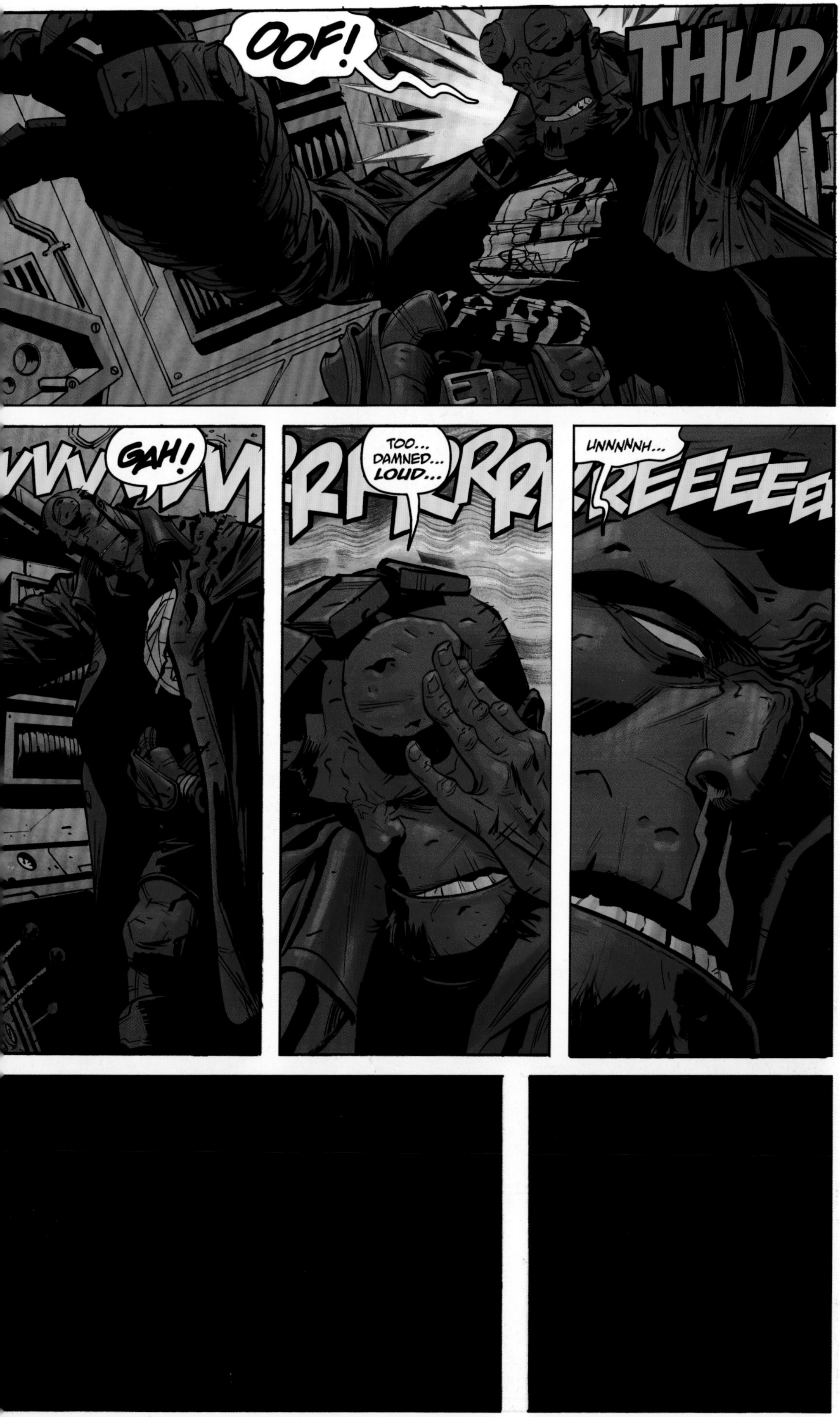
OOF!
THUD
GAH!
TOO... DAMNED... LOUD...
UNNNNNH...

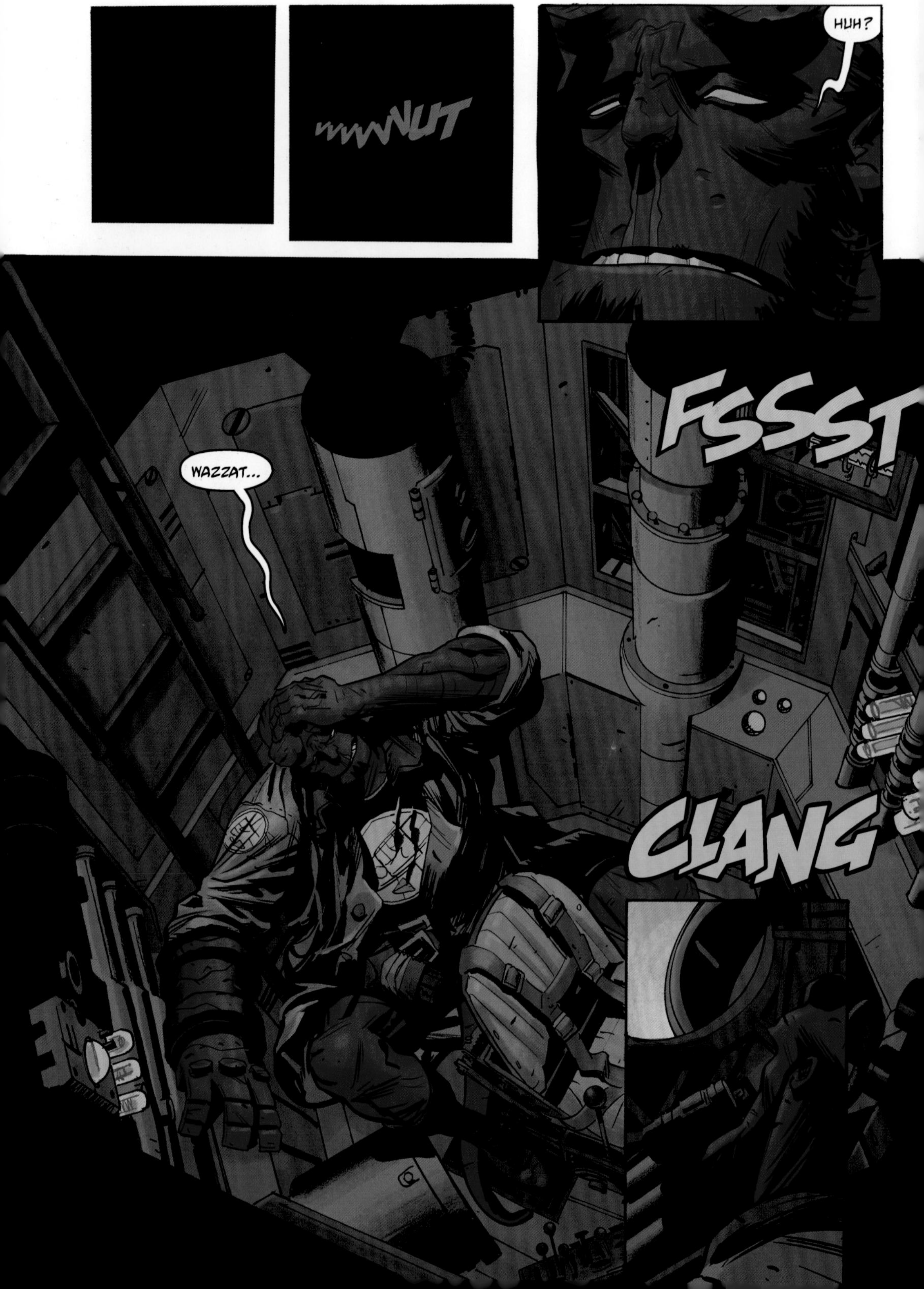
vvvvNUT
HUH?
WAZZAT...
FSSST
CLANG

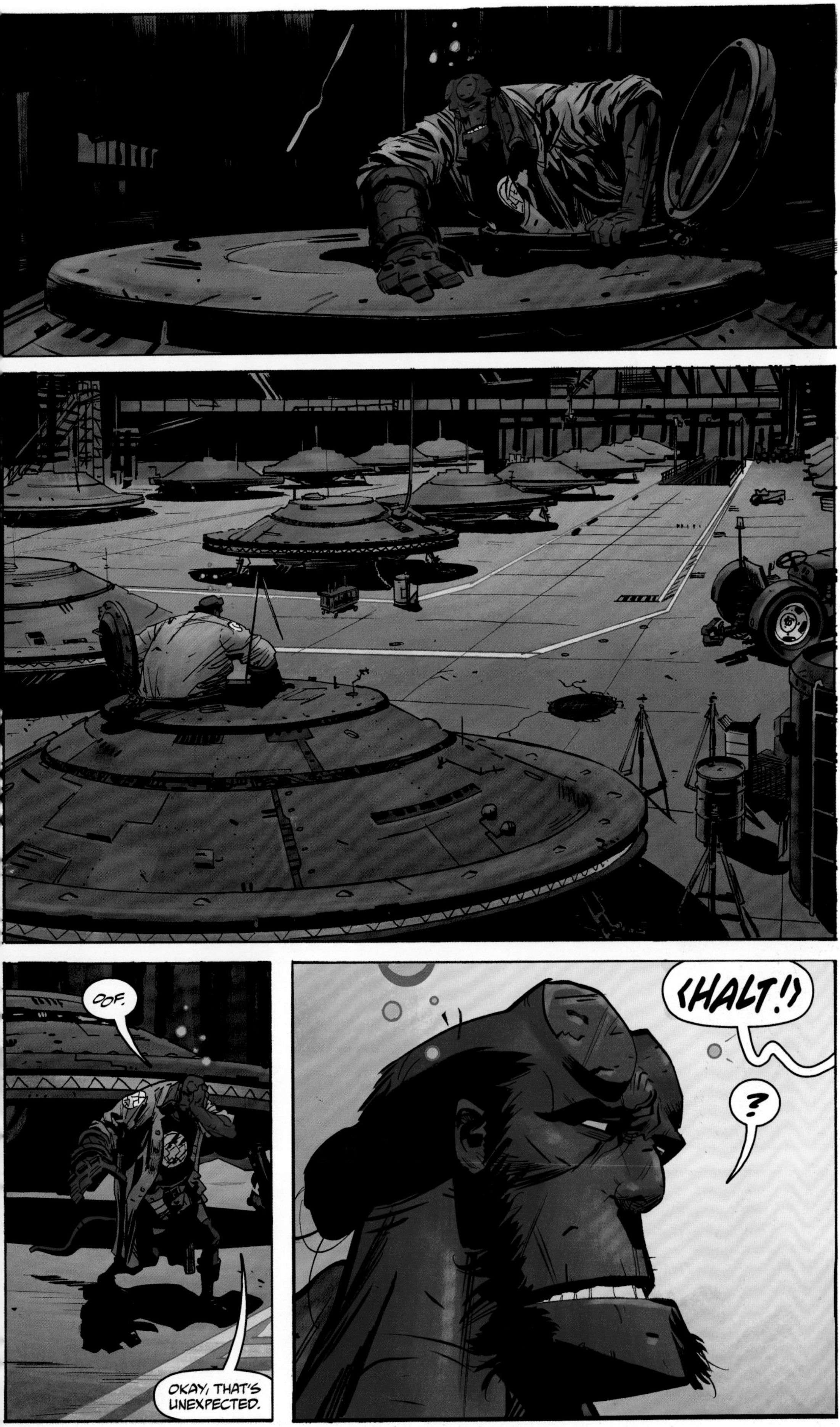
OOF.
OKAY, THAT'S UNEXPECTED.
‹HALT!›
?

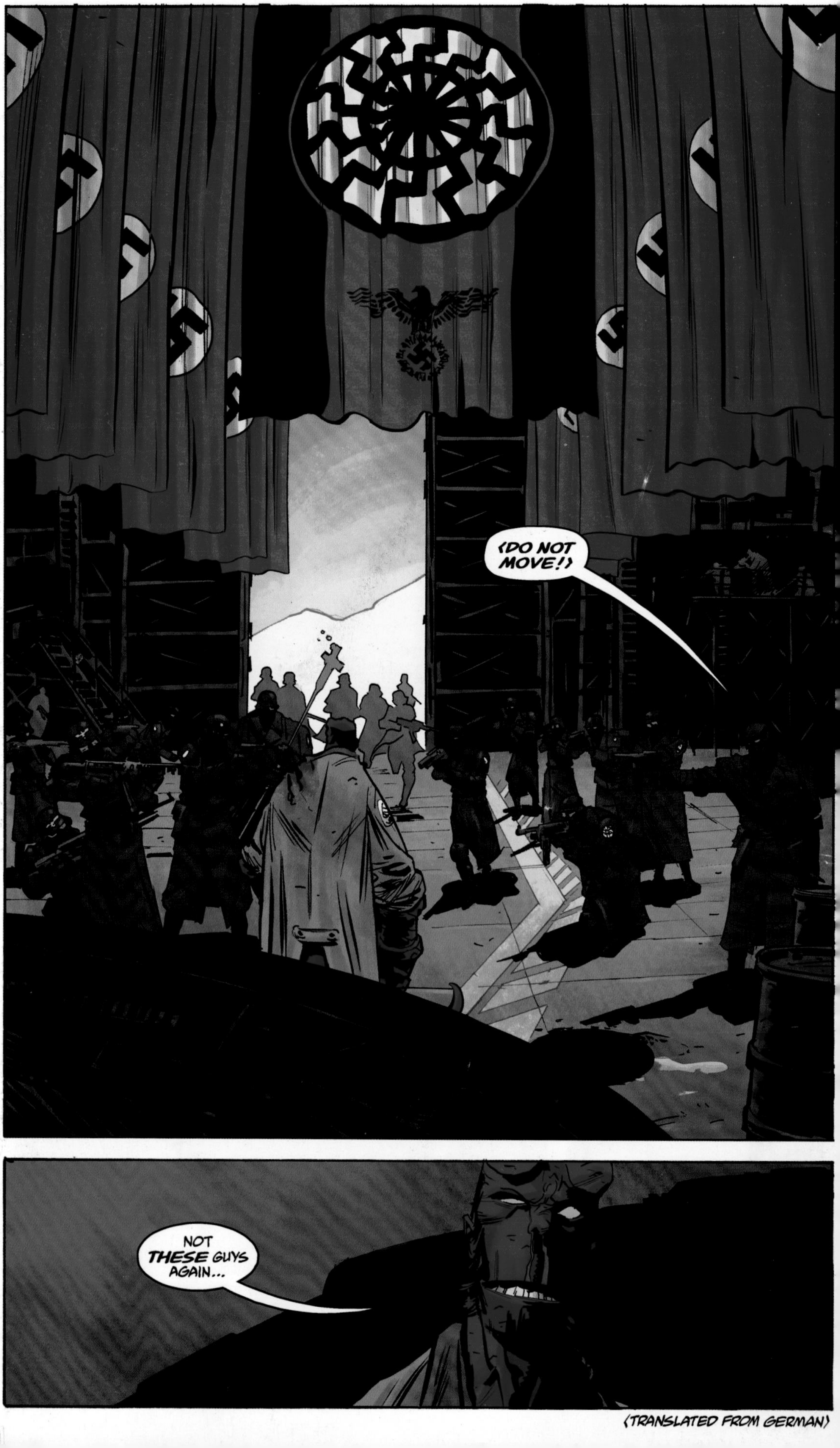
‹DO NOT MOVE!›
NOT ***THESE*** GUYS AGAIN...

‹TRANSLATED FROM GERMAN›

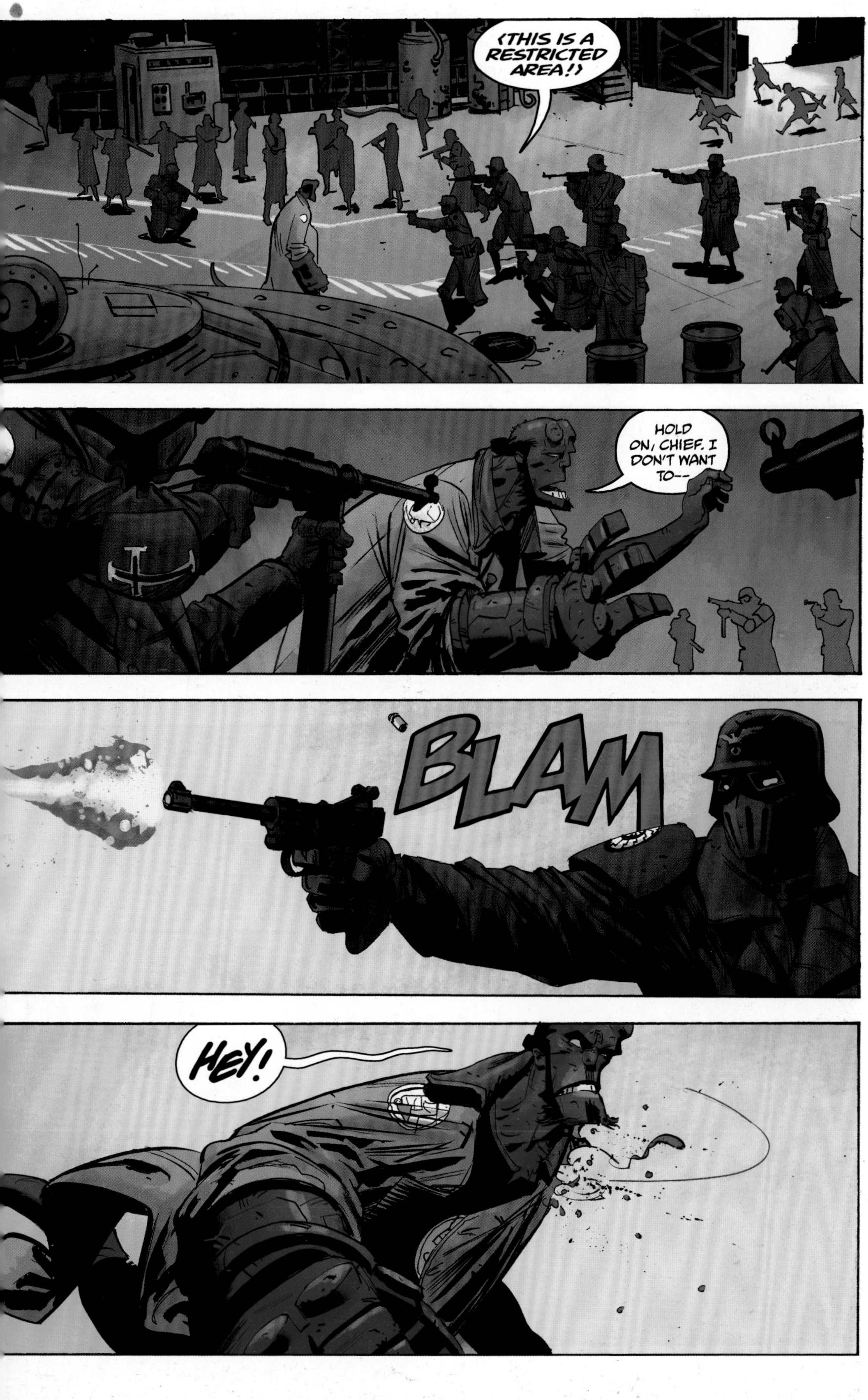
‹THIS IS A RESTRICTED AREA!›
HOLD ON, CHIEF. I DON'T WANT TO--
BLAM
HEY!

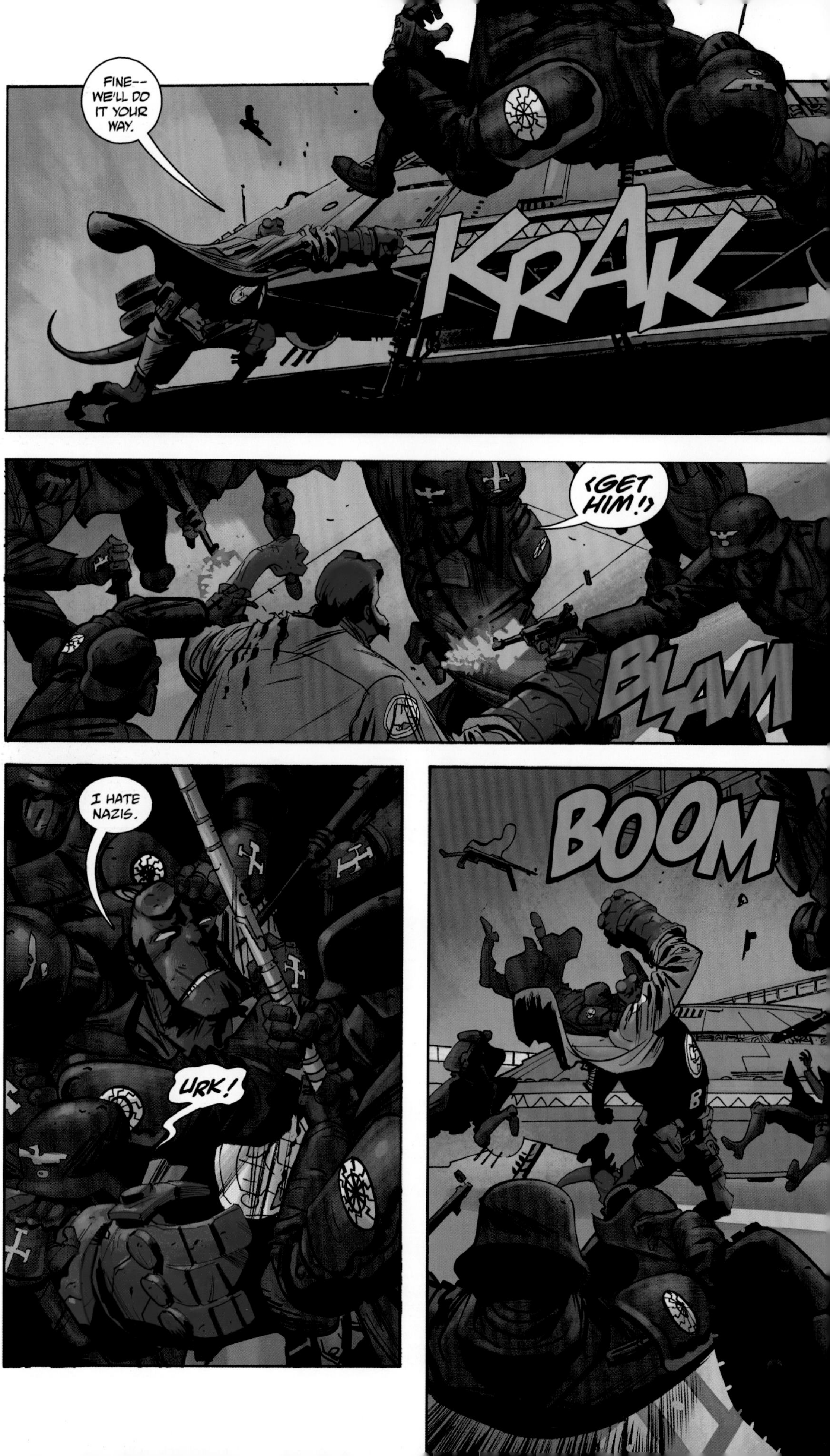
FINE--
WE'LL DO IT YOUR WAY.
KRAK
‹GET HIM!›
BLAM
I HATE NAZIS.
URK!
BOOM

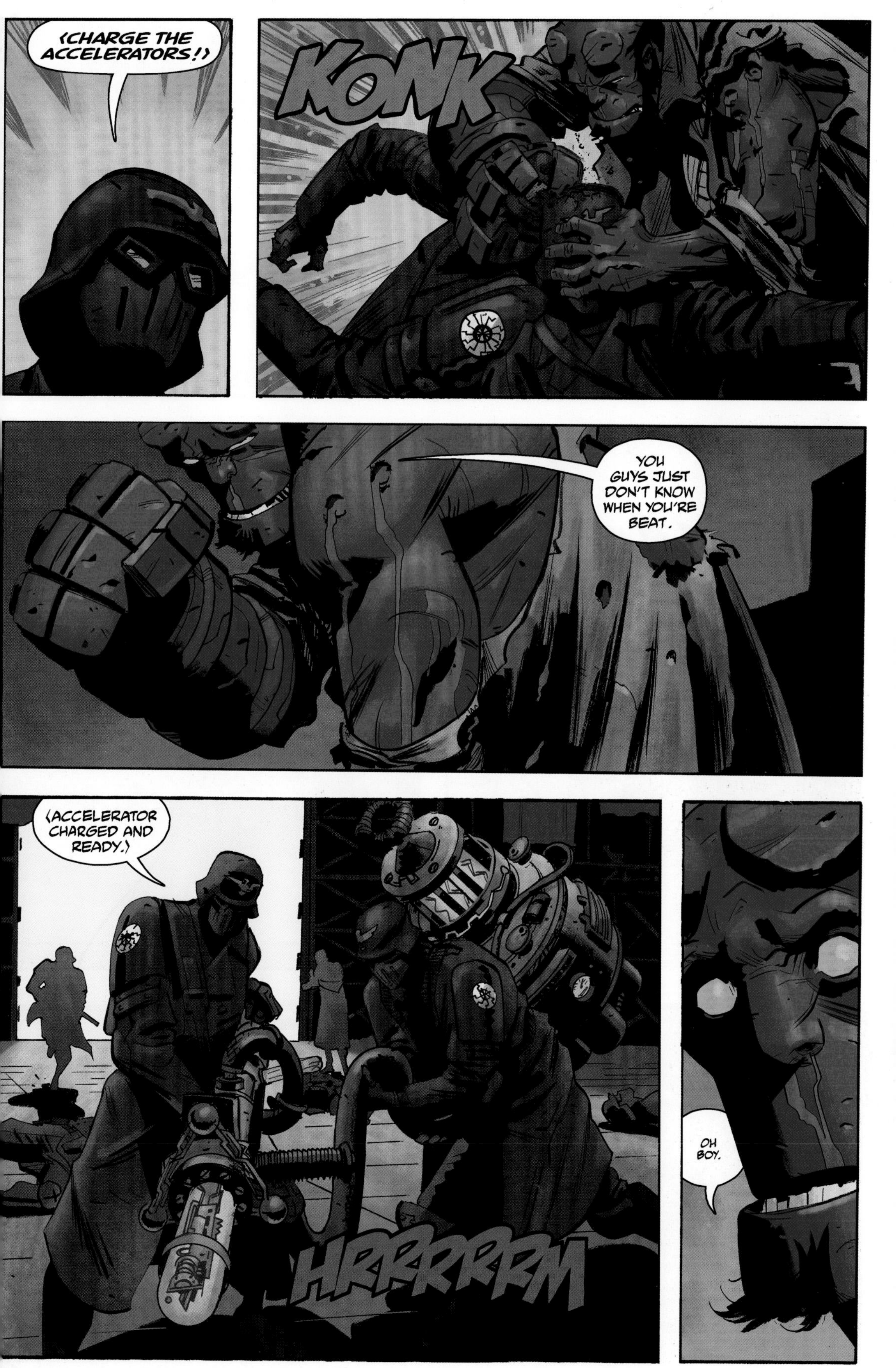
‹CHARGE THE ACCELERATORS!›
KONK
YOU GUYS JUST DON'T KNOW WHEN YOU'RE BEAT.
‹ACCELERATOR CHARGED AND READY.›
HRRRRRM
OH BOY.

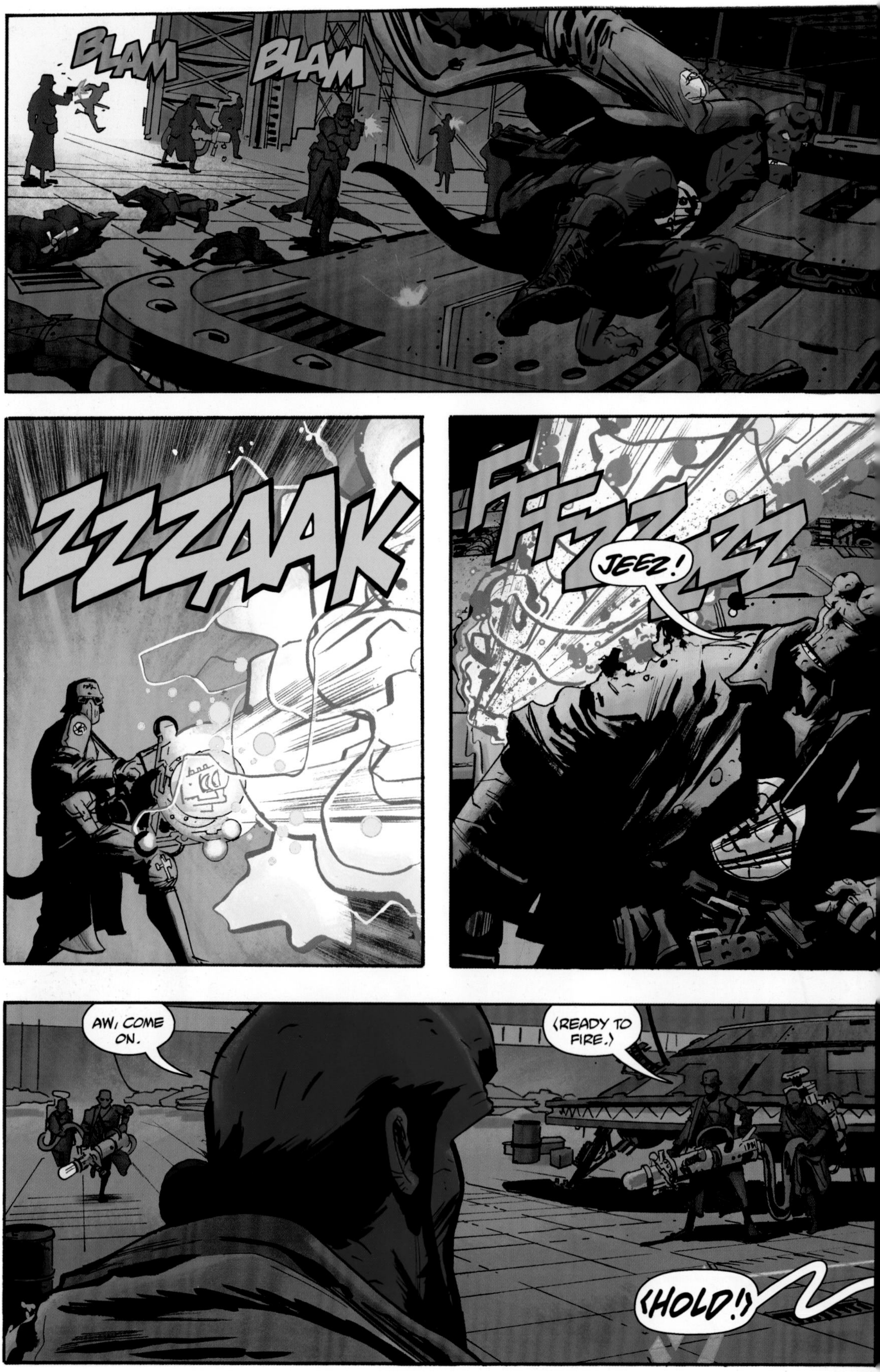
BLAM
BLAM
ZZZAAK
FFFZZZZZ
JEEZ!
AW, COME ON.
‹READY TO FIRE.›
‹HOLD!›

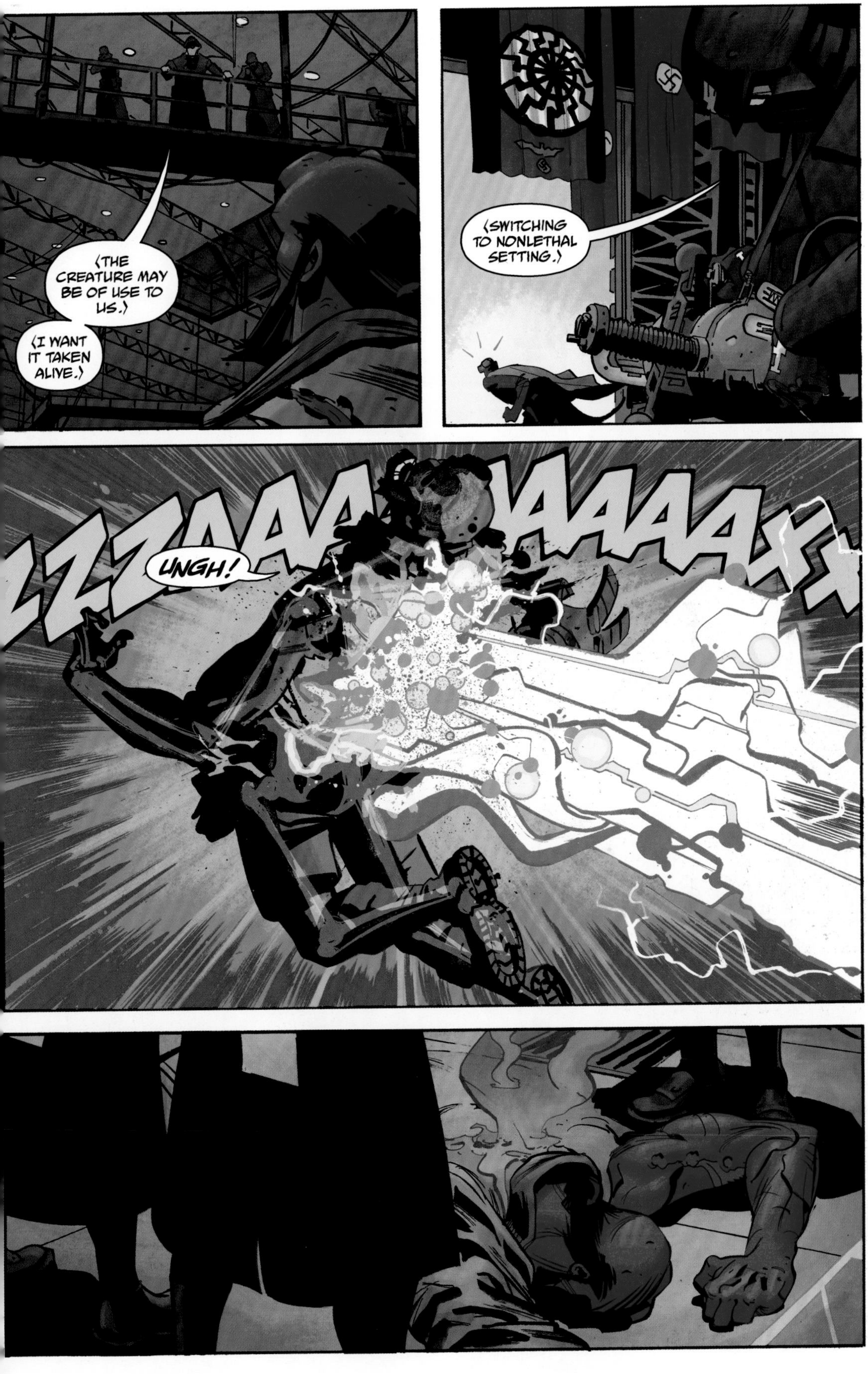
‹THE CREATURE MAY BE OF USE TO US.›
‹I WANT IT TAKEN ALIVE.›
‹SWITCHING TO NONLETHAL SETTING.›
ZZZAAAAAAAAAAAXX
UNGH!

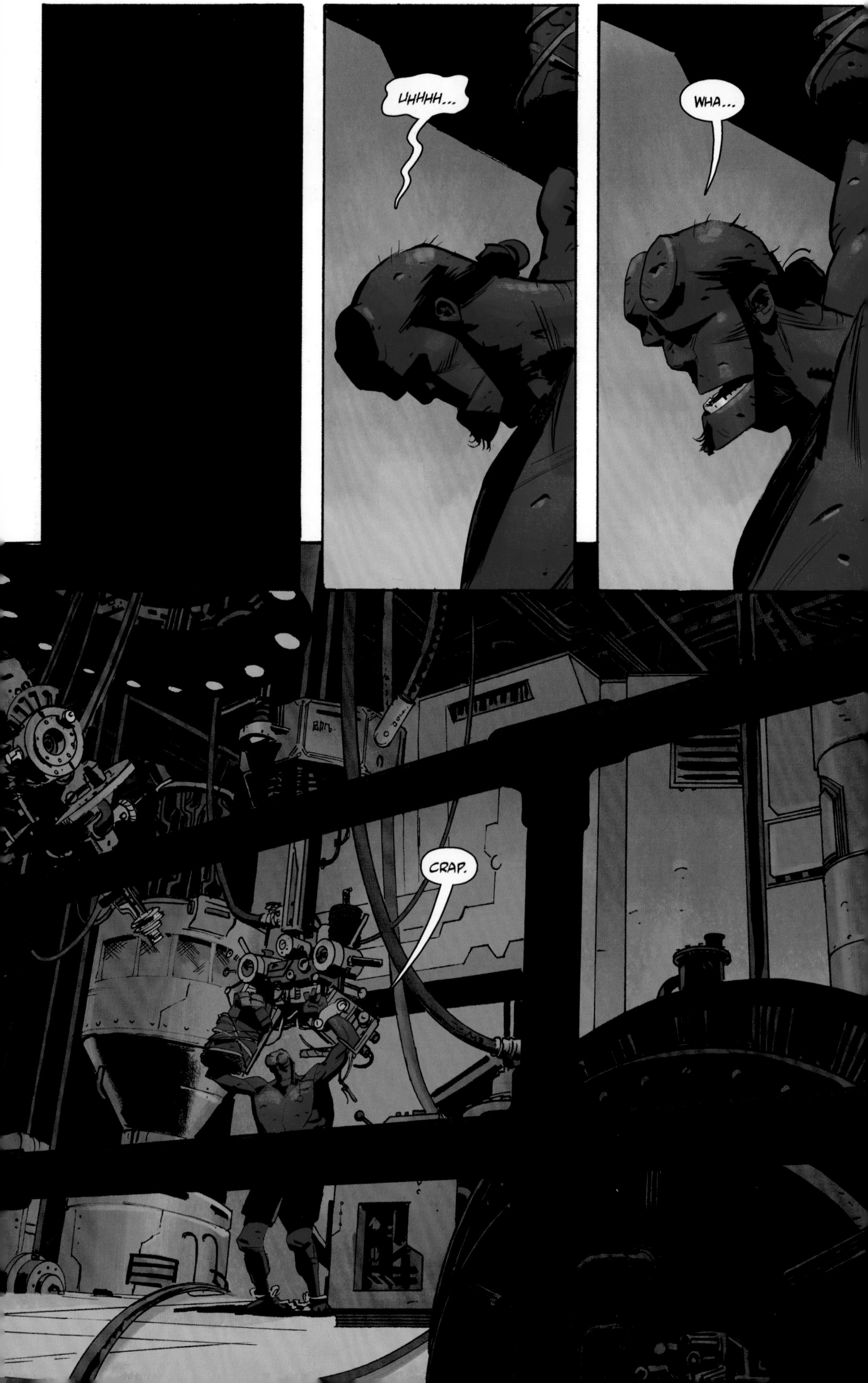
UHHHH...
WHA...
CRAP.

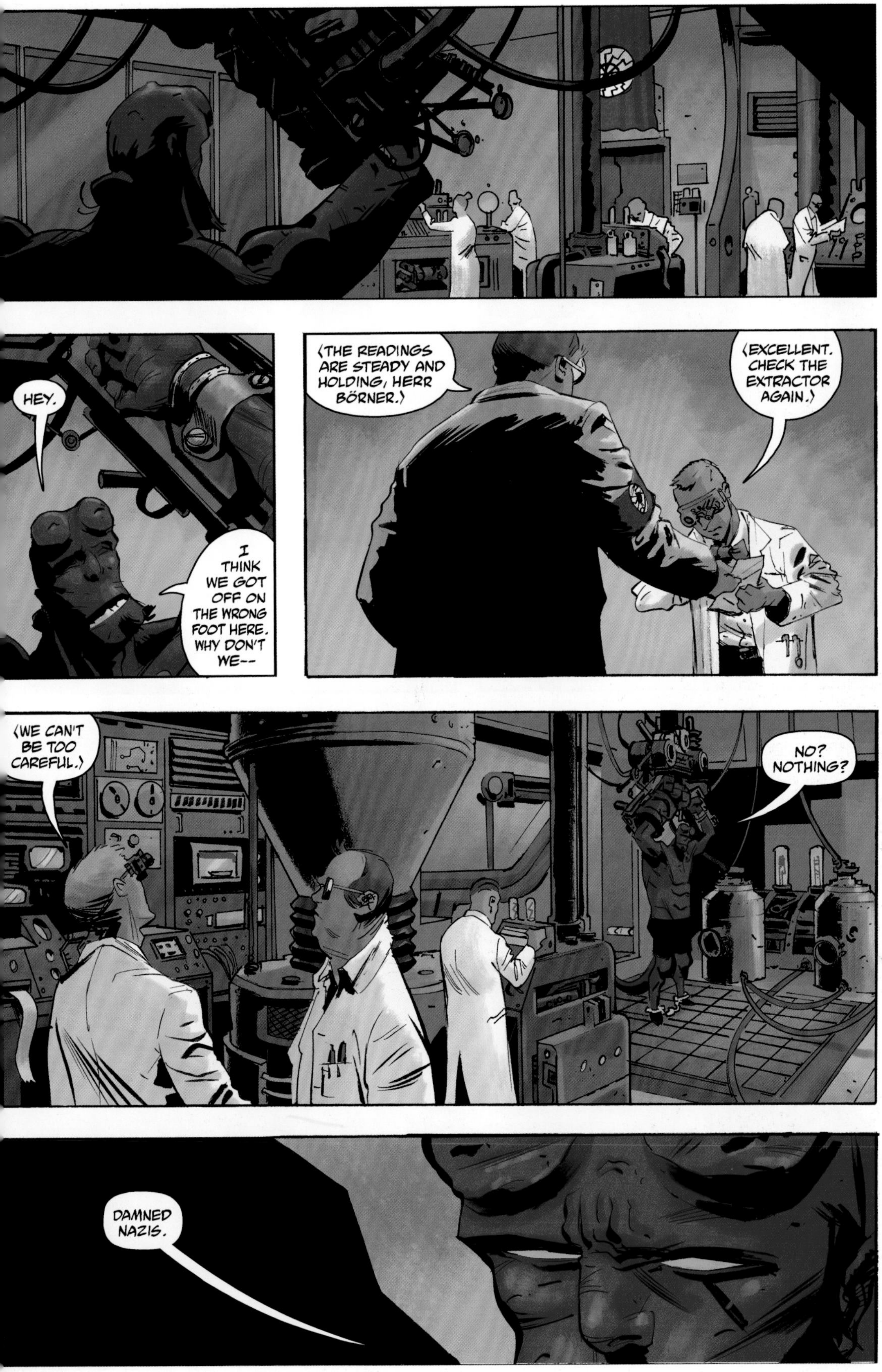
HEY.
I THINK WE GOT OFF ON THE WRONG FOOT HERE. WHY DON'T WE--
‹THE READINGS ARE STEADY AND HOLDING, HERR BÖRNER.›
‹EXCELLENT. CHECK THE EXTRACTOR AGAIN.›
‹WE CAN'T BE TOO CAREFUL.›
NO? NOTHING?
DAMNED NAZIS.

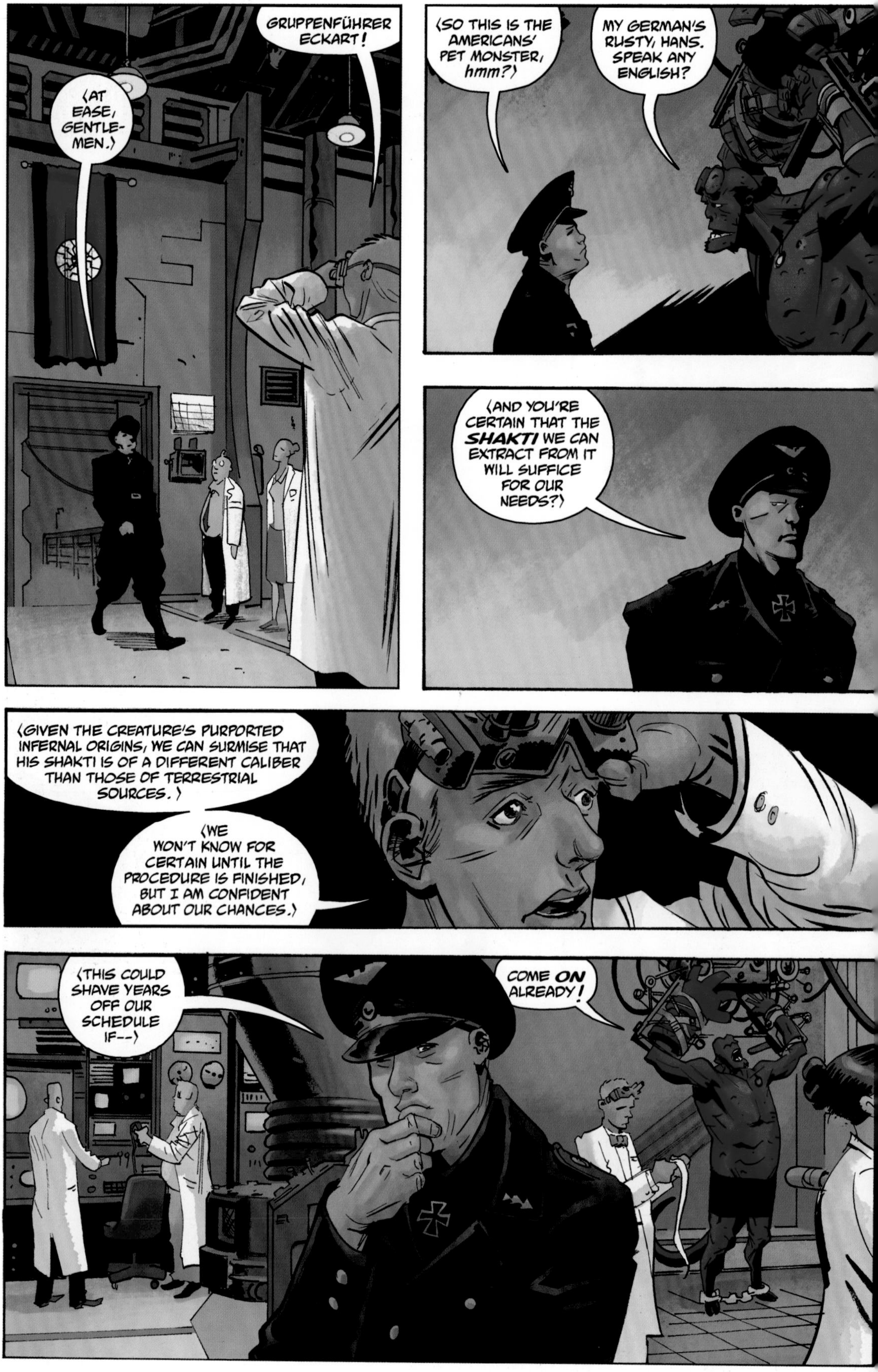
GRUPPENFÜHRER ECKART!
⟨AT EASE, GENTLEMEN.⟩
⟨SO THIS IS THE AMERICANS' PET MONSTER, hmm?⟩
MY GERMAN'S RUSTY, HANS. SPEAK ANY ENGLISH?
⟨AND YOU'RE CERTAIN THAT THE SHAKTI WE CAN EXTRACT FROM IT WILL SUFFICE FOR OUR NEEDS?⟩
⟨GIVEN THE CREATURE'S PURPORTED INFERNAL ORIGINS, WE CAN SURMISE THAT HIS SHAKTI IS OF A DIFFERENT CALIBER THAN THOSE OF TERRESTRIAL SOURCES.⟩
⟨WE WON'T KNOW FOR CERTAIN UNTIL THE PROCEDURE IS FINISHED, BUT I AM CONFIDENT ABOUT OUR CHANCES.⟩
⟨THIS COULD SHAVE YEARS OFF OUR SCHEDULE IF--⟩
COME ON ALREADY!

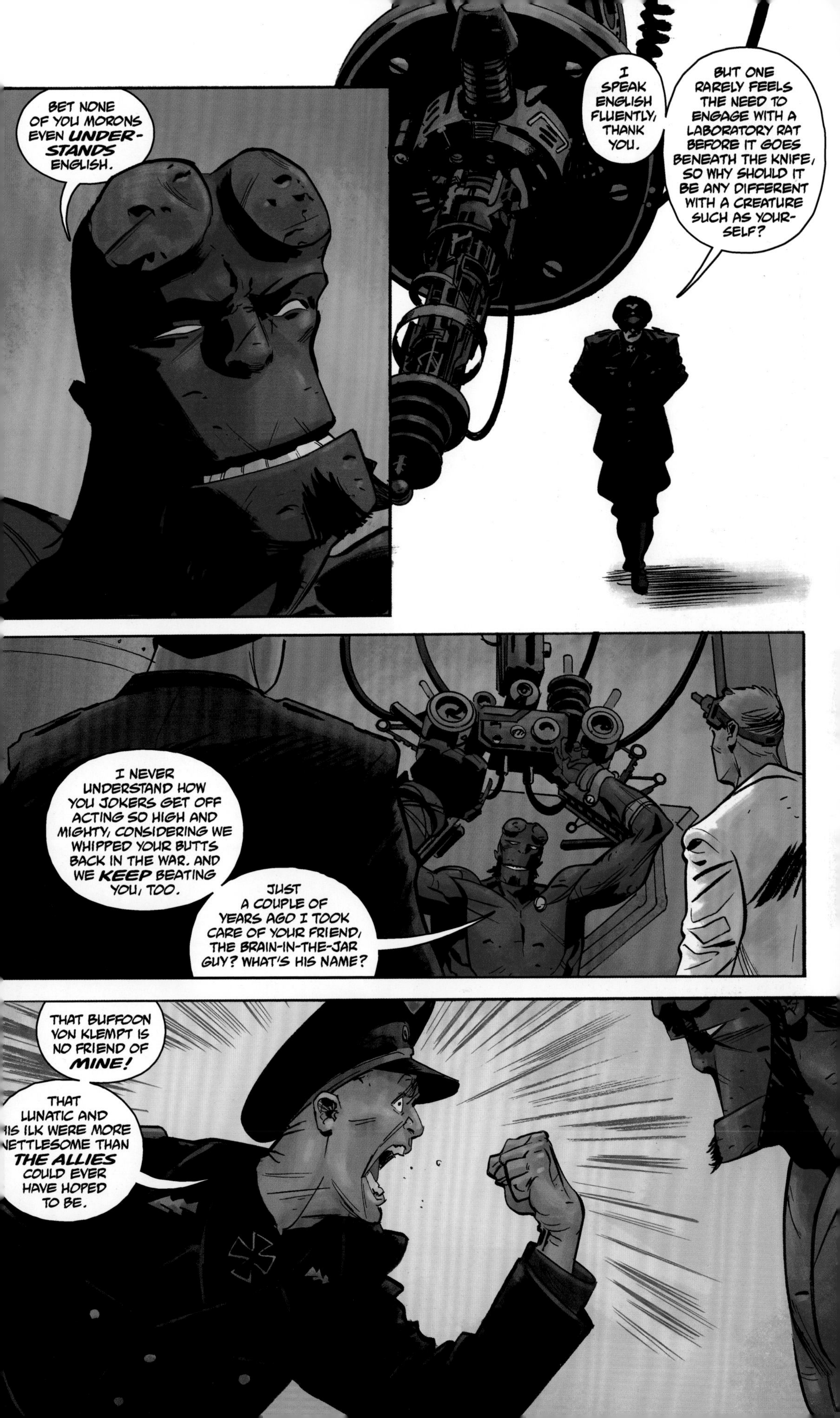
BET NONE OF YOU MORONS EVEN UNDER-STANDS ENGLISH.
I SPEAK ENGLISH FLUENTLY, THANK YOU.
BUT ONE RARELY FEELS THE NEED TO ENGAGE WITH A LABORATORY RAT BEFORE IT GOES BENEATH THE KNIFE, SO WHY SHOULD IT BE ANY DIFFERENT WITH A CREATURE SUCH AS YOUR-SELF?
I NEVER UNDERSTAND HOW YOU JOKERS GET OFF ACTING SO HIGH AND MIGHTY, CONSIDERING WE WHIPPED YOUR BUTTS BACK IN THE WAR. AND WE KEEP BEATING YOU, TOO.
JUST A COUPLE OF YEARS AGO I TOOK CARE OF YOUR FRIEND, THE BRAIN-IN-THE-JAR GUY? WHAT'S HIS NAME?
THAT BUFFOON VON KLEMPT IS NO FRIEND OF MINE!
THAT LUNATIC AND HIS ILK WERE MORE NETTLESOME THAN THE ALLIES COULD EVER HAVE HOPED TO BE.

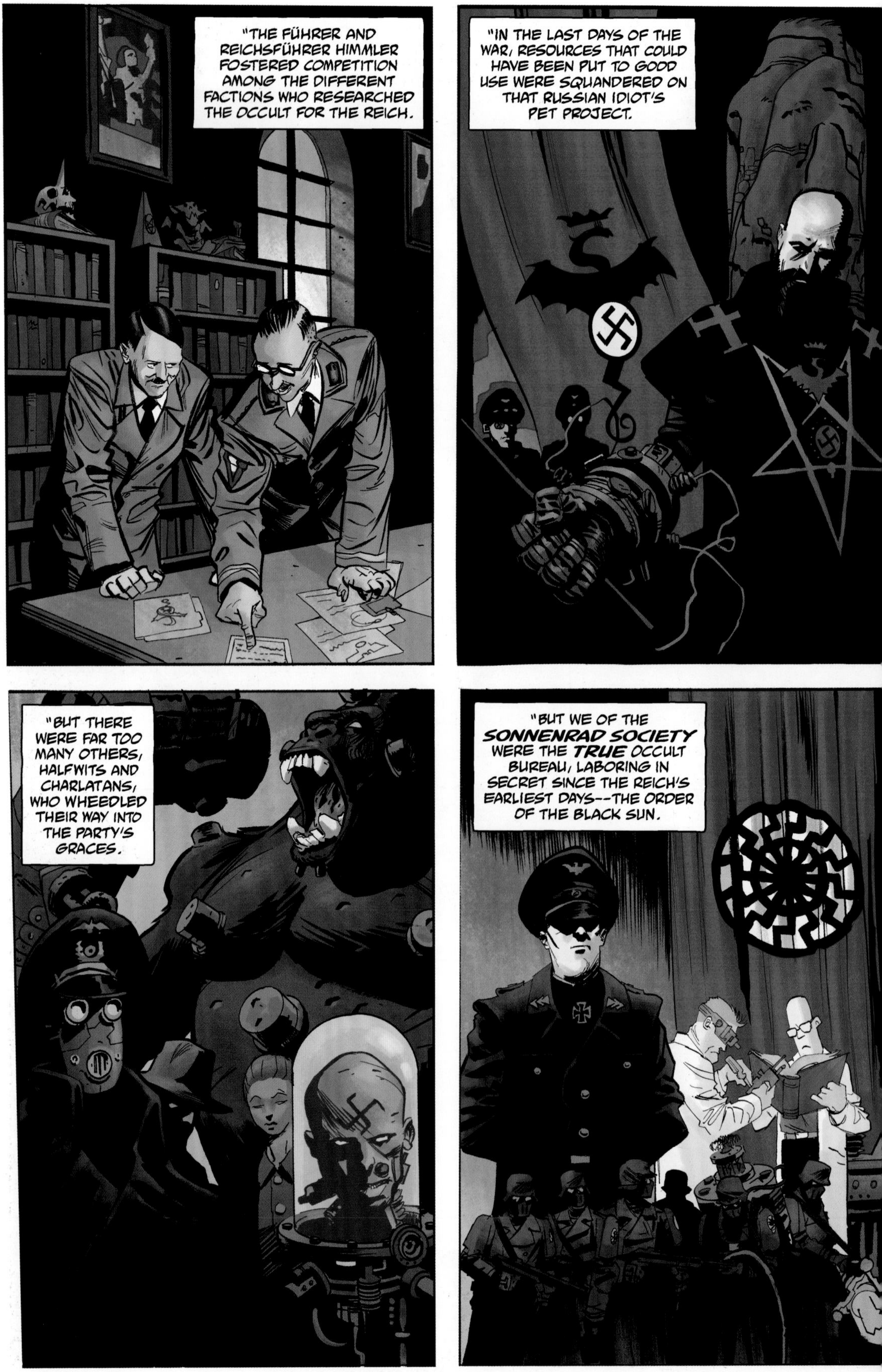
"THE FÜHRER AND REICHSFÜHRER HIMMLER FOSTERED COMPETITION AMONG THE DIFFERENT FACTIONS WHO RESEARCHED THE OCCULT FOR THE REICH.
"IN THE LAST DAYS OF THE WAR, RESOURCES THAT COULD HAVE BEEN PUT TO GOOD USE WERE SQUANDERED ON THAT RUSSIAN IDIOT'S PET PROJECT.
"BUT THERE WERE FAR TOO MANY OTHERS, HALFWITS AND CHARLATANS, WHO WHEEDLED THEIR WAY INTO THE PARTY'S GRACES.
"BUT WE OF THE SONNENRAD SOCIETY WERE THE TRUE OCCULT BUREAU, LABORING IN SECRET SINCE THE REICH'S EARLIEST DAYS--THE ORDER OF THE BLACK SUN.

"WE WERE SCIENTISTS AND RESEARCHERS, TASKED WITH INVESTIGATING ANYTHING OF OCCULT POWER WHICH THE PARTY ENCOUNTERED.

"THINGS HIDDEN DEEP IN THE EARTH OR FROM THE DAWN OF HISTORY, FROM LOST CITIES OR OTHER PLANES OF EXISTENCE.

"AND WE CARRIED OUT OUR OWN SEARCHES FOR SUCH ITEMS, BURIED BY THE SANDS OF TIME.

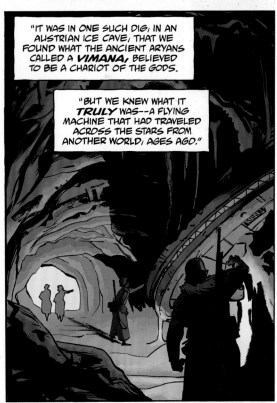

"IT WAS IN ONE SUCH DIG, IN AN AUSTRIAN ICE CAVE, THAT WE FOUND WHAT THE ANCIENT ARYANS CALLED A *VIMANA,* BELIEVED TO BE A CHARIOT OF THE GODS.

"BUT WE KNEW WHAT IT *TRULY* WAS--A FLYING MACHINE THAT HAD TRAVELED ACROSS THE STARS FROM ANOTHER WORLD, AGES AGO."

FLYING SAUCERS FROM OUTER SPACE?

PULL THE OTHER ONE.

THERE WERE THOSE IN THE PARTY WHO DOUBTED US AS WELL, THE FOOLS!

THE EVIDENCE WAS RIGHT BEFORE THEIR EYES, HAD THEY ONLY THE MENTAL CAPACITY TO UNDERSTAND.

SADLY, THE ORIGINAL IS NOW IN THE POSSESSION OF THE SOVIETS. THEY WILL FAIL TO COMPREHEND THE TECHNOLOGY BEHIND ITS WORKINGS, OF COURSE.

BUT STILL, IT IS A SHAME THAT SUCH A WORK OF BEAUTY SHOULD BE SOILED BY THEIR GRUBBY HANDS.

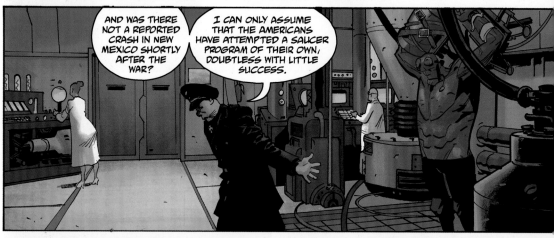

AND WAS THERE NOT A REPORTED CRASH IN NEW MEXICO SHORTLY AFTER THE WAR?

I CAN ONLY ASSUME THAT THE AMERICANS HAVE ATTEMPTED A SAUCER PROGRAM OF THEIR OWN, DOUBTLESS WITH LITTLE SUCCESS.

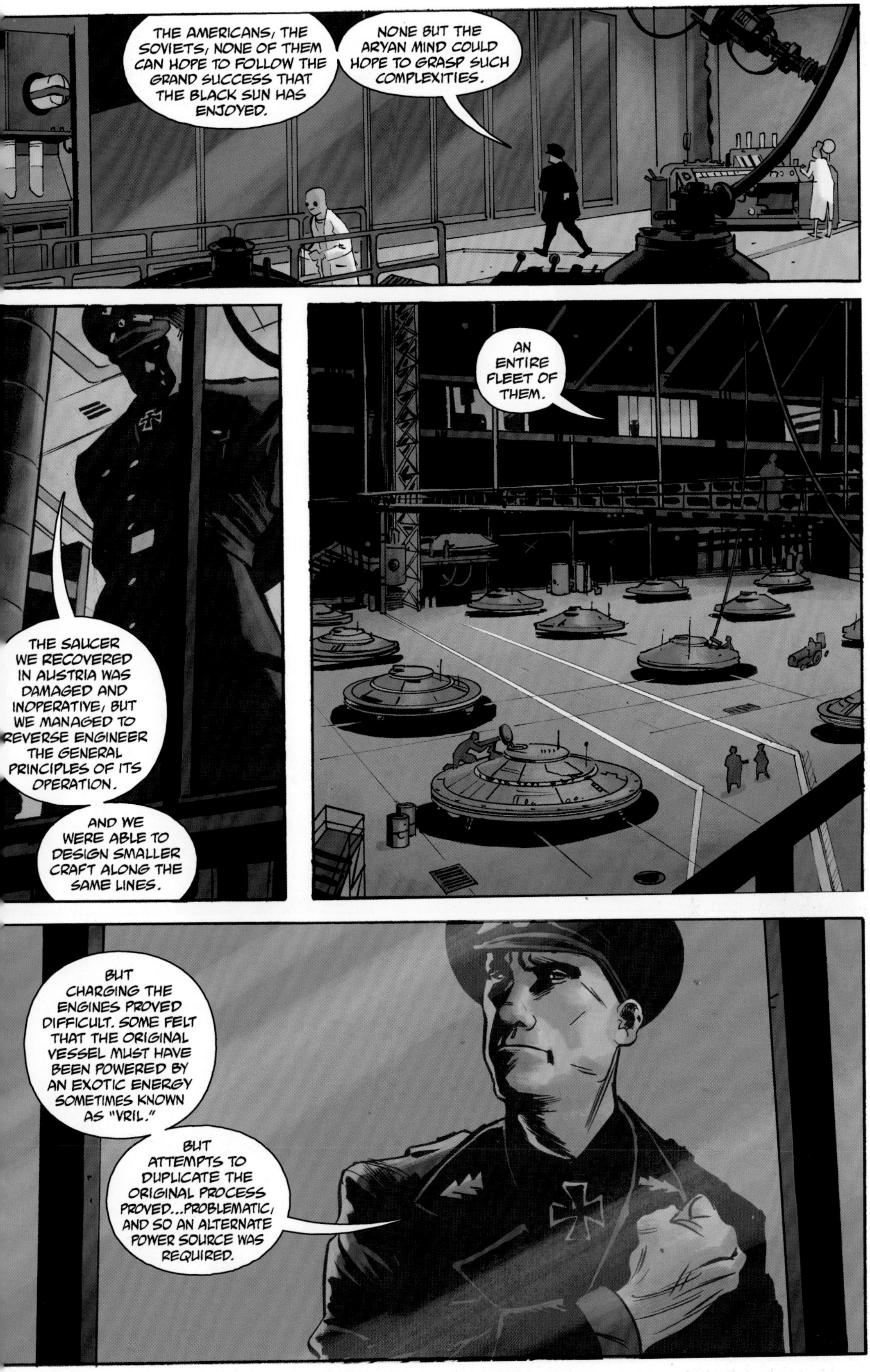
THE AMERICANS, THE SOVIETS, NONE OF THEM CAN HOPE TO FOLLOW THE GRAND SUCCESS THAT THE BLACK SUN HAS ENJOYED.
NONE BUT THE ARYAN MIND COULD HOPE TO GRASP SUCH COMPLEXITIES.
THE SAUCER WE RECOVERED IN AUSTRIA WAS DAMAGED AND INOPERATIVE, BUT WE MANAGED TO REVERSE ENGINEER THE GENERAL PRINCIPLES OF ITS OPERATION.
AND WE WERE ABLE TO DESIGN SMALLER CRAFT ALONG THE SAME LINES.
AN ENTIRE FLEET OF THEM.
BUT CHARGING THE ENGINES PROVED DIFFICULT. SOME FELT THAT THE ORIGINAL VESSEL MUST HAVE BEEN POWERED BY AN EXOTIC ENERGY SOMETIMES KNOWN AS "VRIL."
BUT ATTEMPTS TO DUPLICATE THE ORIGINAL PROCESS PROVED...PROBLEMATIC, AND SO AN ALTERNATE POWER SOURCE WAS REQUIRED.

THANKFULLY, THE SOLUTION WAS BEFORE US THE ENTIRE TIME, HIDDEN IN PLAIN SIGHT ON ANCIENT STONE TABLETS UNEARTHED IN THE NEAR EAST BY GERMAN ARCHAEOLOGISTS.

THESE TABLETS SPOKE OF ANOTHER FORM OF ENERGY, ALMOST THE COUNTER-POINT TO VRIL, A BLACK FLAME CALLED "SHAKTI," HIDDEN DEEP WITHIN ALL LIVING THINGS.

"THE ANCIENTS POSSESSED A MEANS BY WHICH SHAKTI COULD BE HARVESTED. BUT THE AMOUNT WHICH COULD BE DRAWN FROM ANY SINGLE BEING WOULD BE MINUSCULE."

THANKFULLY, OUR SCIENTISTS HAD ACCESS TO AN AMPLE NUMBER OF LIVING BEINGS THAT COULD BE USED FOR THIS PURPOSE.

AND PROFESSOR BÖRNER HIMSELF DEVISED A METHOD OF STORING THE EXTRACTED SHAKTI FOR LATER USE.

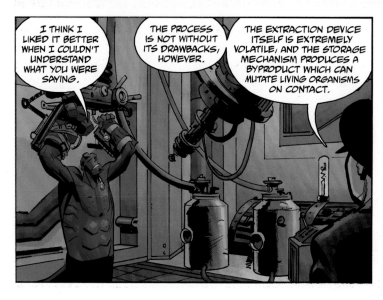

I THINK I LIKED IT BETTER WHEN I COULDN'T UNDERSTAND WHAT YOU WERE SAYING.

THE PROCESS IS NOT WITHOUT ITS DRAWBACKS, HOWEVER.

THE EXTRACTION DEVICE ITSELF IS EXTREMELY VOLATILE, AND THE STORAGE MECHANISM PRODUCES A BYPRODUCT WHICH CAN MUTATE LIVING ORGANISMS ON CONTACT.

"THERE WERE... SETBACKS."

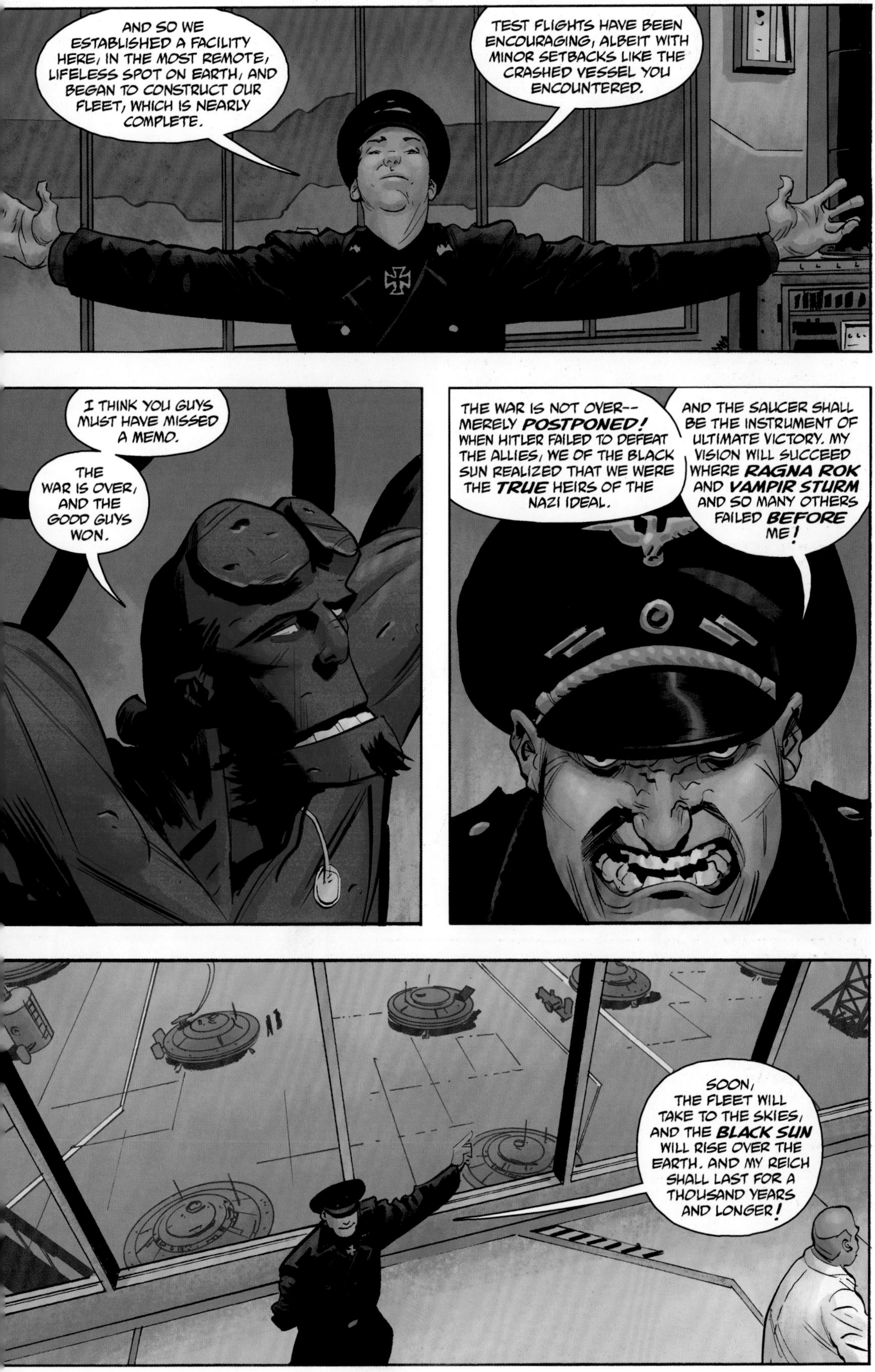
AND SO WE ESTABLISHED A FACILITY HERE, IN THE MOST REMOTE, LIFELESS SPOT ON EARTH, AND BEGAN TO CONSTRUCT OUR FLEET, WHICH IS NEARLY COMPLETE.
TEST FLIGHTS HAVE BEEN ENCOURAGING, ALBEIT WITH MINOR SETBACKS LIKE THE CRASHED VESSEL YOU ENCOUNTERED.
I THINK YOU GUYS MUST HAVE MISSED A MEMO.
THE WAR IS OVER, AND THE GOOD GUYS WON.
THE WAR IS NOT OVER--MERELY POSTPONED! WHEN HITLER FAILED TO DEFEAT THE ALLIES, WE OF THE BLACK SUN REALIZED THAT WE WERE THE TRUE HEIRS OF THE NAZI IDEAL.
AND THE SAUCER SHALL BE THE INSTRUMENT OF ULTIMATE VICTORY. MY VISION WILL SUCCEED WHERE RAGNA ROK AND VAMPIR STURM AND SO MANY OTHERS FAILED BEFORE ME!
SOON, THE FLEET WILL TAKE TO THE SKIES, AND THE BLACK SUN WILL RISE OVER THE EARTH. AND MY REICH SHALL LAST FOR A THOUSAND YEARS AND LONGER!

⟨EVERYTHING IS CHECKED AND READY, GRUPPENFÜHRER. WE NEED ONLY POSITION THE EXTRACTOR.⟩

⟨THANK YOU, HERR DOKTOR, YOU MAY PROCEED.⟩

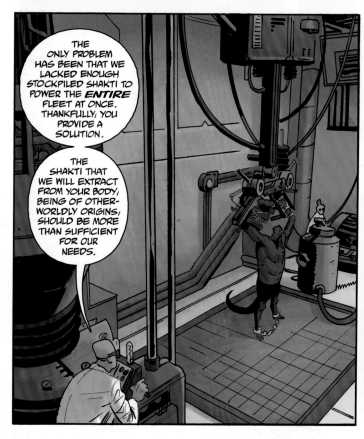

THE ONLY PROBLEM HAS BEEN THAT WE LACKED ENOUGH STOCKPILED SHAKTI TO POWER THE *ENTIRE* FLEET AT ONCE. THANKFULLY, YOU PROVIDE A SOLUTION.

THE SHAKTI THAT WE WILL EXTRACT FROM YOUR BODY, BEING OF OTHER-WORLDLY ORIGINS, SHOULD BE MORE THAN SUFFICIENT FOR OUR NEEDS.

⟨THE EXTRACTOR IS READY.⟩

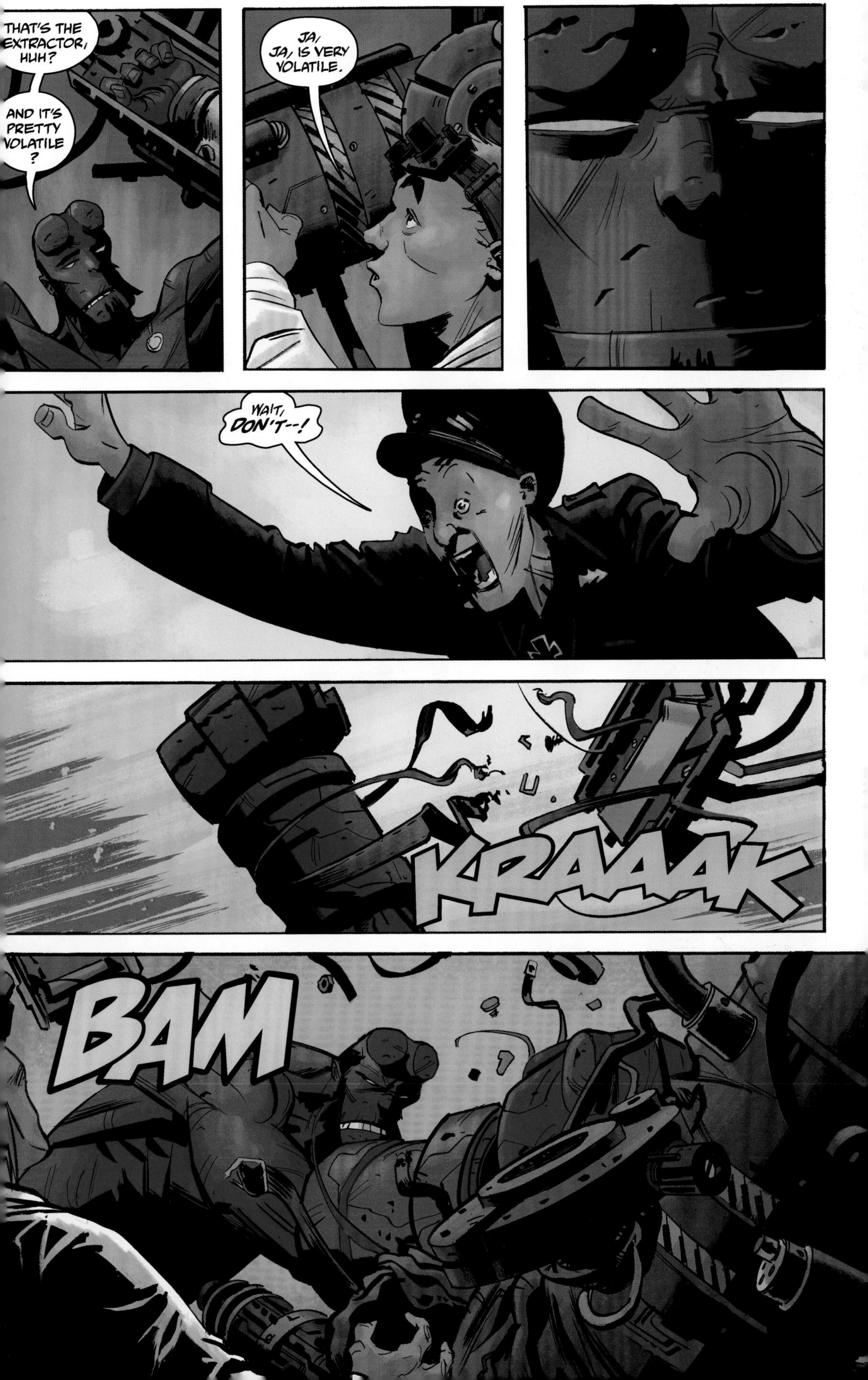
THAT'S THE EXTRACTOR, HUH?
AND IT'S PRETTY VOLATILE ?
JA, JA, IS VERY VOLATILE.
WAIT, DON'T--!
KRAAAK
BAM

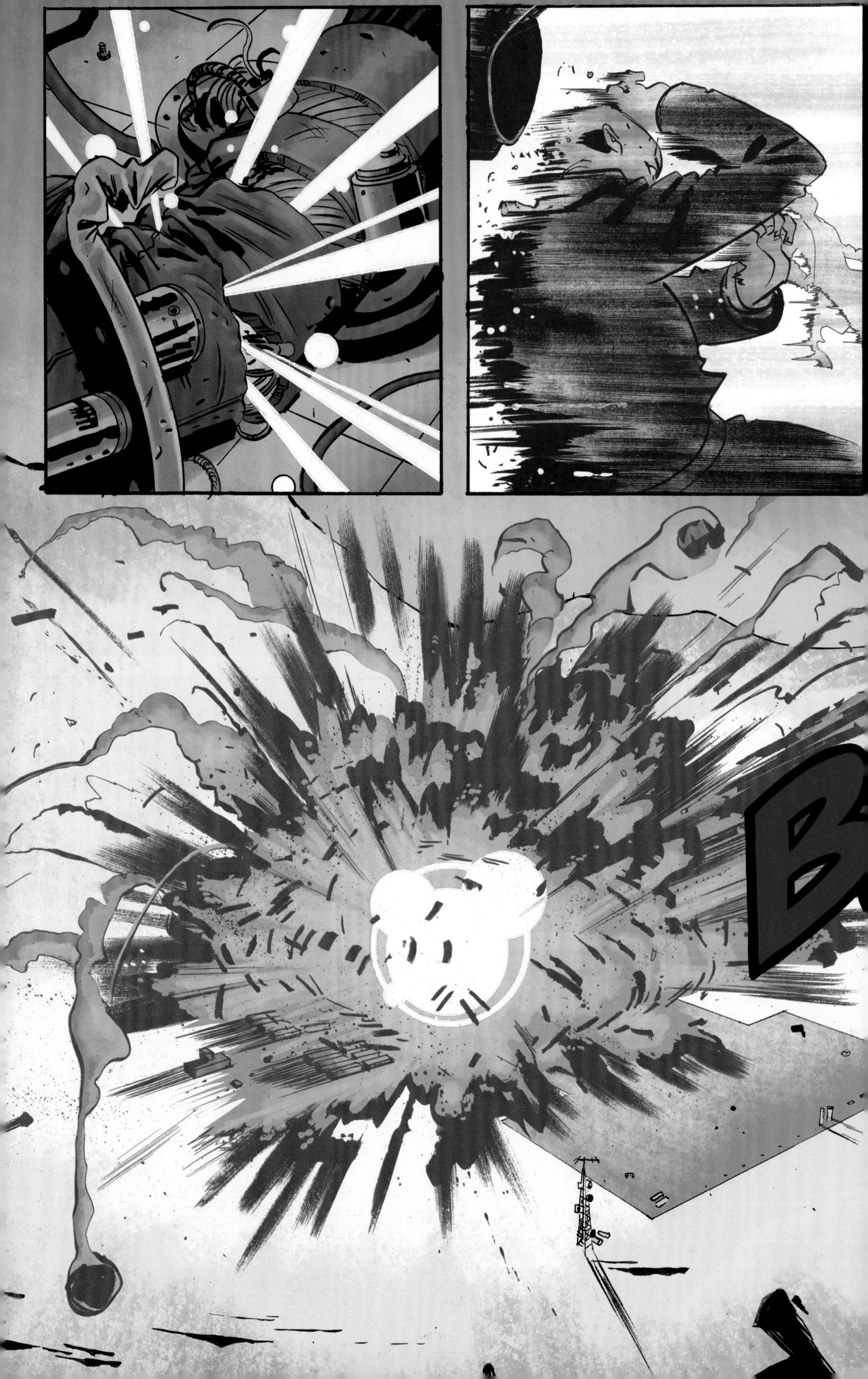
B

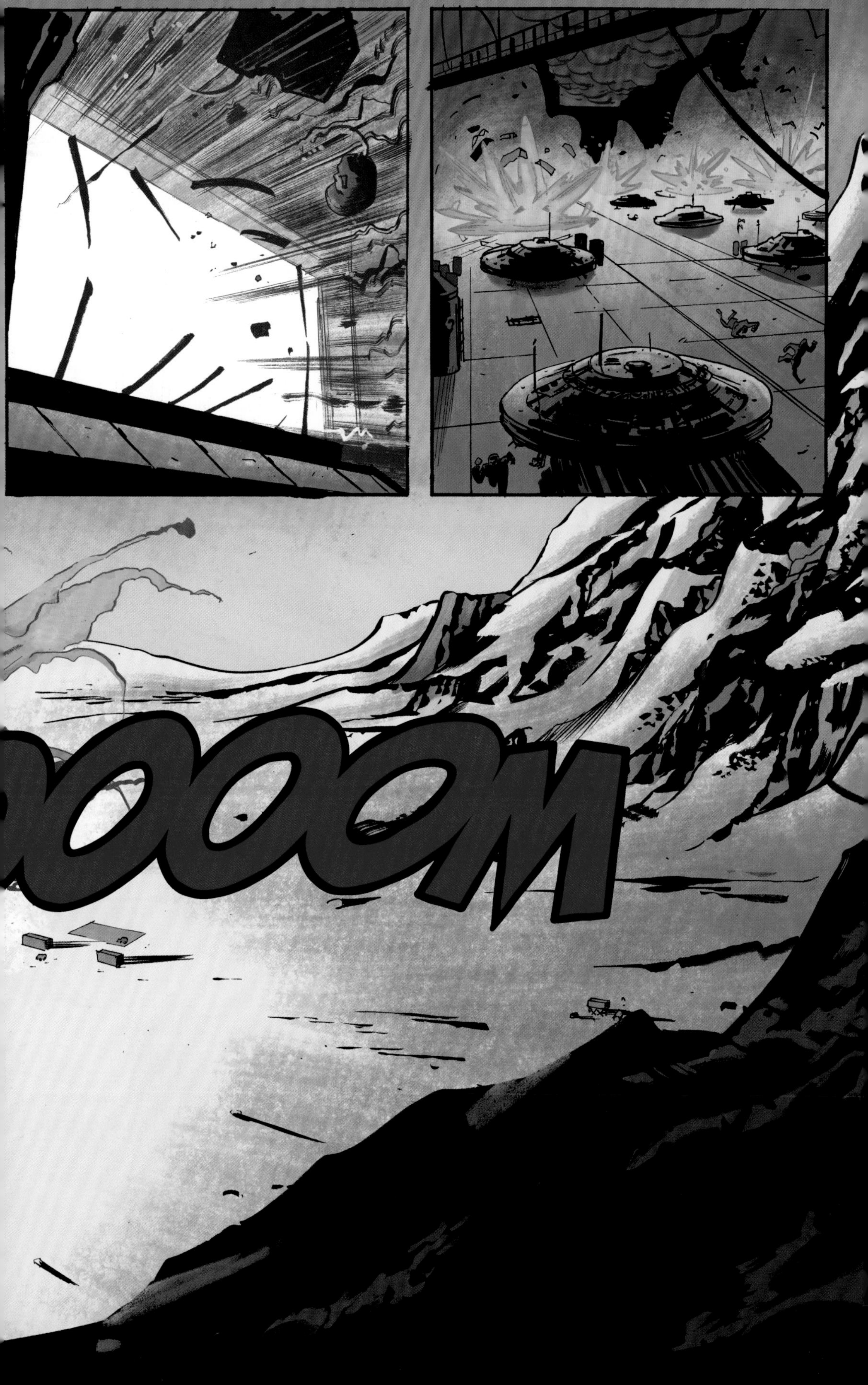
OOOM

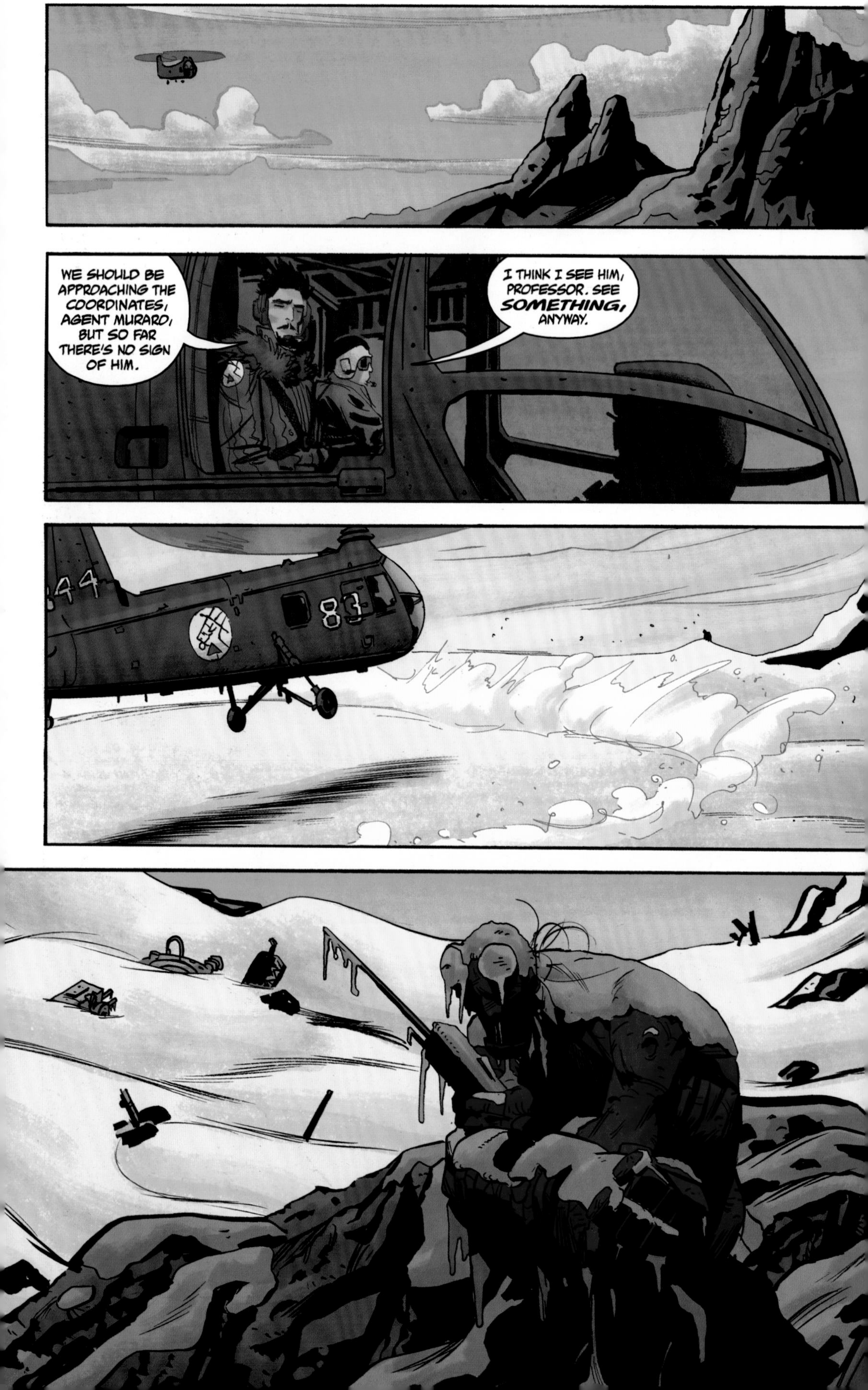
WE SHOULD BE APPROACHING THE COORDINATES, AGENT MURARO, BUT SO FAR THERE'S NO SIGN OF HIM.
I THINK I SEE HIM, PROFESSOR. SEE SOMETHING, ANYWAY.

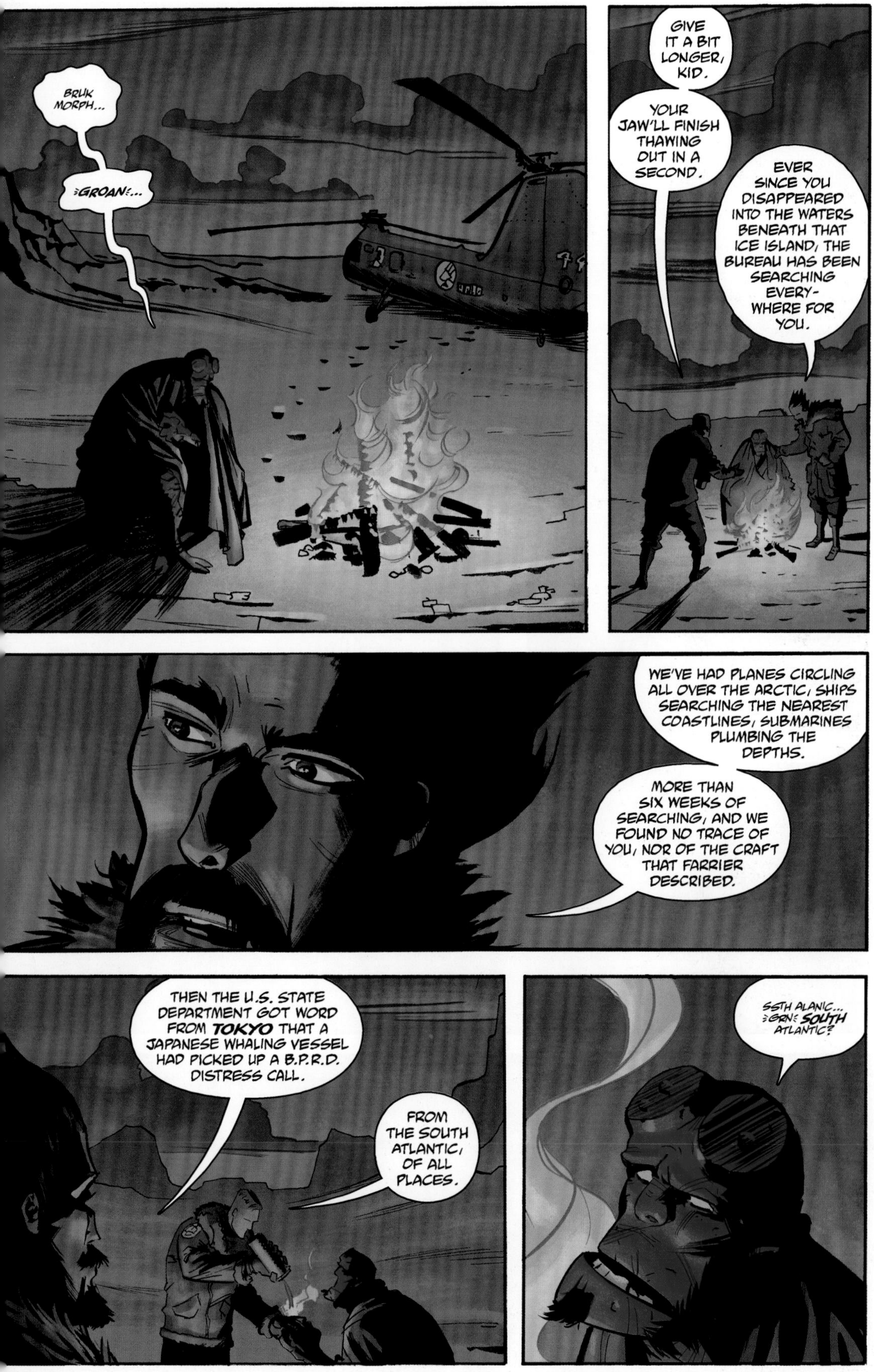
BRUK MORPH...
GROAN...
GIVE IT A BIT LONGER, KID.
YOUR JAW'LL FINISH THAWING OUT IN A SECOND.
EVER SINCE YOU DISAPPEARED INTO THE WATERS BENEATH THAT ICE ISLAND, THE BUREAU HAS BEEN SEARCHING EVERY-WHERE FOR YOU.
WE'VE HAD PLANES CIRCLING ALL OVER THE ARCTIC, SHIPS SEARCHING THE NEAREST COASTLINES, SUBMARINES PLUMBING THE DEPTHS.
MORE THAN SIX WEEKS OF SEARCHING, AND WE FOUND NO TRACE OF YOU, NOR OF THE CRAFT THAT FARRIER DESCRIBED.
THEN THE U.S. STATE DEPARTMENT GOT WORD FROM TOKYO THAT A JAPANESE WHALING VESSEL HAD PICKED UP A B.P.R.D. DISTRESS CALL.
FROM THE SOUTH ATLANTIC, OF ALL PLACES.
SSTH ALANIC... GRN SOUTH ATLANTIC?

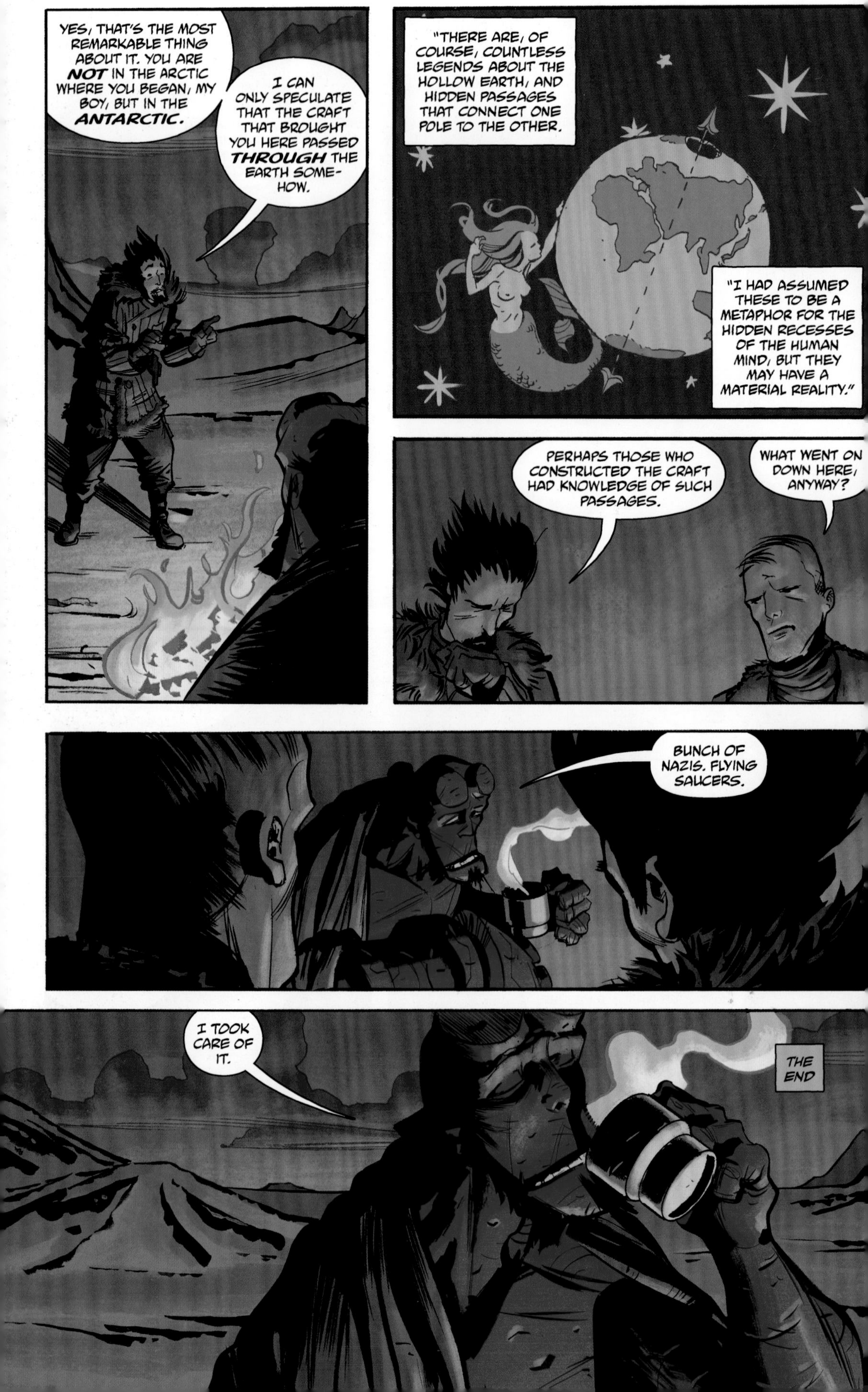

YES, THAT'S THE MOST REMARKABLE THING ABOUT IT. YOU ARE **NOT** IN THE ARCTIC WHERE YOU BEGAN, MY BOY, BUT IN THE **ANTARCTIC.**
I CAN ONLY SPECULATE THAT THE CRAFT THAT BROUGHT YOU HERE PASSED **THROUGH** THE EARTH SOME-HOW.
"THERE ARE, OF COURSE, COUNTLESS LEGENDS ABOUT THE HOLLOW EARTH, AND HIDDEN PASSAGES THAT CONNECT ONE POLE TO THE OTHER.
"I HAD ASSUMED THESE TO BE A METAPHOR FOR THE HIDDEN RECESSES OF THE HUMAN MIND, BUT THEY MAY HAVE A MATERIAL REALITY."
PERHAPS THOSE WHO CONSTRUCTED THE CRAFT HAD KNOWLEDGE OF SUCH PASSAGES.
WHAT WENT ON DOWN HERE, ANYWAY?
BUNCH OF NAZIS. FLYING SAUCERS.
I TOOK CARE OF IT.
THE END

THE UNREASONING BEAST

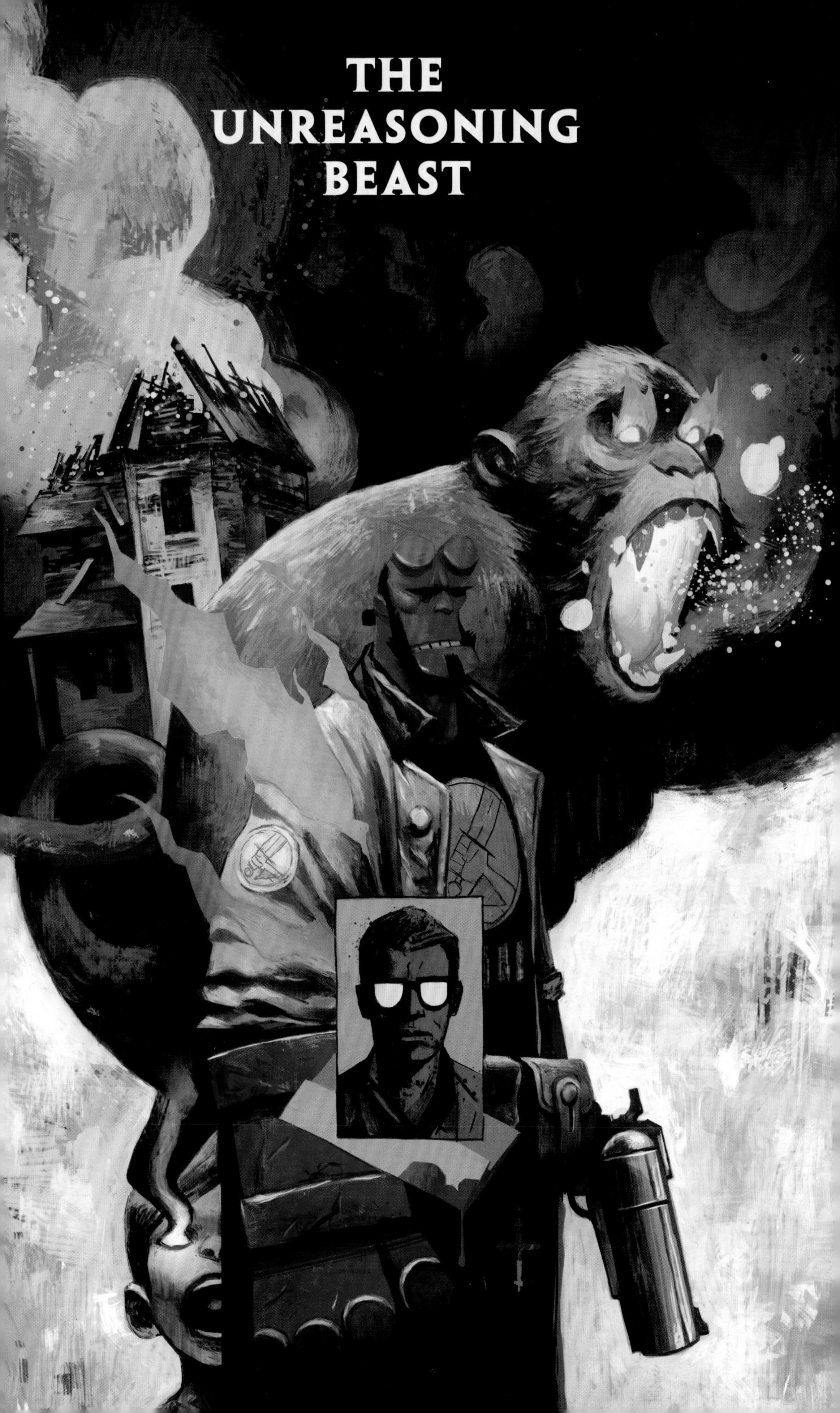

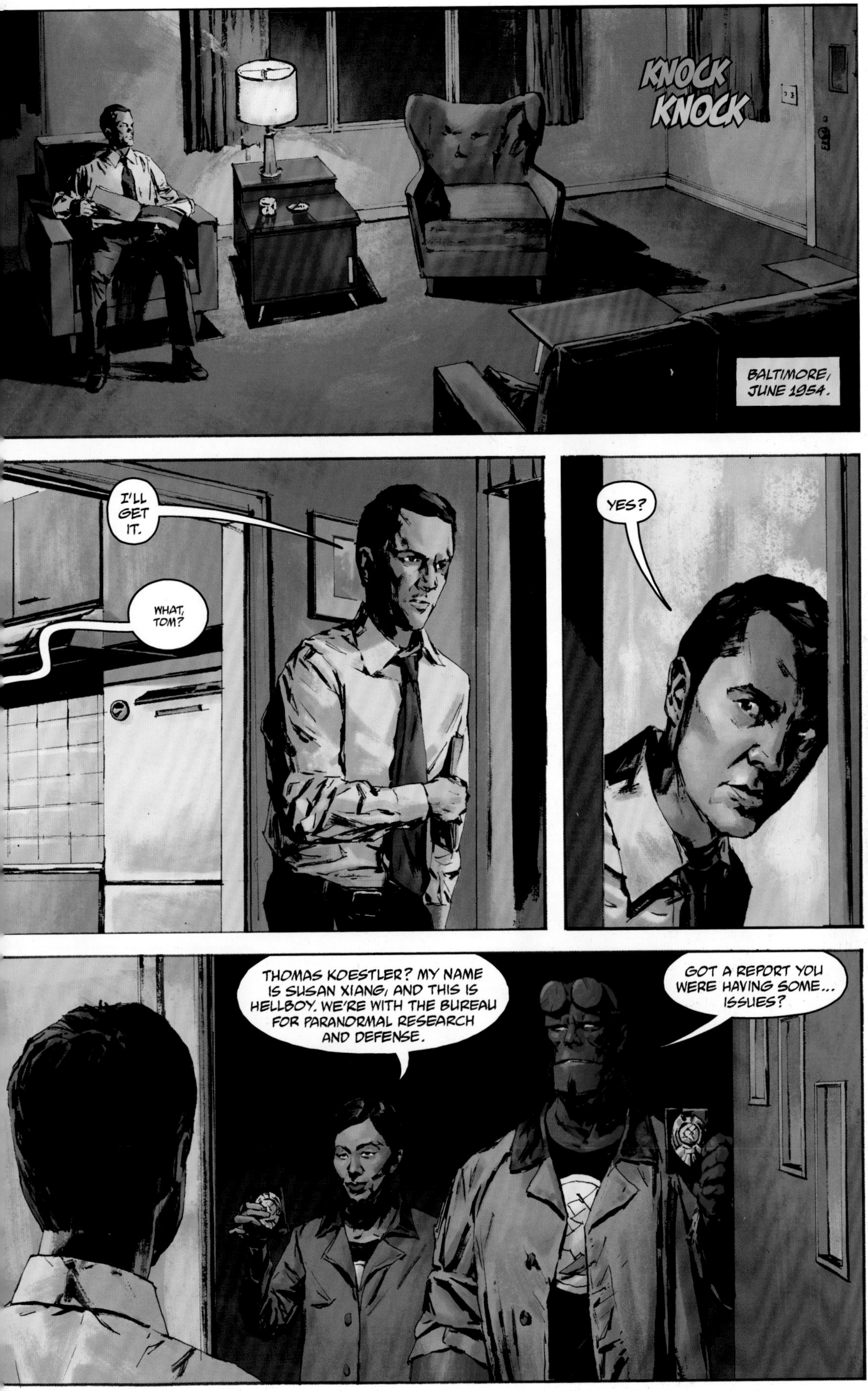
KNOCK KNOCK
BALTIMORE, JUNE 1954.
I'LL GET IT.
WHAT, TOM?
YES?
THOMAS KOESTLER? MY NAME IS SUSAN XIANG, AND THIS IS HELLBOY. WE'RE WITH THE BUREAU FOR PARANORMAL RESEARCH AND DEFENSE.
GOT A REPORT YOU WERE HAVING SOME... ISSUES?

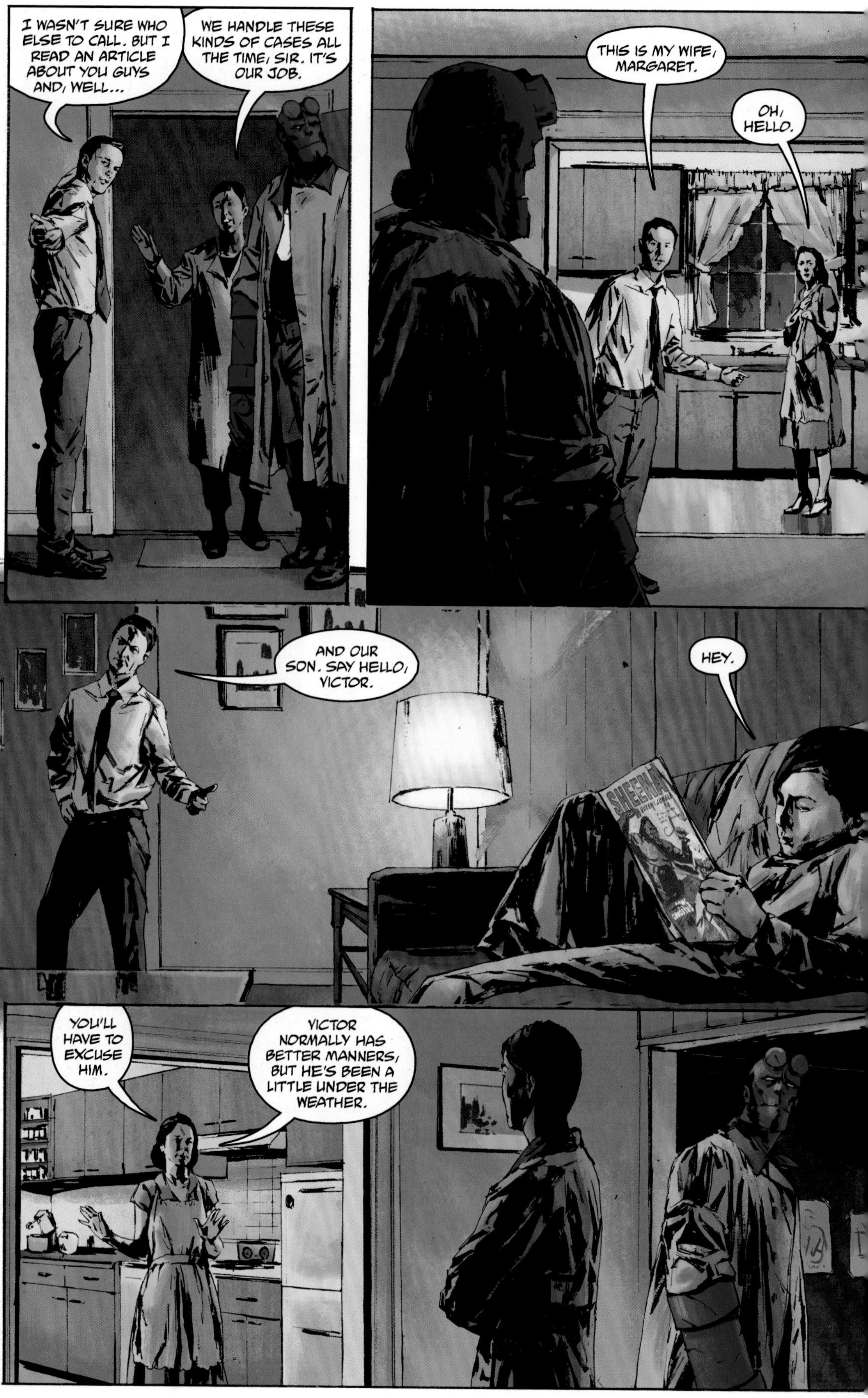
I WASN'T SURE WHO ELSE TO CALL. BUT I READ AN ARTICLE ABOUT YOU GUYS AND, WELL...
WE HANDLE THESE KINDS OF CASES ALL THE TIME, SIR. IT'S OUR JOB.
THIS IS MY WIFE, MARGARET.
OH, HELLO.
AND OUR SON. SAY HELLO, VICTOR.
HEY.
YOU'LL HAVE TO EXCUSE HIM.
VICTOR NORMALLY HAS BETTER MANNERS, BUT HE'S BEEN A LITTLE UNDER THE WEATHER.

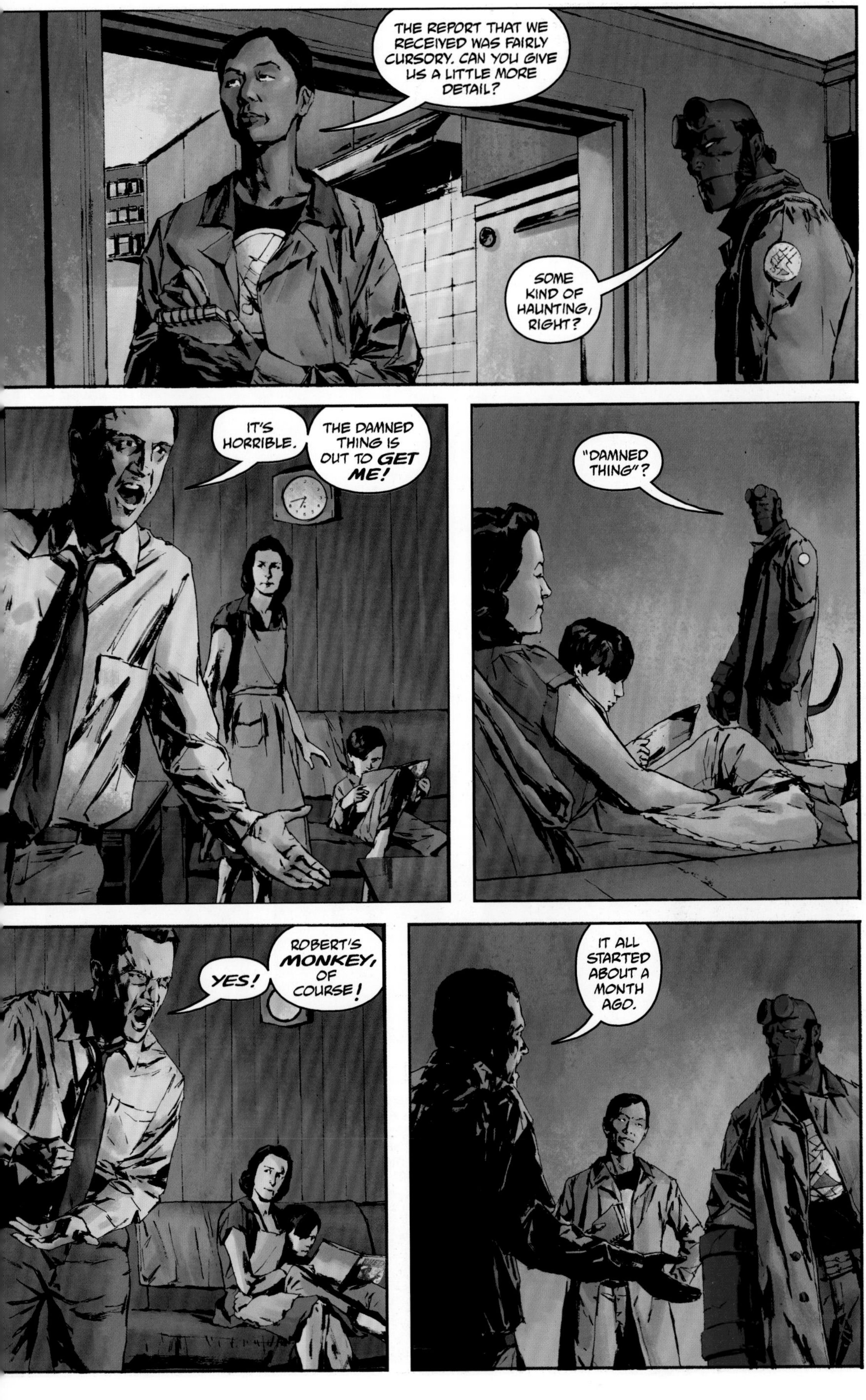
THE REPORT THAT WE RECEIVED WAS FAIRLY CURSORY. CAN YOU GIVE US A LITTLE MORE DETAIL?
SOME KIND OF HAUNTING, RIGHT?
IT'S HORRIBLE.
THE DAMNED THING IS OUT TO GET ME!
"DAMNED THING"?
YES!
ROBERT'S MONKEY, OF COURSE!
IT ALL STARTED ABOUT A MONTH AGO.

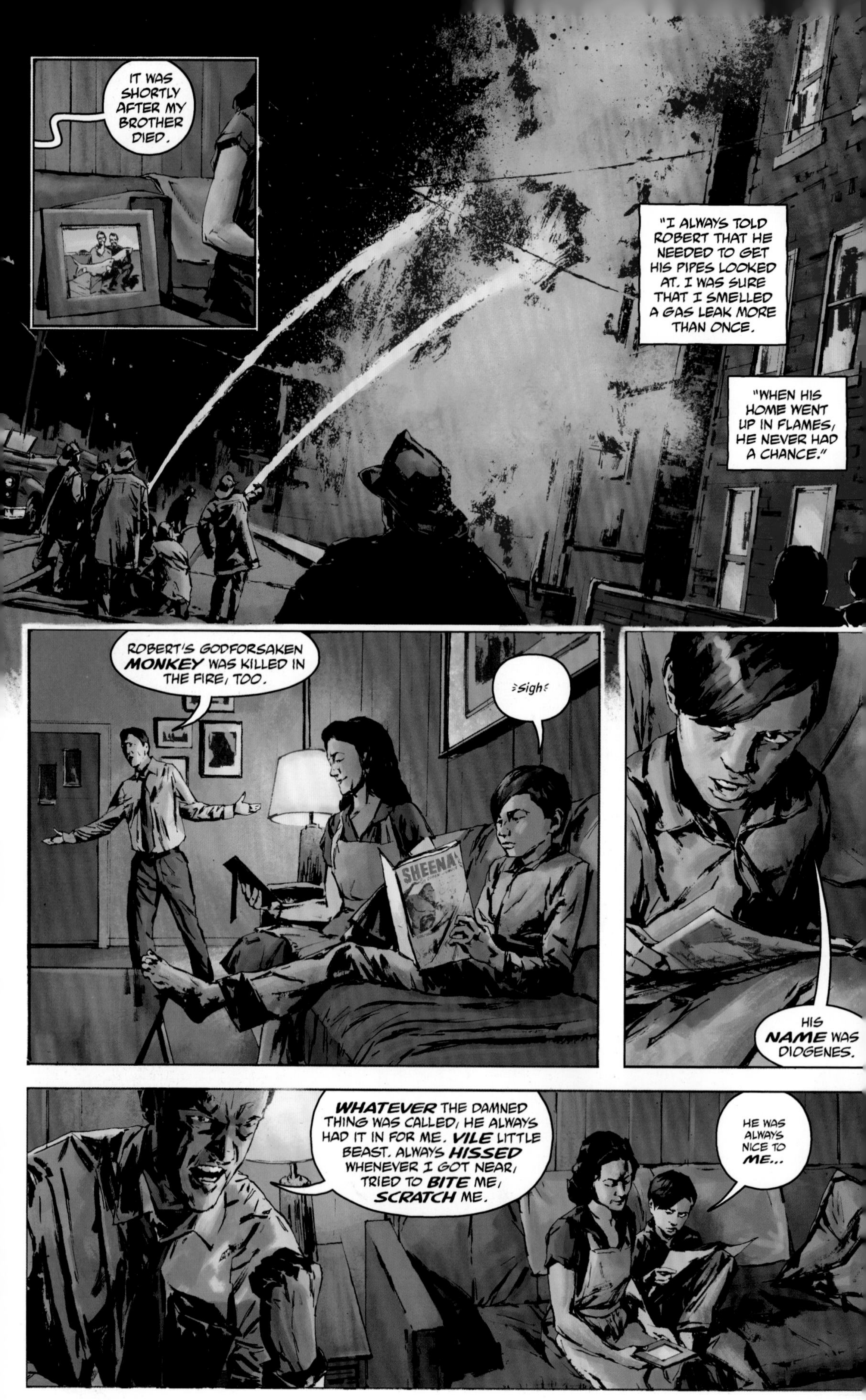
IT WAS SHORTLY AFTER MY BROTHER DIED.
"I ALWAYS TOLD ROBERT THAT HE NEEDED TO GET HIS PIPES LOOKED AT. I WAS SURE THAT I SMELLED A GAS LEAK MORE THAN ONCE.
"WHEN HIS HOME WENT UP IN FLAMES, HE NEVER HAD A CHANCE."
ROBERT'S GODFORSAKEN **MONKEY** WAS KILLED IN THE FIRE, TOO.
Sigh
SHEENA
HIS **NAME** WAS DIOGENES.
WHATEVER THE DAMNED THING WAS CALLED, HE ALWAYS HAD IT IN FOR ME. ***VILE*** LITTLE BEAST. ALWAYS ***HISSED*** WHENEVER I GOT NEAR, TRIED TO ***BITE*** ME, ***SCRATCH*** ME.
HE WAS ALWAYS NICE TO ***ME...***

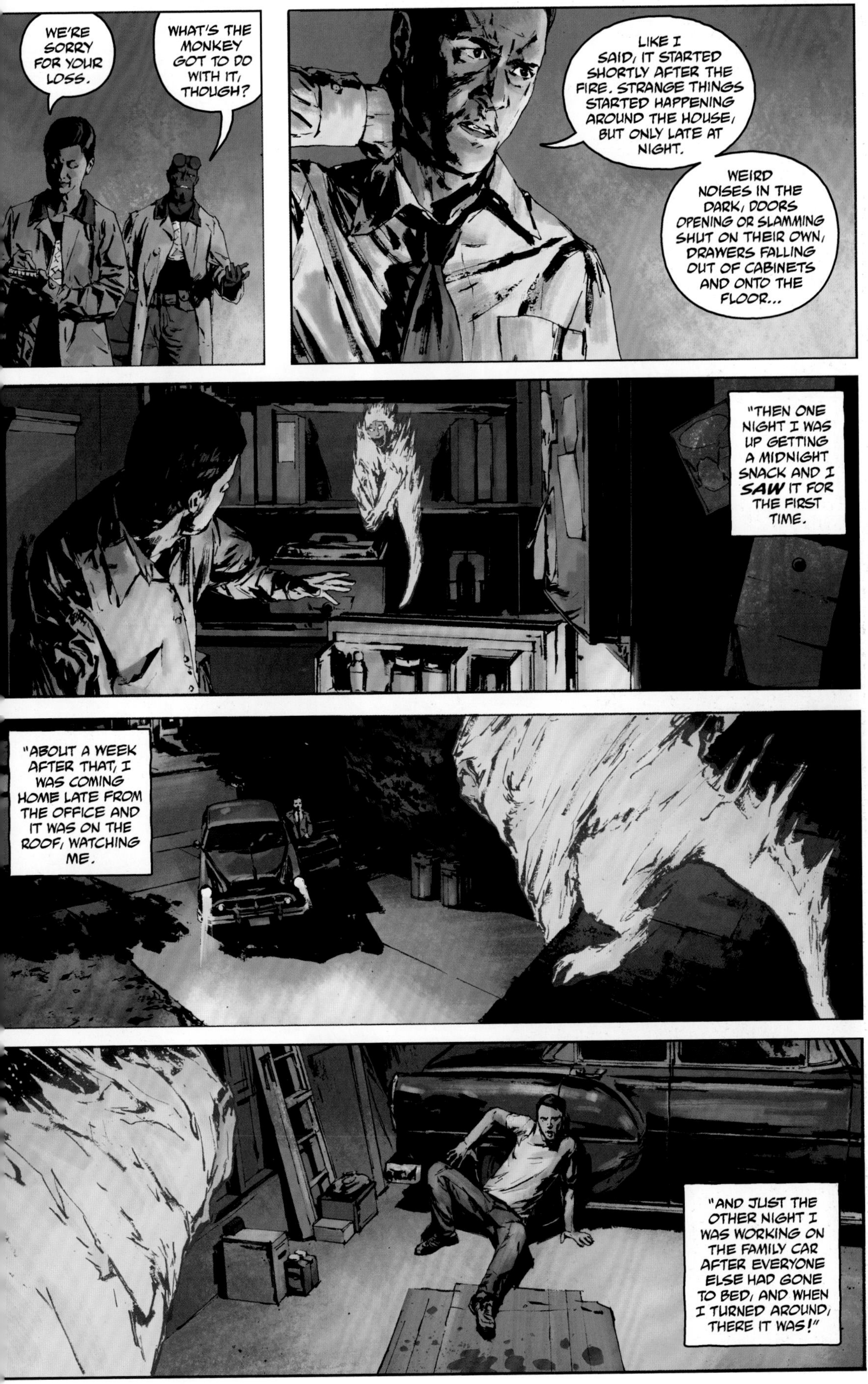
WE'RE SORRY FOR YOUR LOSS.
WHAT'S THE MONKEY GOT TO DO WITH IT, THOUGH?
LIKE I SAID, IT STARTED SHORTLY AFTER THE FIRE. STRANGE THINGS STARTED HAPPENING AROUND THE HOUSE, BUT ONLY LATE AT NIGHT.
WEIRD NOISES IN THE DARK, DOORS OPENING OR SLAMMING SHUT ON THEIR OWN, DRAWERS FALLING OUT OF CABINETS AND ONTO THE FLOOR...
"THEN ONE NIGHT I WAS UP GETTING A MIDNIGHT SNACK AND I **SAW** IT FOR THE FIRST TIME.
"ABOUT A WEEK AFTER THAT, I WAS COMING HOME LATE FROM THE OFFICE AND IT WAS ON THE ROOF, WATCHING ME.
"AND JUST THE OTHER NIGHT I WAS WORKING ON THE FAMILY CAR AFTER EVERYONE ELSE HAD GONE TO BED, AND WHEN I TURNED AROUND, THERE IT WAS!"

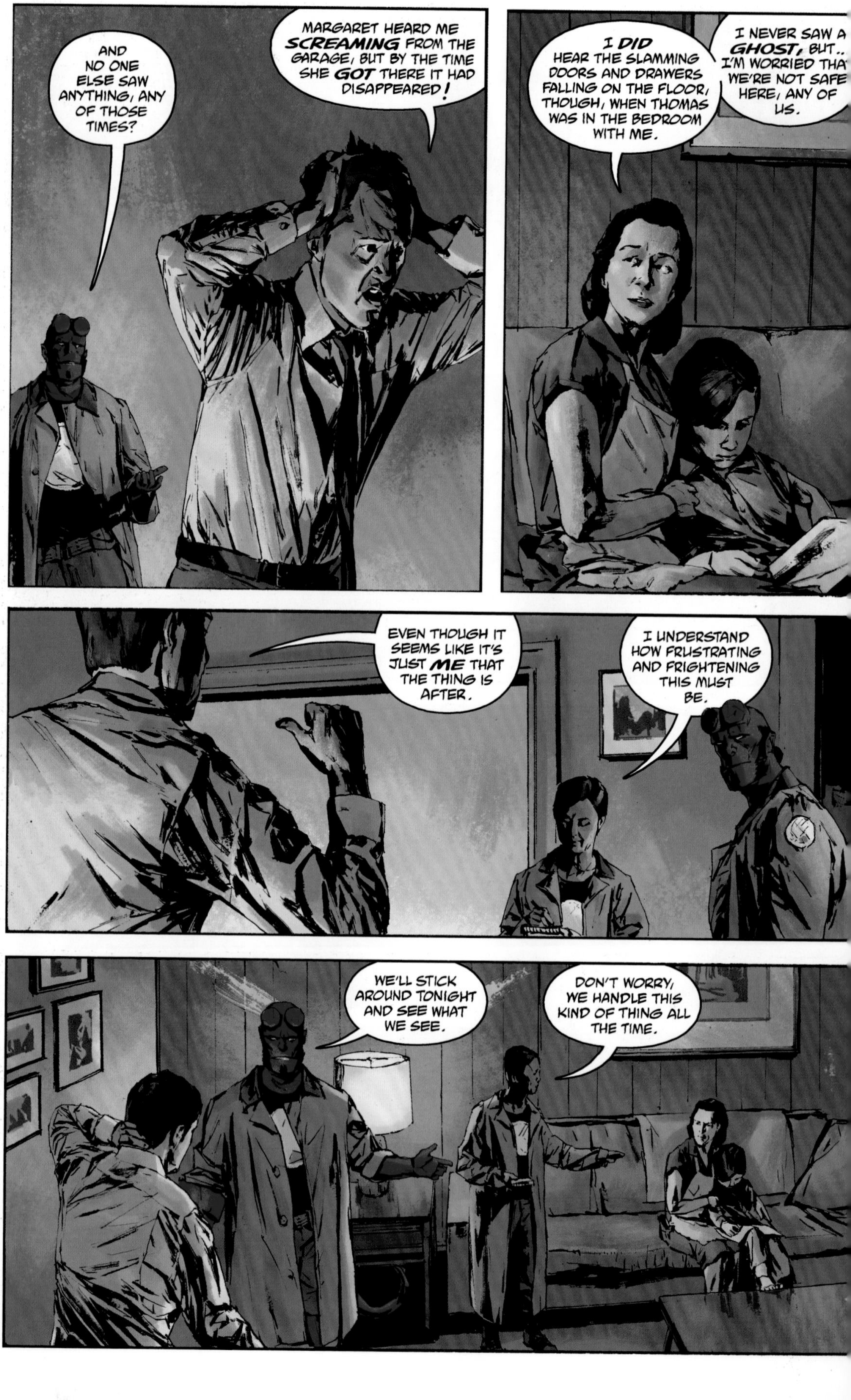
AND NO ONE ELSE SAW ANYTHING, ANY OF THOSE TIMES?
MARGARET HEARD ME SCREAMING FROM THE GARAGE, BUT BY THE TIME SHE GOT THERE IT HAD DISAPPEARED!
I DID HEAR THE SLAMMING DOORS AND DRAWERS FALLING ON THE FLOOR, THOUGH, WHEN THOMAS WAS IN THE BEDROOM WITH ME.
I NEVER SAW A GHOST, BUT.. I'M WORRIED THA WE'RE NOT SAFE HERE, ANY OF US.
EVEN THOUGH IT SEEMS LIKE IT'S JUST ME THAT THE THING IS AFTER.
I UNDERSTAND HOW FRUSTRATING AND FRIGHTENING THIS MUST BE.
WE'LL STICK AROUND TONIGHT AND SEE WHAT WE SEE.
DON'T WORRY, WE HANDLE THIS KIND OF THING ALL THE TIME.

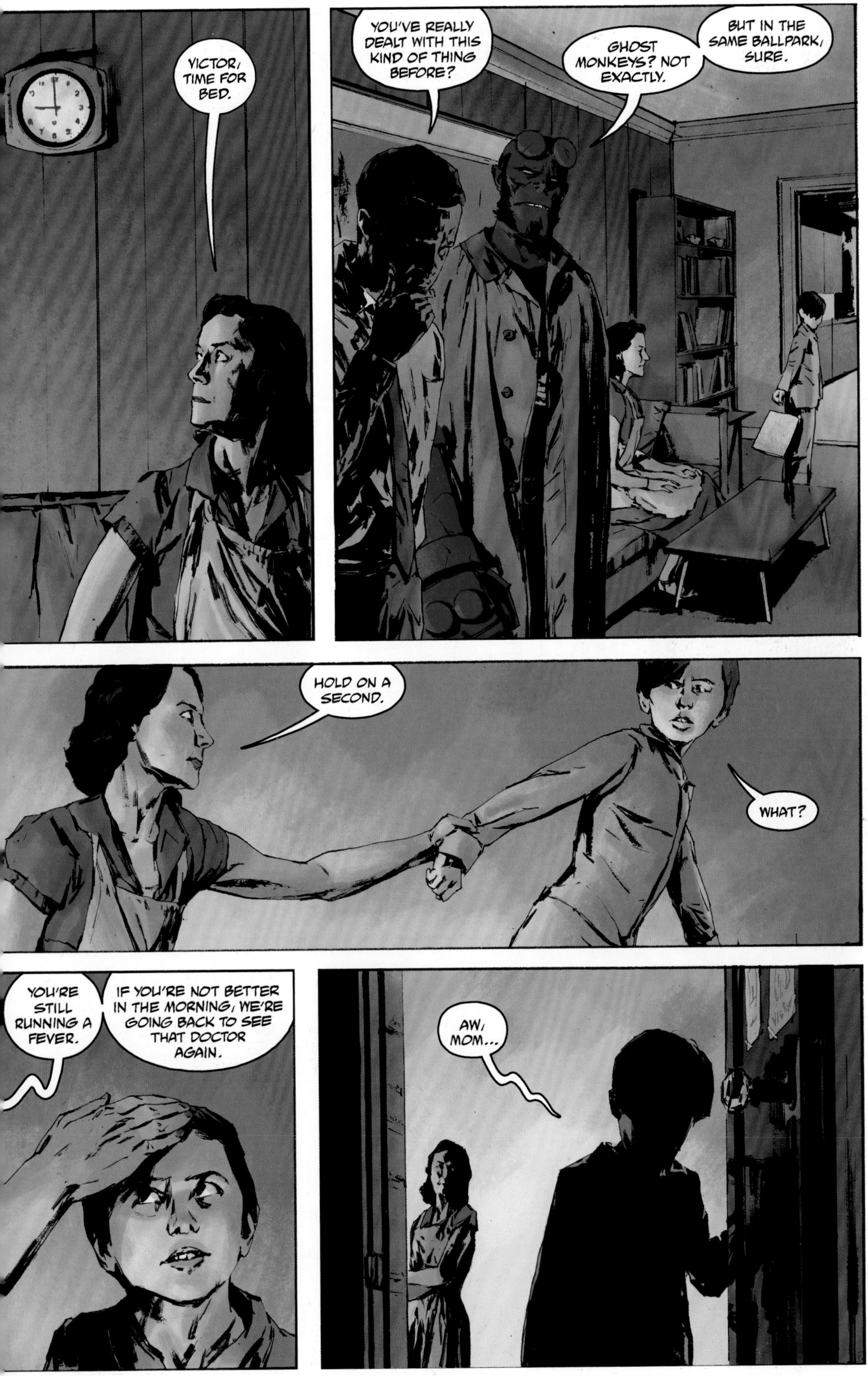
VICTOR, TIME FOR BED.
YOU'VE REALLY DEALT WITH THIS KIND OF THING BEFORE?
GHOST MONKEYS? NOT EXACTLY.
BUT IN THE SAME BALLPARK, SURE.
HOLD ON A SECOND.
WHAT?
YOU'RE STILL RUNNING A FEVER.
IF YOU'RE NOT BETTER IN THE MORNING, WE'RE GOING BACK TO SEE THAT DOCTOR AGAIN.
AW, MOM...

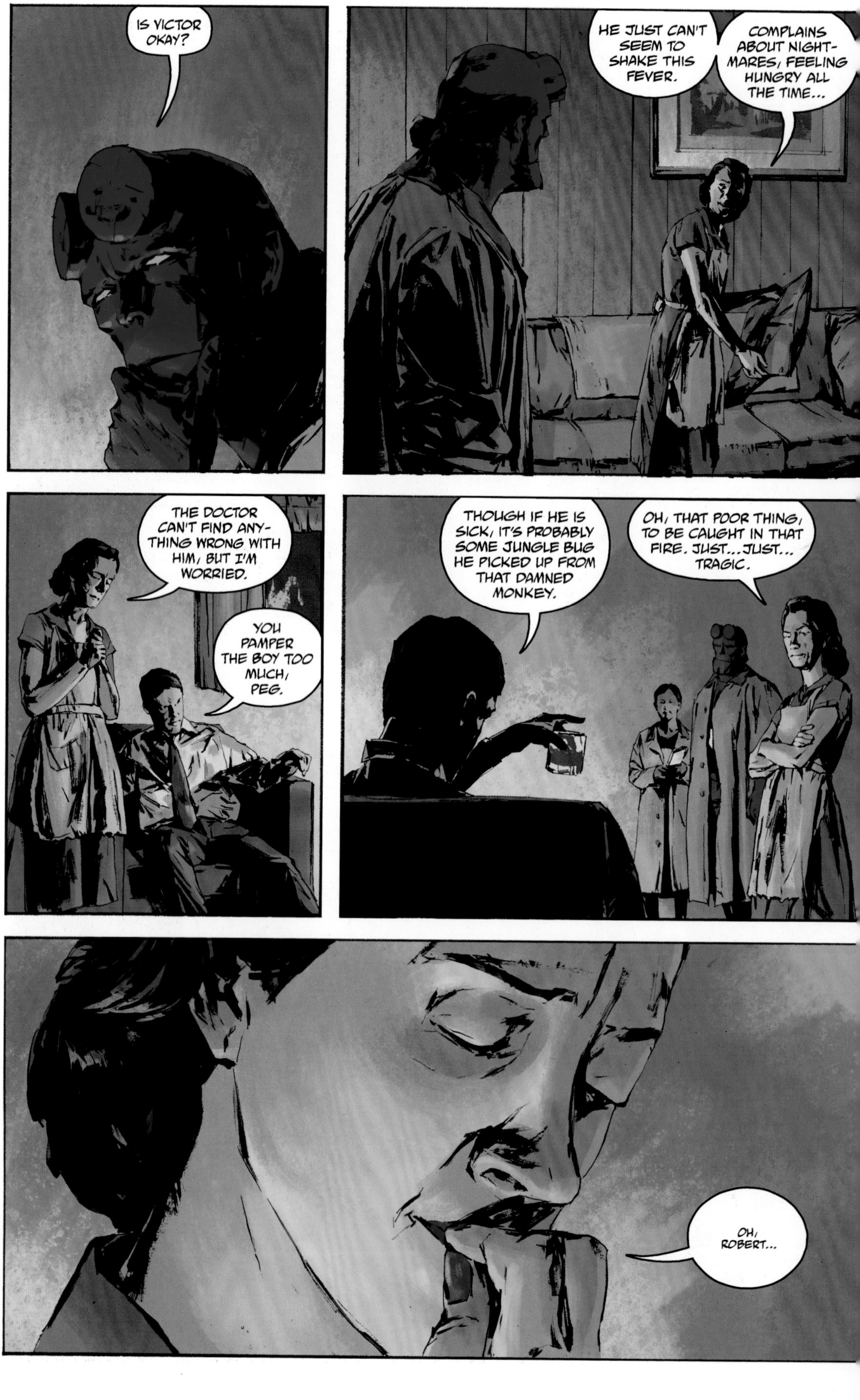
IS VICTOR OKAY?
HE JUST CAN'T SEEM TO SHAKE THIS FEVER.
COMPLAINS ABOUT NIGHT-MARES, FEELING HUNGRY ALL THE TIME...
THE DOCTOR CAN'T FIND ANY-THING WRONG WITH HIM, BUT I'M WORRIED.
YOU PAMPER THE BOY TOO MUCH, PEG.
THOUGH IF HE IS SICK, IT'S PROBABLY SOME JUNGLE BUG HE PICKED UP FROM THAT DAMNED MONKEY.
OH, THAT POOR THING, TO BE CAUGHT IN THAT FIRE. JUST... JUST... TRAGIC.
OH, ROBERT...

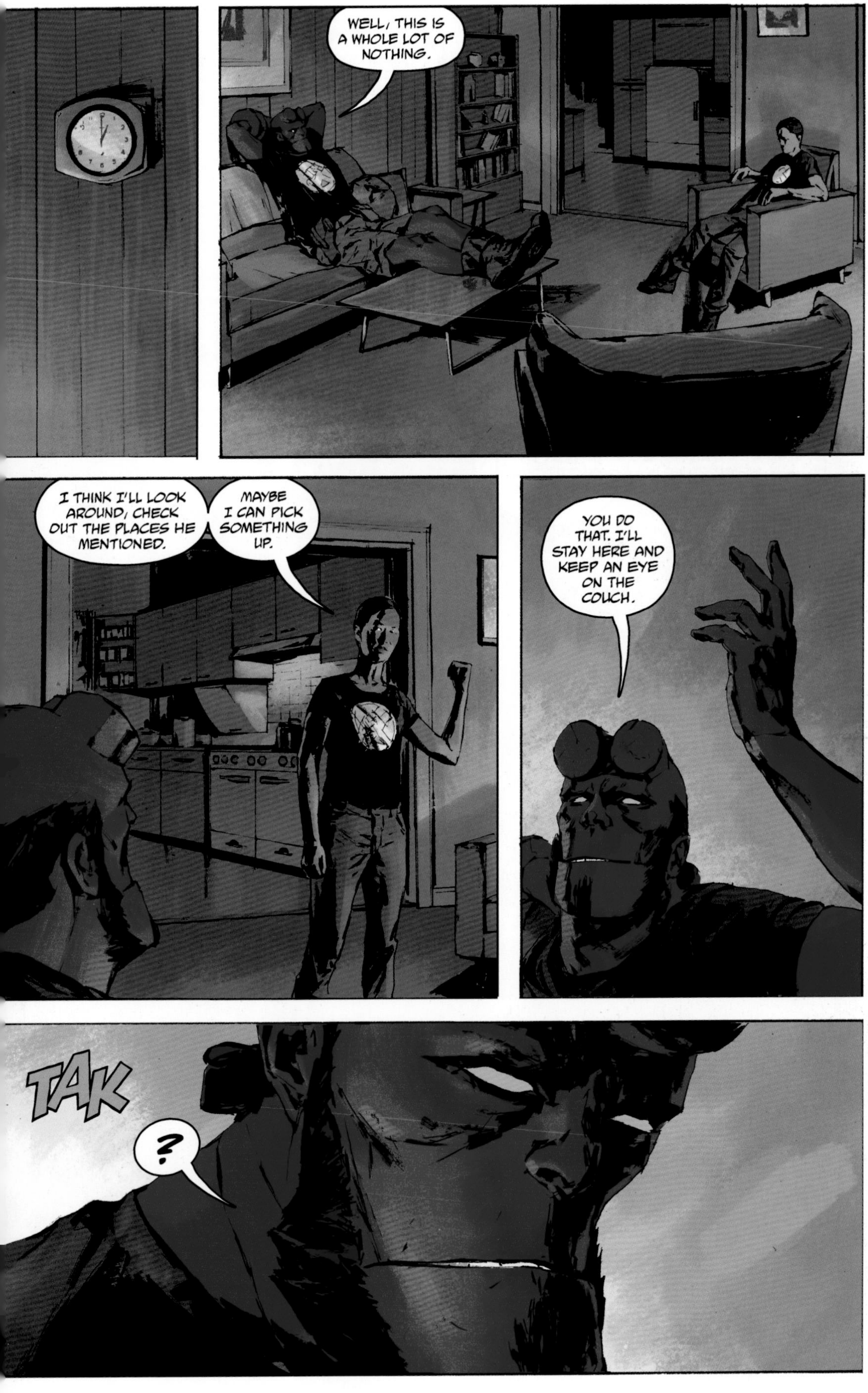

WELL, THIS IS A WHOLE LOT OF NOTHING.
I THINK I'LL LOOK AROUND, CHECK OUT THE PLACES HE MENTIONED.
MAYBE I CAN PICK SOMETHING UP.
YOU DO THAT. I'LL STAY HERE AND KEEP AN EYE ON THE COUCH.
TAK
?

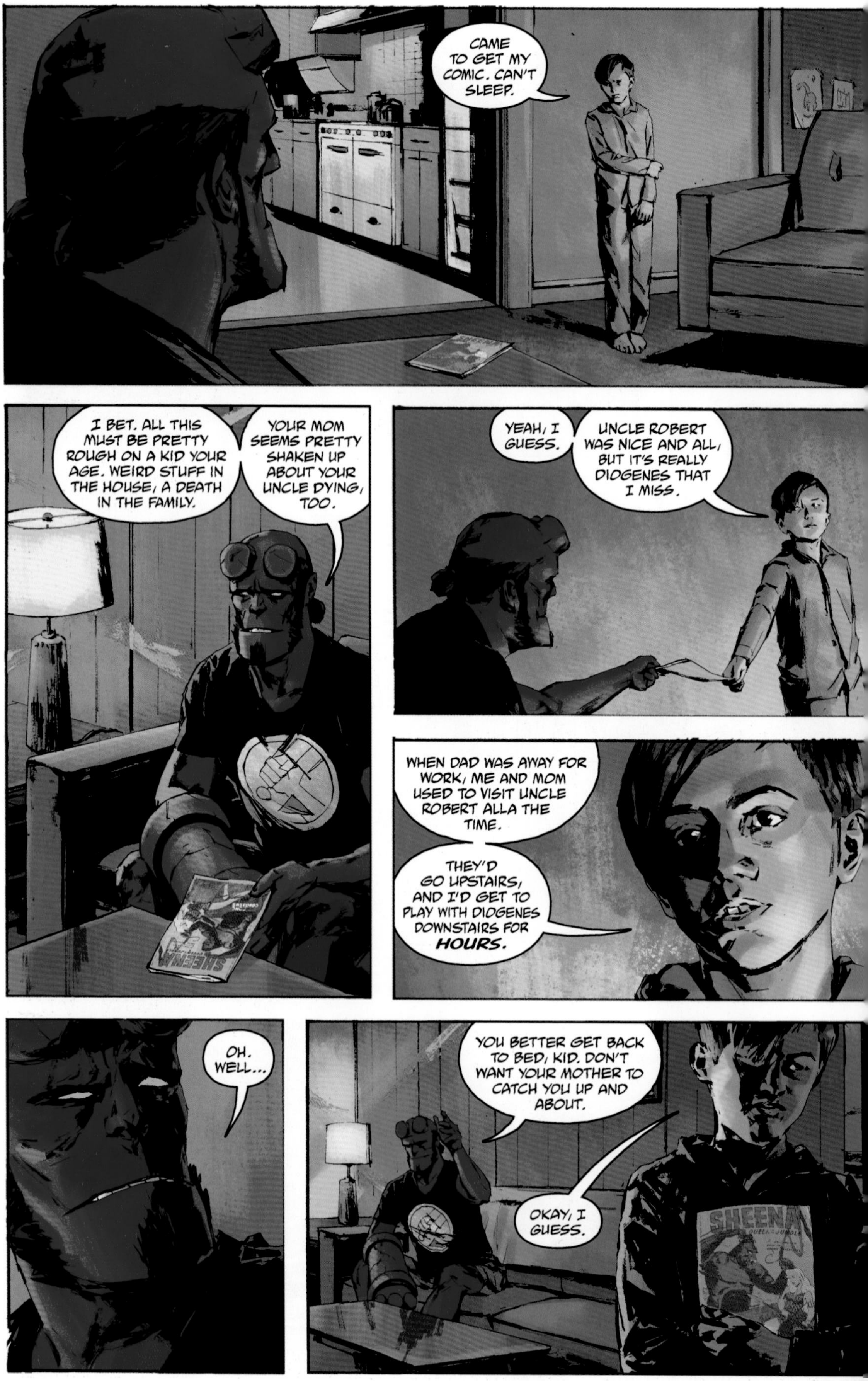
CAME TO GET MY COMIC. CAN'T SLEEP.
I BET. ALL THIS MUST BE PRETTY ROUGH ON A KID YOUR AGE. WEIRD STUFF IN THE HOUSE, A DEATH IN THE FAMILY.
YOUR MOM SEEMS PRETTY SHAKEN UP ABOUT YOUR UNCLE DYING, TOO.
YEAH, I GUESS.
UNCLE ROBERT WAS NICE AND ALL, BUT IT'S REALLY DIOGENES THAT I MISS.
WHEN DAD WAS AWAY FOR WORK, ME AND MOM USED TO VISIT UNCLE ROBERT ALLA THE TIME.
THEY'D GO UPSTAIRS, AND I'D GET TO PLAY WITH DIOGENES DOWNSTAIRS FOR HOURS.
OH. WELL...
YOU BETTER GET BACK TO BED, KID. DON'T WANT YOUR MOTHER TO CATCH YOU UP AND ABOUT.
OKAY, I GUESS.
SHEENA

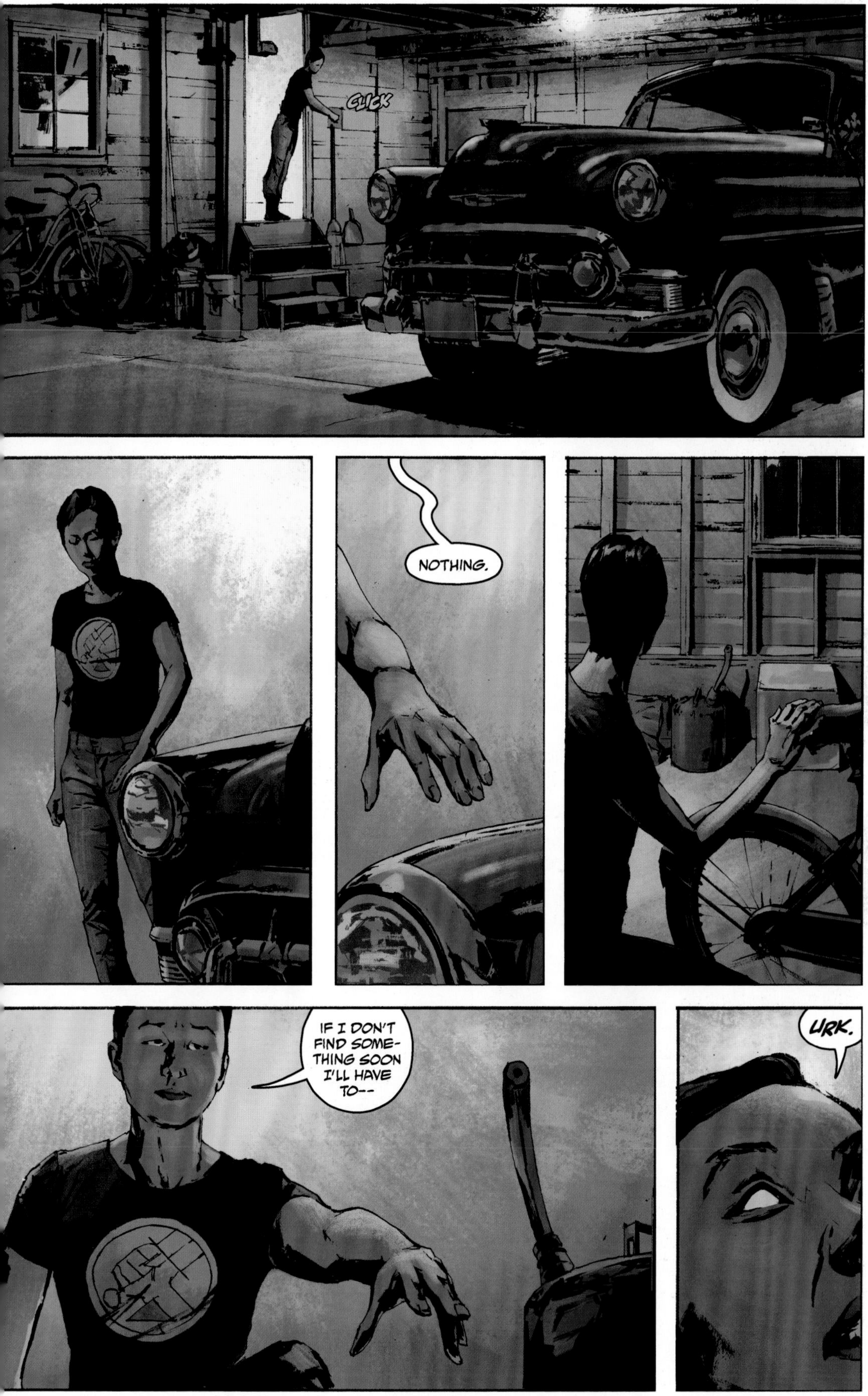
CLICK
NOTHING.
IF I DON'T FIND SOME-THING SOON I'LL HAVE TO--
URK.

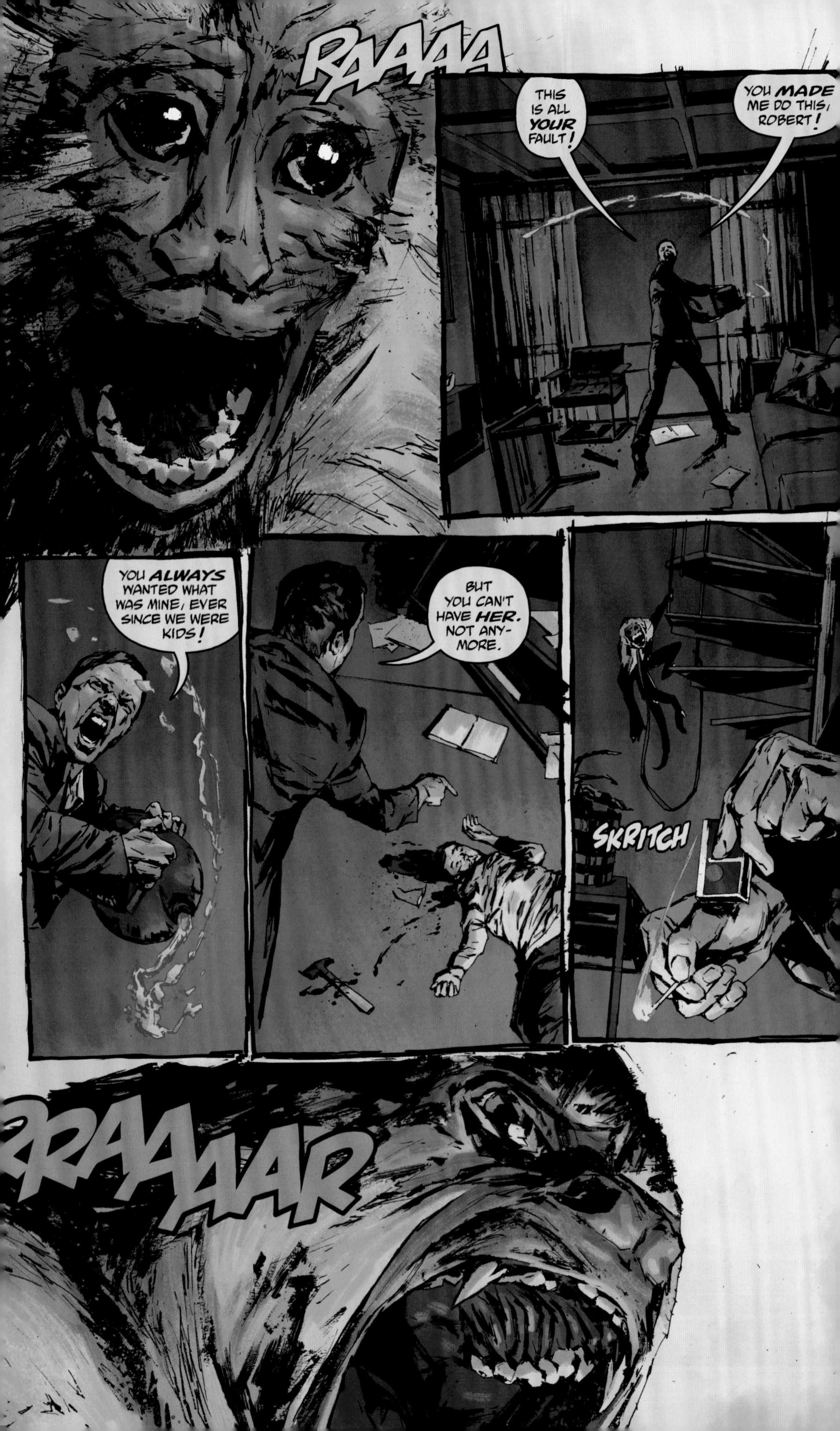
RAAAA
THIS IS ALL YOUR FAULT!
YOU MADE ME DO THIS, ROBERT!
YOU ALWAYS WANTED WHAT WAS MINE, EVER SINCE WE WERE KIDS!
BUT YOU CAN'T HAVE HER. NOT ANY-MORE.
SKRITCH
RAAAAR

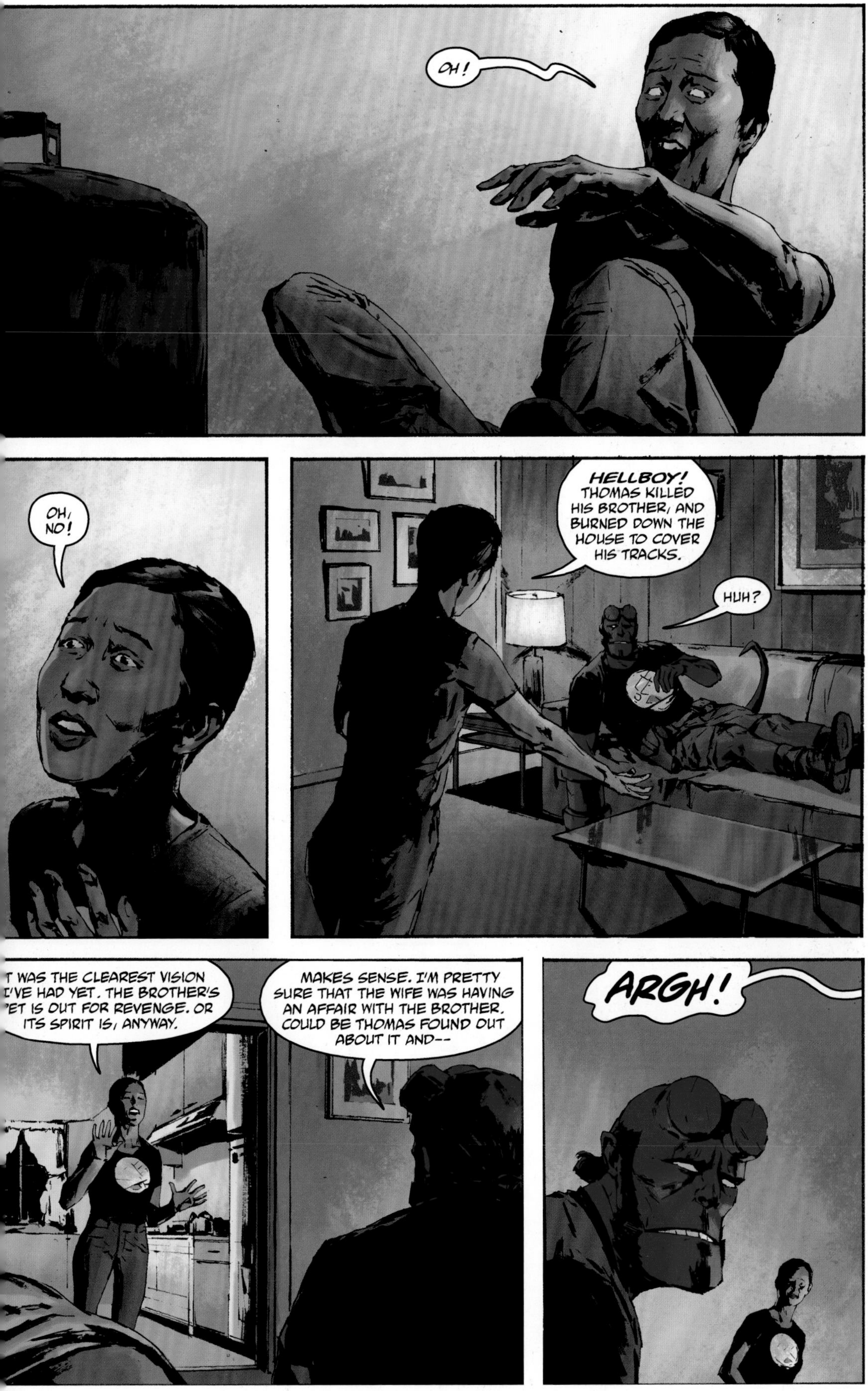
OH!
OH, NO!
HELLBOY! THOMAS KILLED HIS BROTHER, AND BURNED DOWN THE HOUSE TO COVER HIS TRACKS.
HUH?
T WAS THE CLEAREST VISION I'VE HAD YET. THE BROTHER'S 'ET IS OUT FOR REVENGE. OR ITS SPIRIT IS, ANYWAY.
MAKES SENSE. I'M PRETTY SURE THAT THE WIFE WAS HAVING AN AFFAIR WITH THE BROTHER. COULD BE THOMAS FOUND OUT ABOUT IT AND--
ARGH!

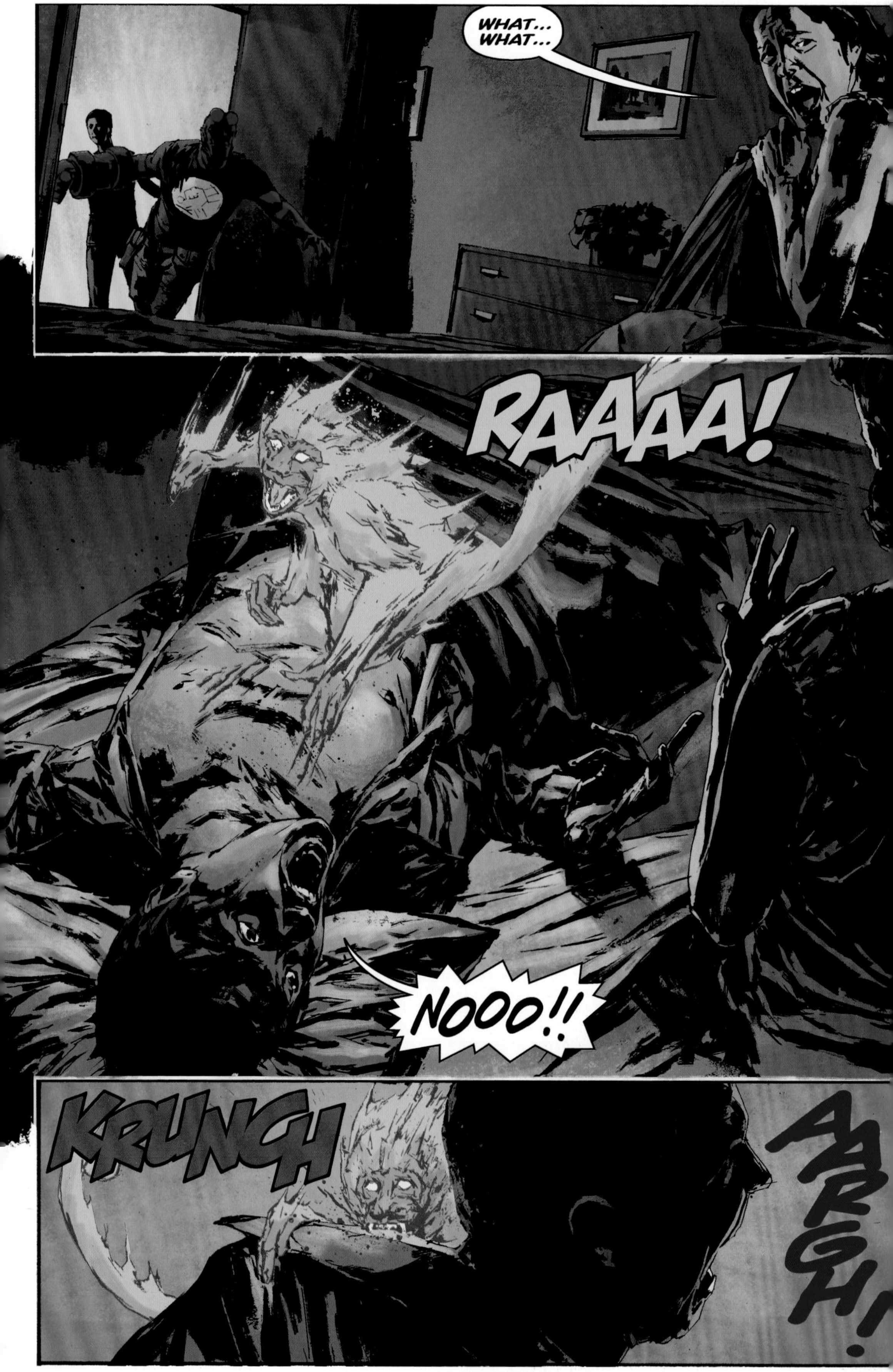
WHAT... WHAT...
RAAAA!
NOOO!!
KRUNCH
AARGH!

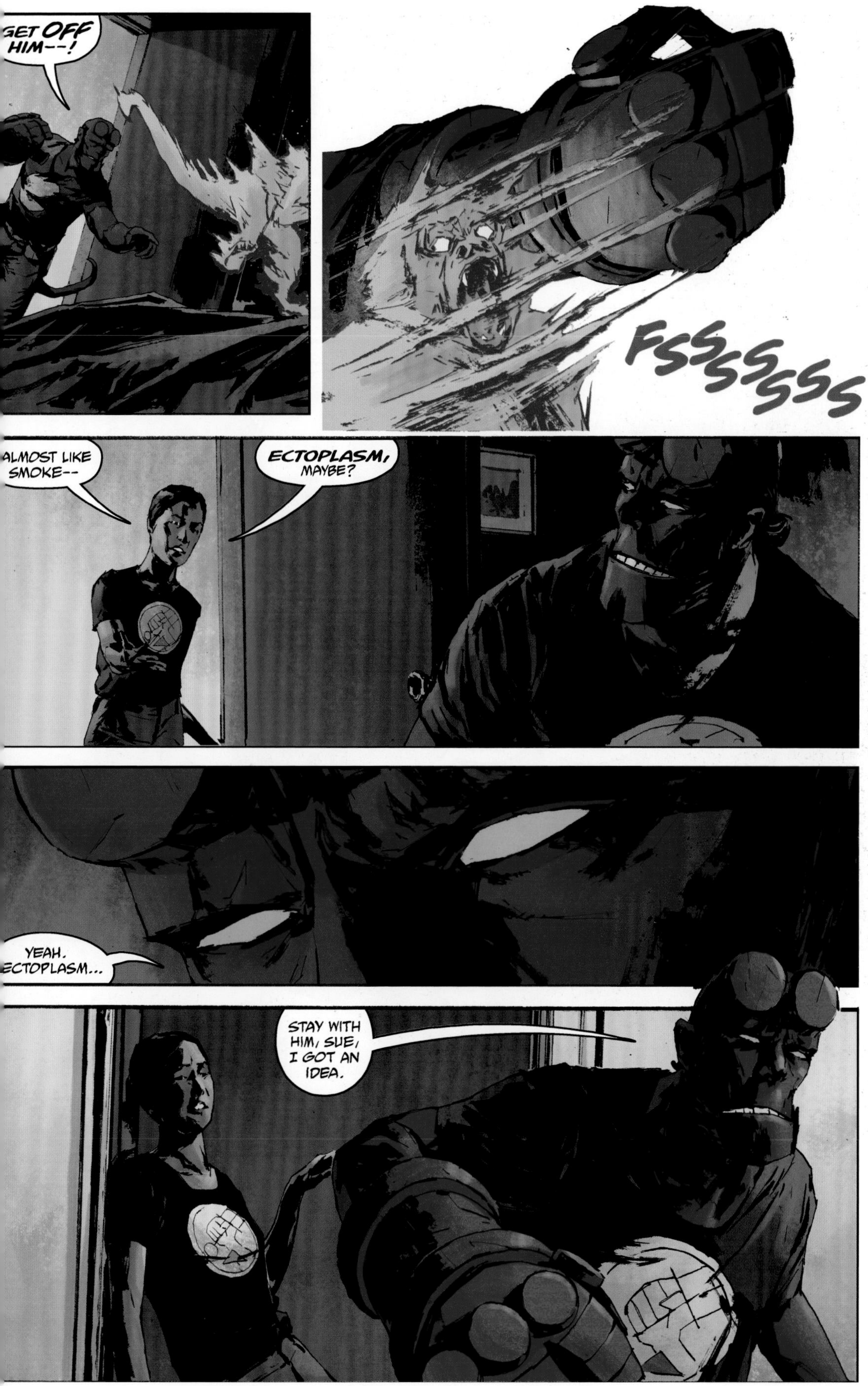
GET OFF HIM--!
FSSSSSSS
ALMOST LIKE SMOKE--
ECTOPLASM, MAYBE?
YEAH. ECTOPLASM...
STAY WITH HIM, SUE, I GOT AN IDEA.

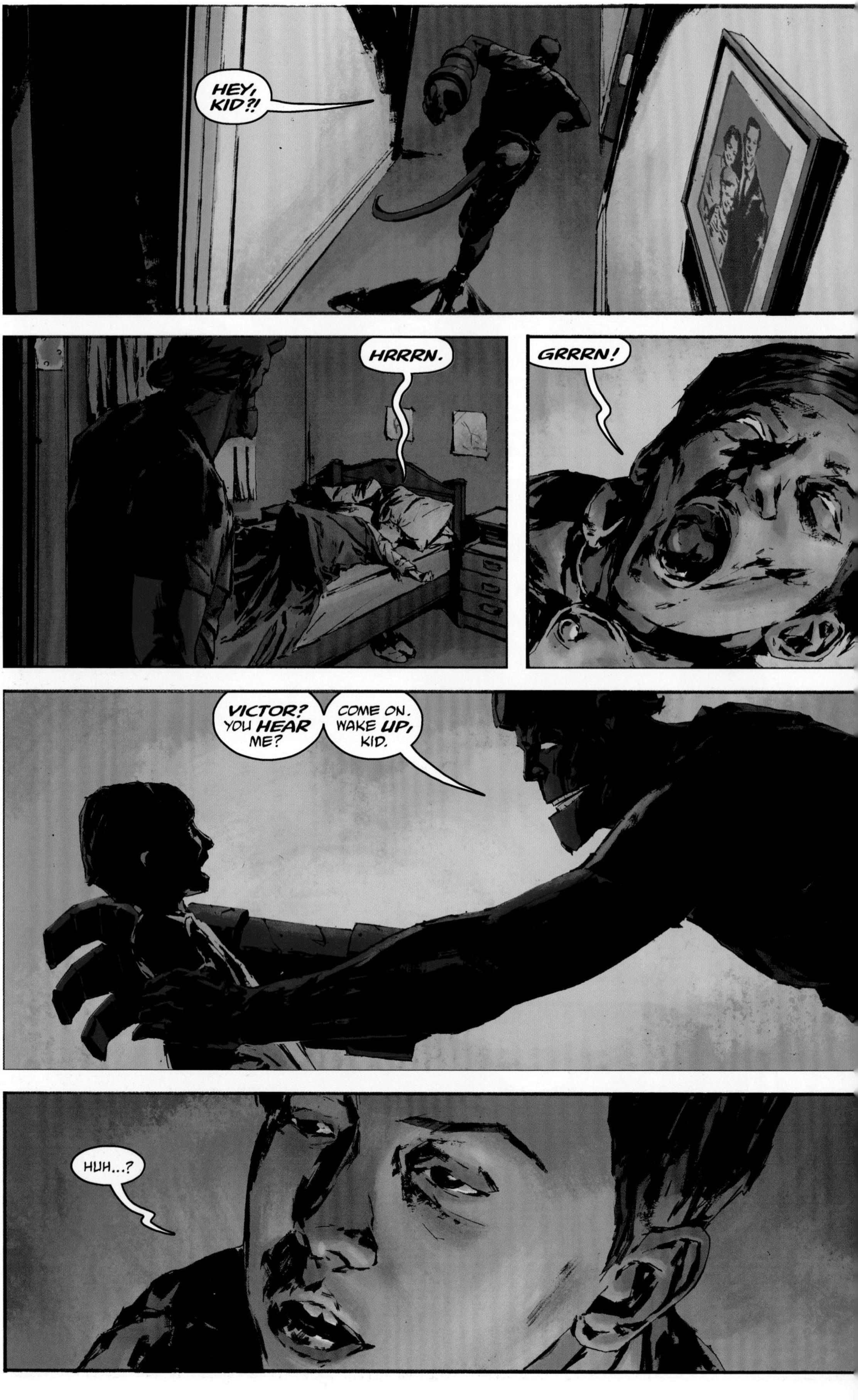
HEY, KID?!
HRRRN.
GRRRN!
VICTOR? YOU HEAR ME?
COME ON. WAKE UP, KID.
HUH...?

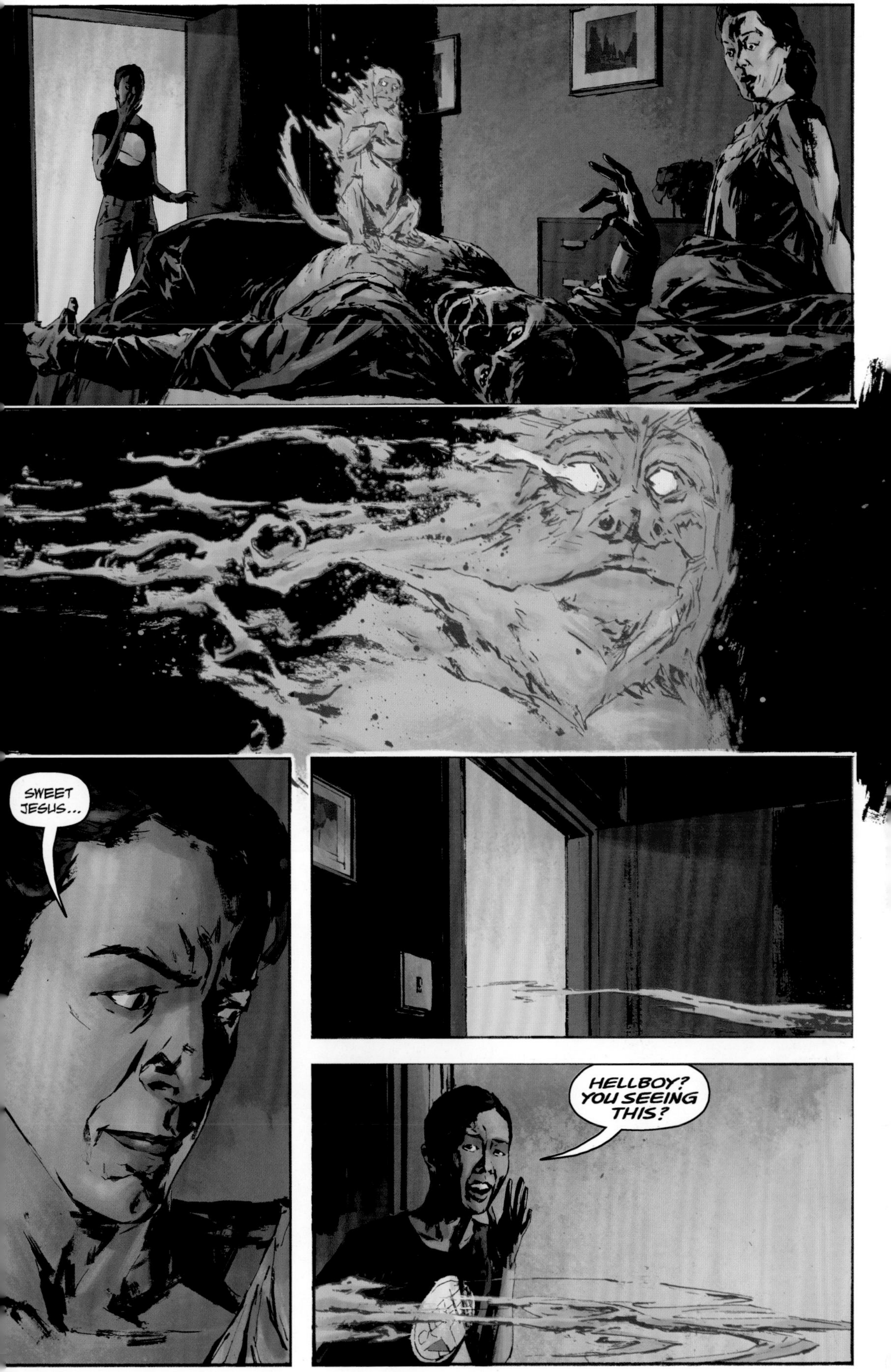
SWEET JESUS...
HELLBOY? YOU SEEING THIS?

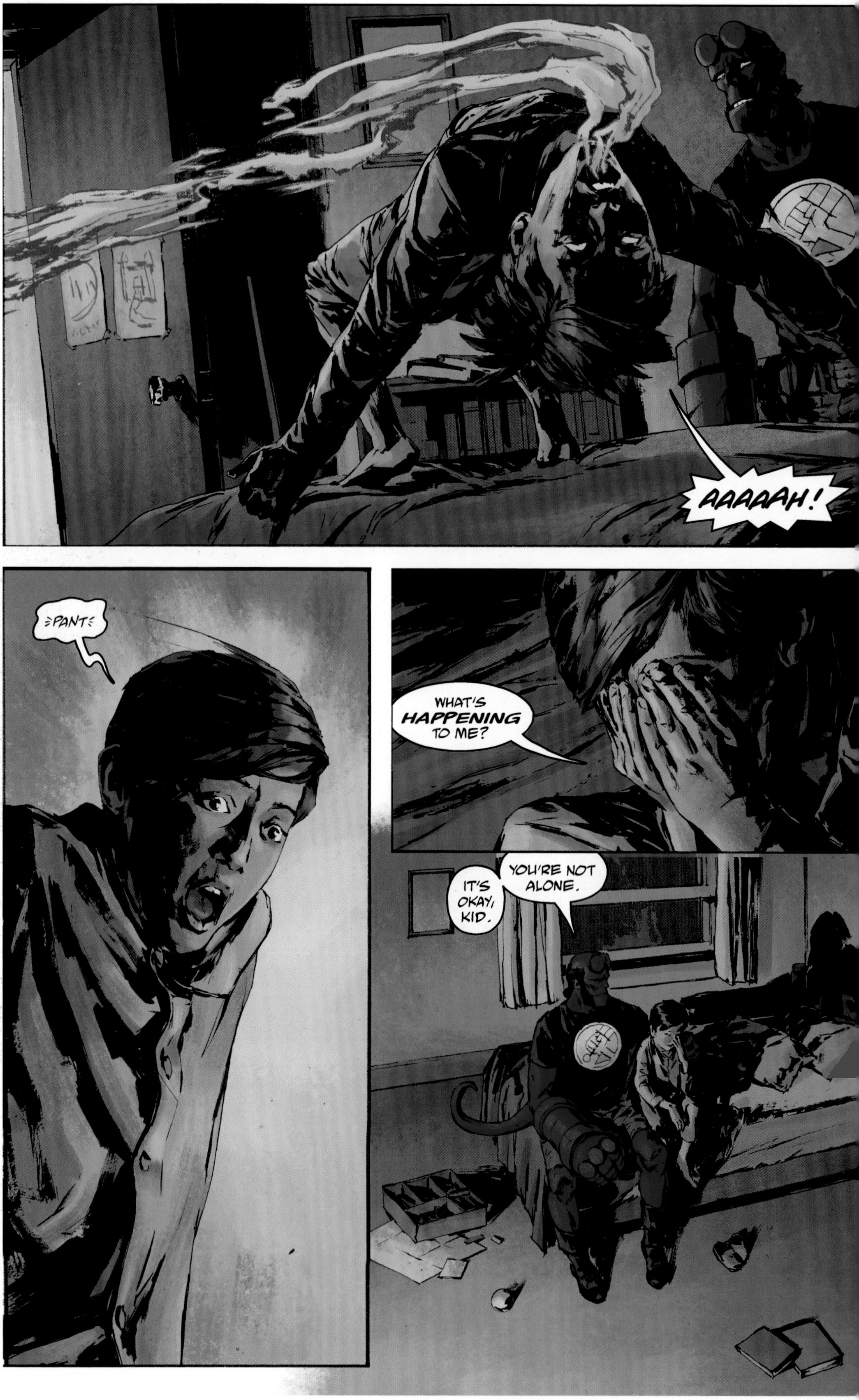
AAAAAH!
PANT
WHAT'S HAPPENING TO ME?
IT'S OKAY, KID.
YOU'RE NOT ALONE.

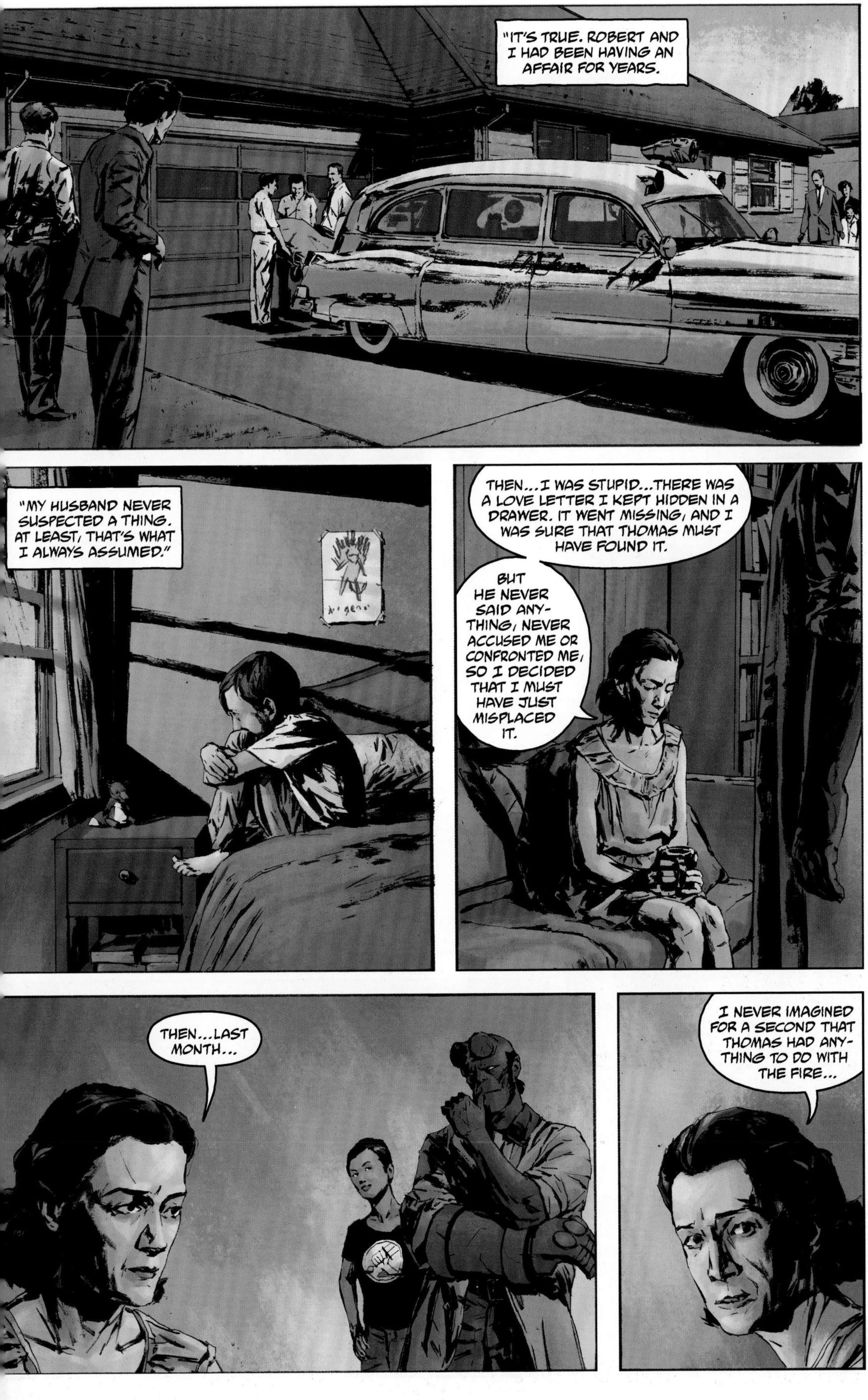
"IT'S TRUE. ROBERT AND I HAD BEEN HAVING AN AFFAIR FOR YEARS.
"MY HUSBAND NEVER SUSPECTED A THING. AT LEAST, THAT'S WHAT I ALWAYS ASSUMED."
THEN... I WAS STUPID... THERE WAS A LOVE LETTER I KEPT HIDDEN IN A DRAWER. IT WENT MISSING, AND I WAS SURE THAT THOMAS MUST HAVE FOUND IT.
BUT HE NEVER SAID ANY-THING, NEVER ACCUSED ME OR CONFRONTED ME, SO I DECIDED THAT I MUST HAVE JUST MISPLACED IT.
THEN... LAST MONTH...
I NEVER IMAGINED FOR A SECOND THAT THOMAS HAD ANY-THING TO DO WITH THE FIRE...

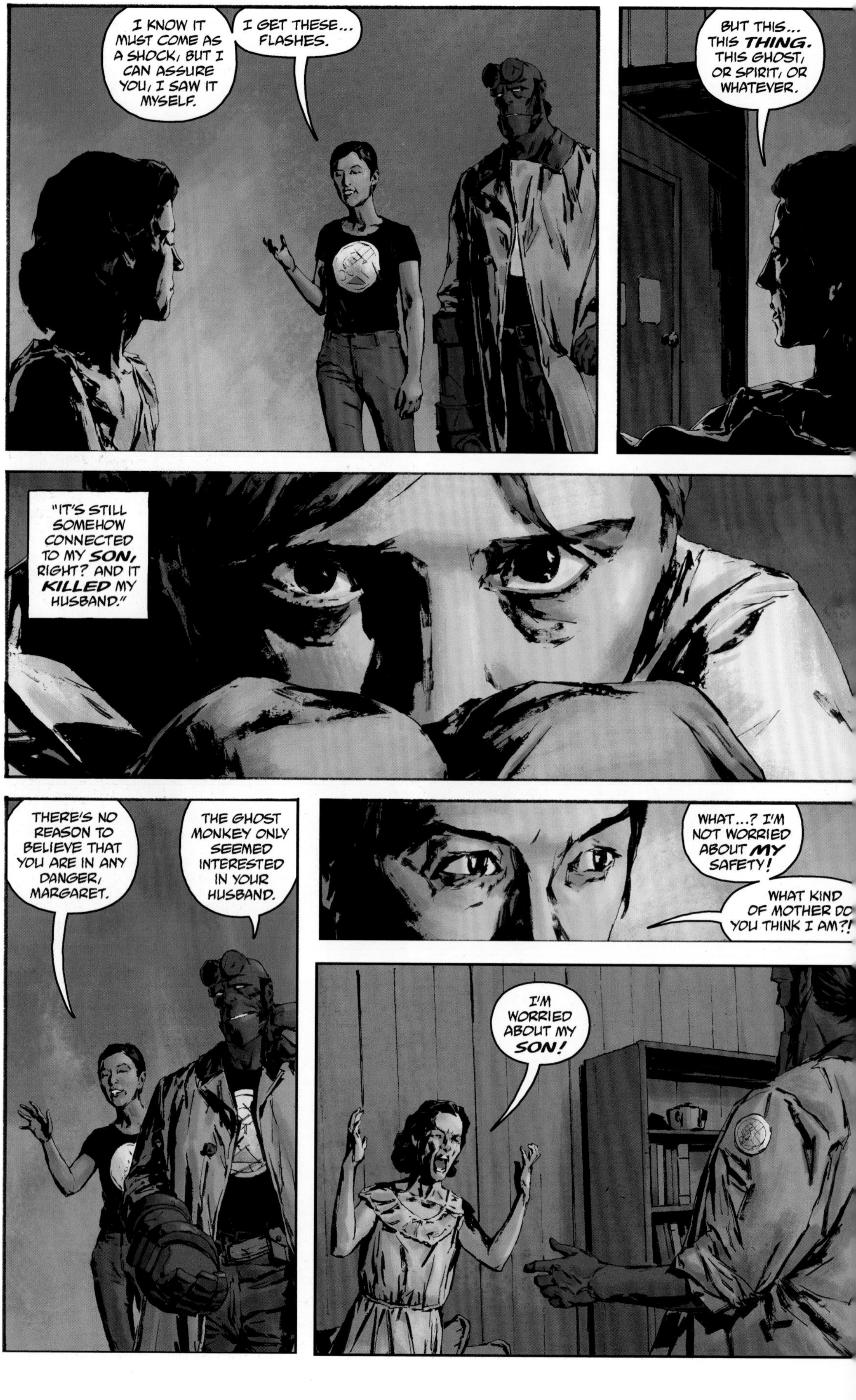

I KNOW IT MUST COME AS A SHOCK, BUT I CAN ASSURE YOU, I SAW IT MYSELF.
I GET THESE... FLASHES.
BUT THIS... THIS THING. THIS GHOST, OR SPIRIT, OR WHATEVER.
"IT'S STILL SOMEHOW CONNECTED TO MY SON, RIGHT? AND IT KILLED MY HUSBAND."
THERE'S NO REASON TO BELIEVE THAT YOU ARE IN ANY DANGER, MARGARET.
THE GHOST MONKEY ONLY SEEMED INTERESTED IN YOUR HUSBAND.
WHAT...? I'M NOT WORRIED ABOUT MY SAFETY!
WHAT KIND OF MOTHER DO YOU THINK I AM?!
I'M WORRIED ABOUT MY SON!

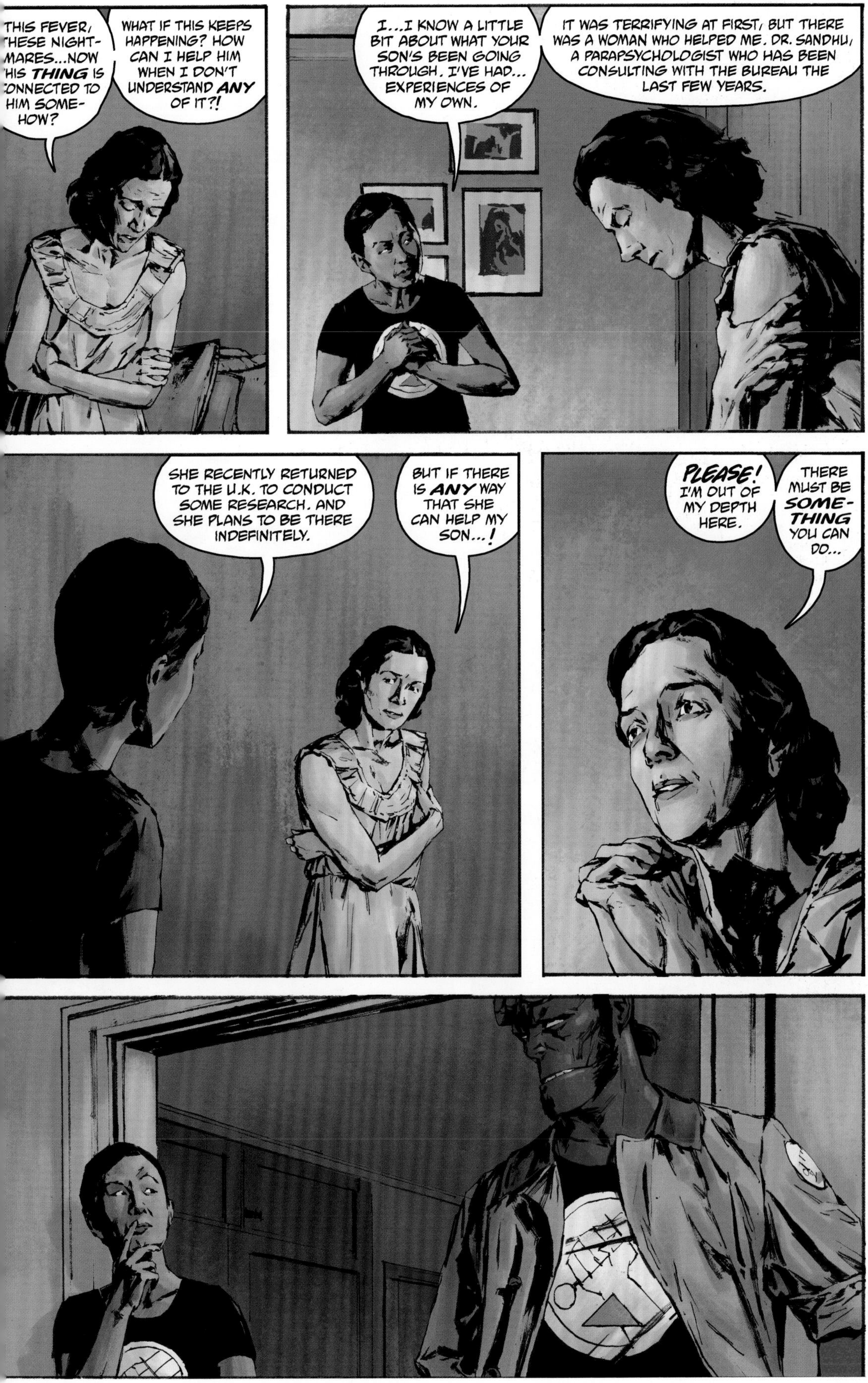
THIS FEVER, THESE NIGHT-MARES...NOW THIS THING IS CONNECTED TO HIM SOME-HOW?
WHAT IF THIS KEEPS HAPPENING? HOW CAN I HELP HIM WHEN I DON'T UNDERSTAND ANY OF IT?!
I...I KNOW A LITTLE BIT ABOUT WHAT YOUR SON'S BEEN GOING THROUGH. I'VE HAD... EXPERIENCES OF MY OWN.
IT WAS TERRIFYING AT FIRST, BUT THERE WAS A WOMAN WHO HELPED ME. DR. SANDHU, A PARAPSYCHOLOGIST WHO HAS BEEN CONSULTING WITH THE BUREAU THE LAST FEW YEARS.
SHE RECENTLY RETURNED TO THE U.K. TO CONDUCT SOME RESEARCH. AND SHE PLANS TO BE THERE INDEFINITELY.
BUT IF THERE IS ANY WAY THAT SHE CAN HELP MY SON...!
PLEASE! I'M OUT OF MY DEPTH HERE.
THERE MUST BE SOME-THING YOU CAN DO...

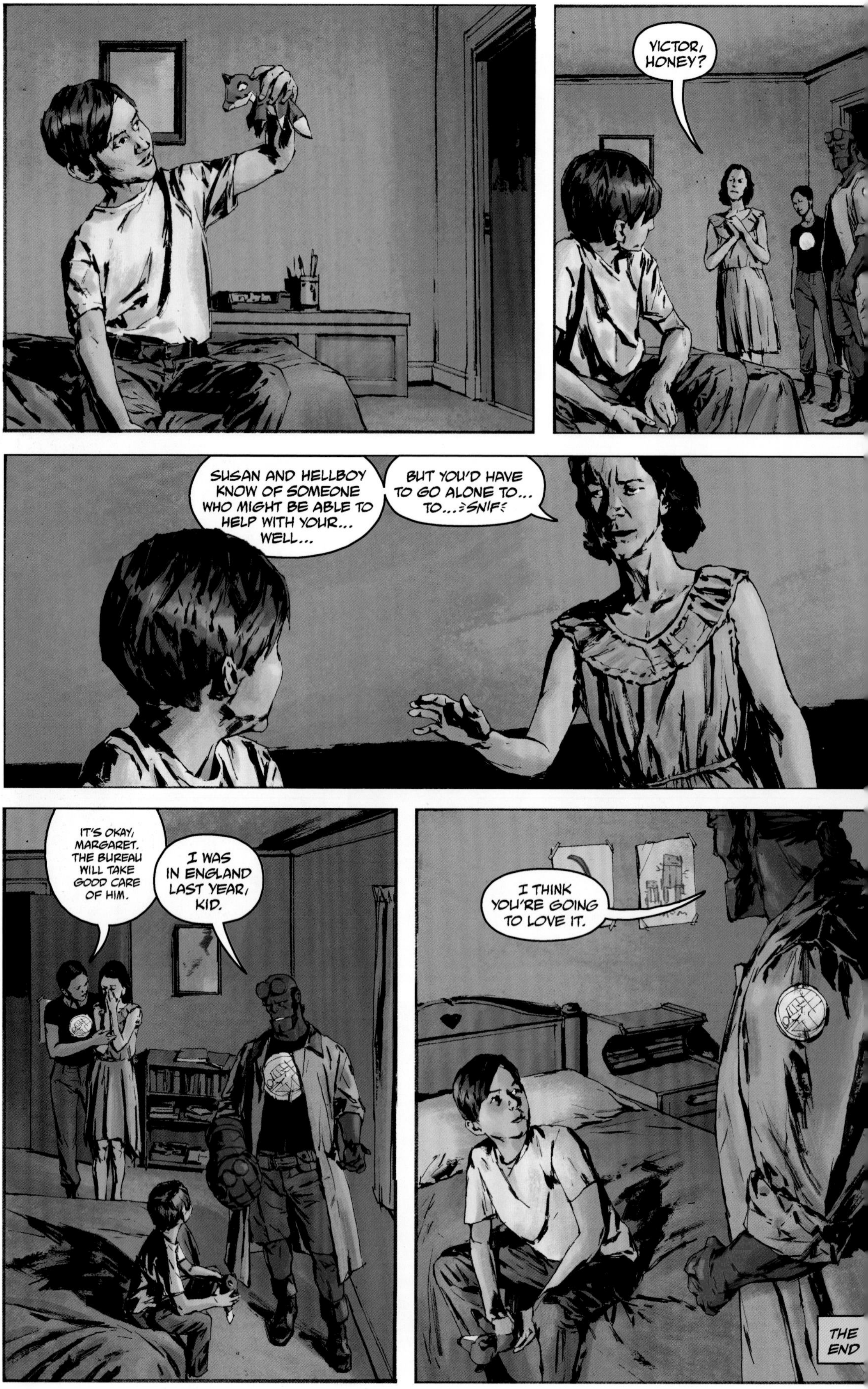
VICTOR, HONEY?
SUSAN AND HELLBOY KNOW OF SOMEONE WHO MIGHT BE ABLE TO HELP WITH YOUR... WELL...
BUT YOU'D HAVE TO GO ALONE TO... TO... SNIF
IT'S OKAY, MARGARET. THE BUREAU WILL TAKE GOOD CARE OF HIM.
I WAS IN ENGLAND LAST YEAR, KID.
I THINK YOU'RE GOING TO LOVE IT.
THE END

GHOST MOON

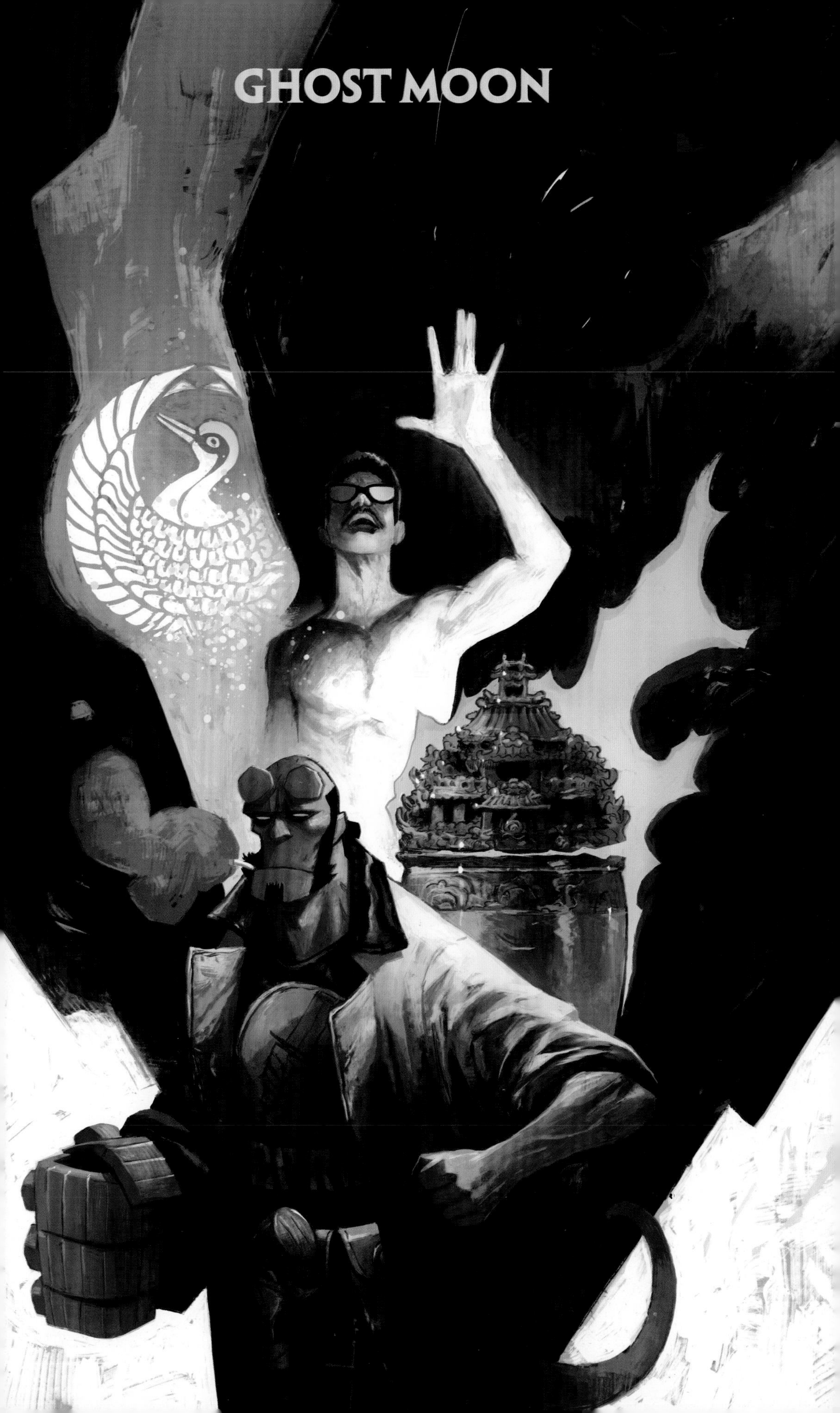

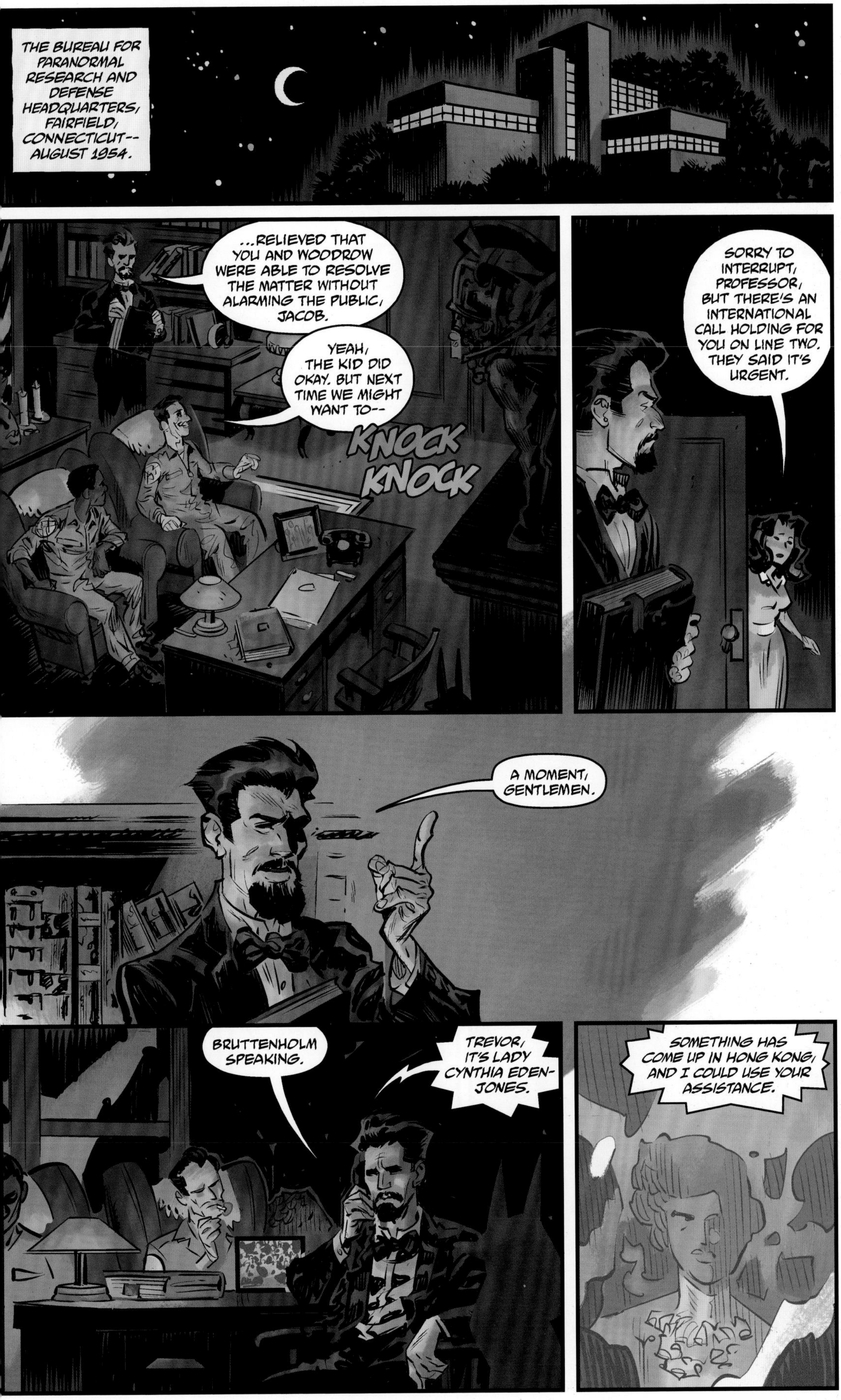
THE BUREAU FOR PARANORMAL RESEARCH AND DEFENSE HEADQUARTERS, FAIRFIELD, CONNECTICUT-- AUGUST 1954.
...RELIEVED THAT YOU AND WOODROW WERE ABLE TO RESOLVE THE MATTER WITHOUT ALARMING THE PUBLIC, JACOB.
YEAH, THE KID DID OKAY. BUT NEXT TIME WE MIGHT WANT TO--
KNOCK KNOCK
SORRY TO INTERRUPT, PROFESSOR, BUT THERE'S AN INTERNATIONAL CALL HOLDING FOR YOU ON LINE TWO. THEY SAID IT'S URGENT.
A MOMENT, GENTLEMEN.
BRUTTENHOLM SPEAKING.
TREVOR, IT'S LADY CYNTHIA EDEN-JONES.
SOMETHING HAS COME UP IN HONG KONG, AND I COULD USE YOUR ASSISTANCE.

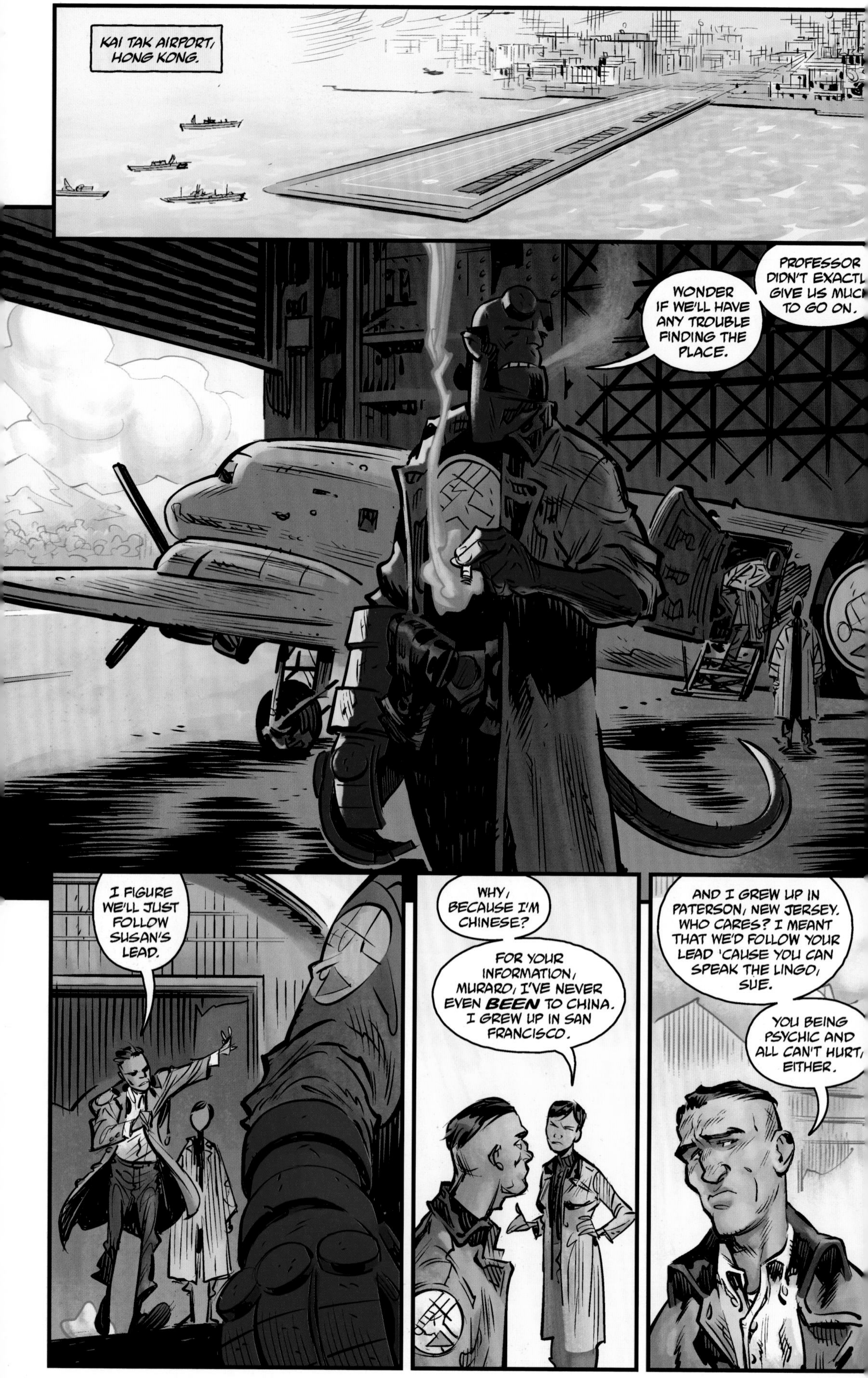
KAI TAK AIRPORT, HONG KONG.
WONDER IF WE'LL HAVE ANY TROUBLE FINDING THE PLACE.
PROFESSOR DIDN'T EXACTL GIVE US MUCI TO GO ON.
I FIGURE WE'LL JUST FOLLOW SUSAN'S LEAD.
WHY, BECAUSE I'M CHINESE?
FOR YOUR INFORMATION, MURARO, I'VE NEVER EVEN BEEN TO CHINA. I GREW UP IN SAN FRANCISCO.
AND I GREW UP IN PATERSON, NEW JERSEY. WHO CARES? I MEANT THAT WE'D FOLLOW YOUR LEAD 'CAUSE YOU CAN SPEAK THE LINGO, SUE.
YOU BEING PSYCHIC AND ALL CAN'T HURT, EITHER.

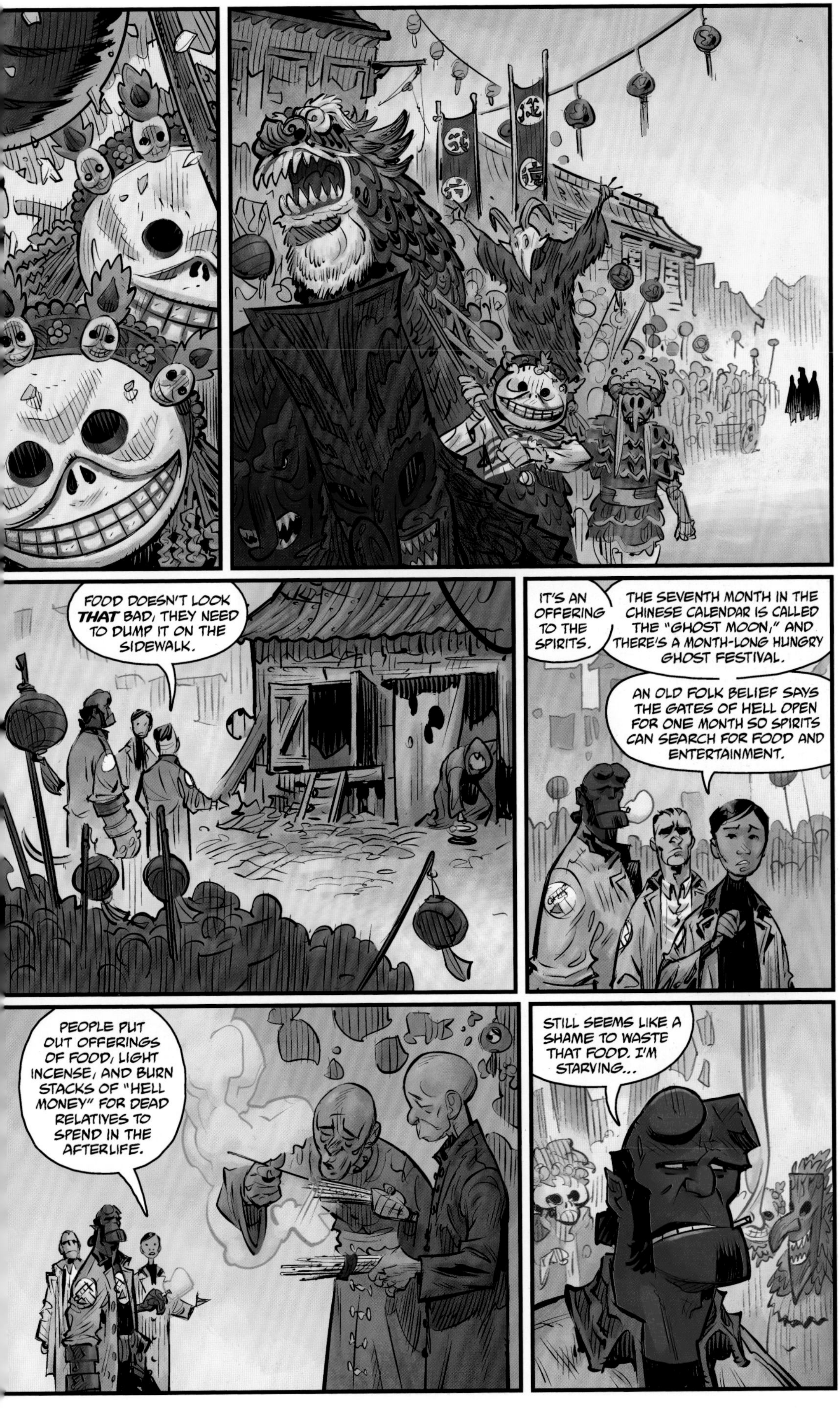
FOOD DOESN'T LOOK **THAT** BAD, THEY NEED TO DUMP IT ON THE SIDEWALK.
IT'S AN OFFERING TO THE SPIRITS.
THE SEVENTH MONTH IN THE CHINESE CALENDAR IS CALLED THE "GHOST MOON," AND THERE'S A MONTH-LONG HUNGRY GHOST FESTIVAL.
AN OLD FOLK BELIEF SAYS THE GATES OF HELL OPEN FOR ONE MONTH SO SPIRITS CAN SEARCH FOR FOOD AND ENTERTAINMENT.
PEOPLE PUT OUT OFFERINGS OF FOOD, LIGHT INCENSE, AND BURN STACKS OF "HELL MONEY" FOR DEAD RELATIVES TO SPEND IN THE AFTERLIFE.
STILL SEEMS LIKE A SHAME TO WASTE THAT FOOD. I'M STARVING...

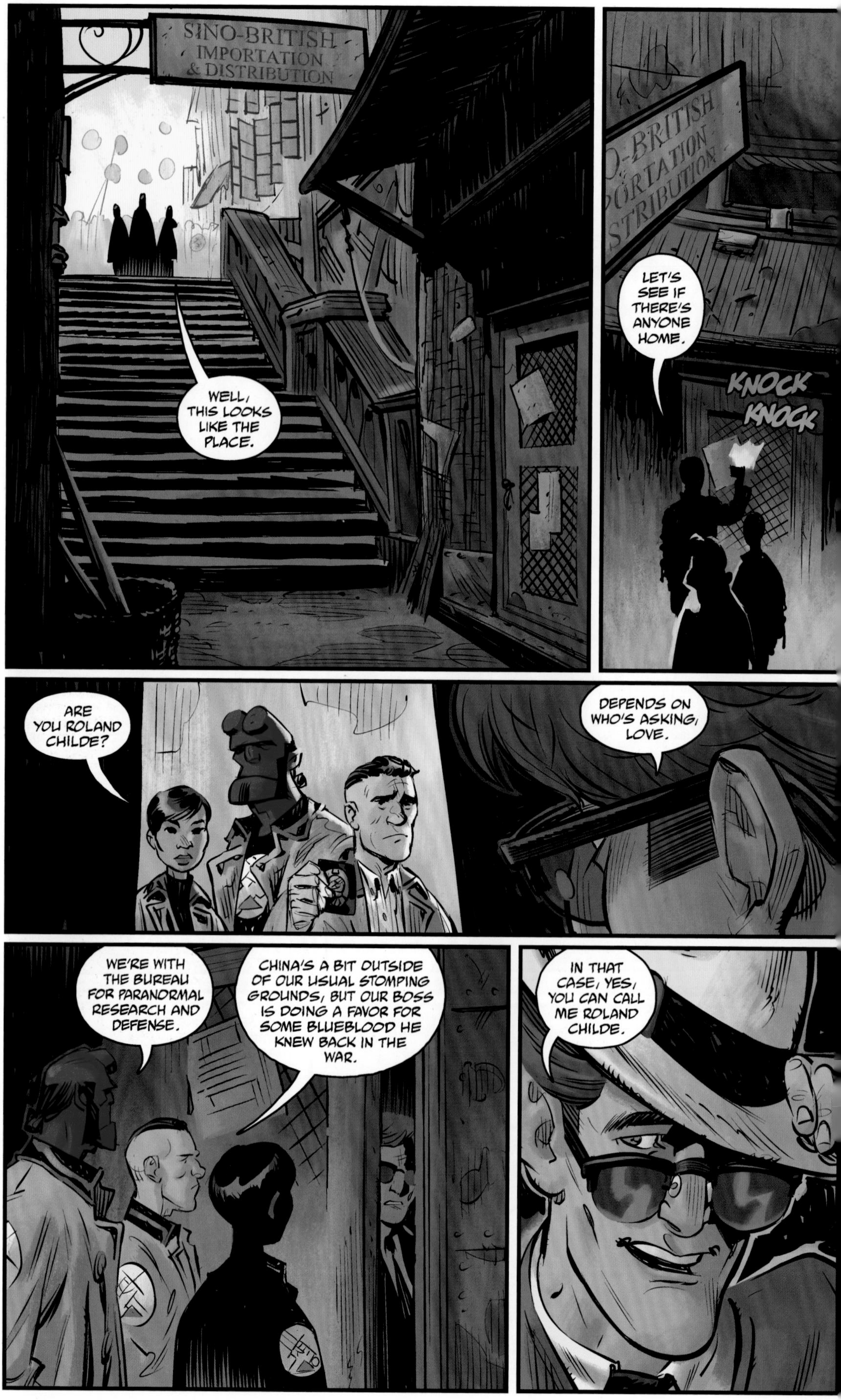
SINO-BRITISH IMPORTATION & DISTRIBUTION
WELL, THIS LOOKS LIKE THE PLACE.
LET'S SEE IF THERE'S ANYONE HOME.
KNOCK KNOCK
ARE YOU ROLAND CHILDE?
DEPENDS ON WHO'S ASKING, LOVE.
WE'RE WITH THE BUREAU FOR PARANORMAL RESEARCH AND DEFENSE.
CHINA'S A BIT OUTSIDE OF OUR USUAL STOMPING GROUNDS, BUT OUR BOSS IS DOING A FAVOR FOR SOME BLUEBLOOD HE KNEW BACK IN THE WAR.
IN THAT CASE, YES, YOU CAN CALL ME ROLAND CHILDE.

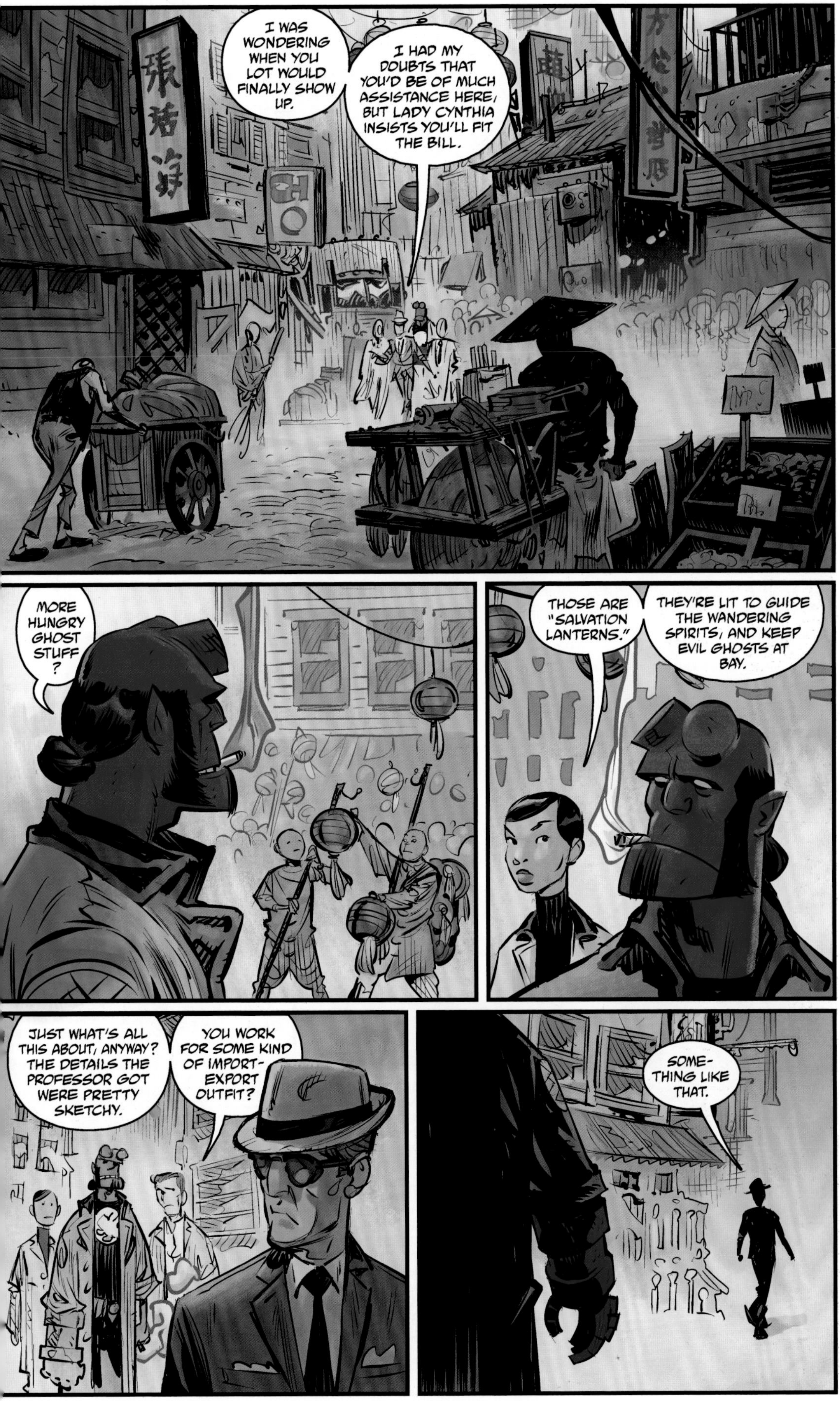
I WAS WONDERING WHEN YOU LOT WOULD FINALLY SHOW UP.
I HAD MY DOUBTS THAT YOU'D BE OF MUCH ASSISTANCE HERE, BUT LADY CYNTHIA INSISTS YOU'LL FIT THE BILL.
MORE HUNGRY GHOST STUFF?
THOSE ARE "SALVATION LANTERNS."
THEY'RE LIT TO GUIDE THE WANDERING SPIRITS, AND KEEP EVIL GHOSTS AT BAY.
JUST WHAT'S ALL THIS ABOUT, ANYWAY? THE DETAILS THE PROFESSOR GOT WERE PRETTY SKETCHY.
YOU WORK FOR SOME KIND OF IMPORT-EXPORT OUTFIT?
SOME-THING LIKE THAT.

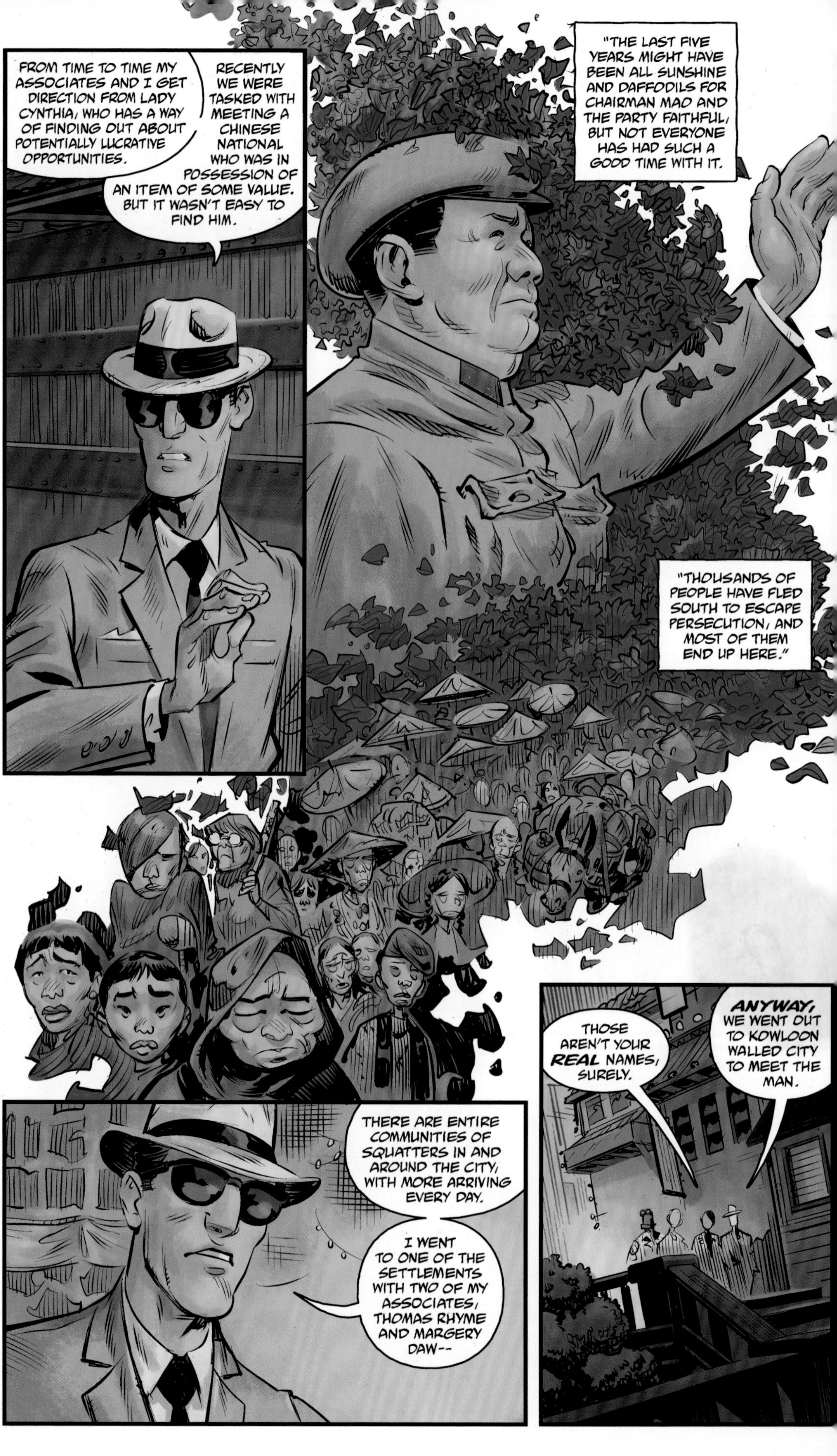
FROM TIME TO TIME MY ASSOCIATES AND I GET DIRECTION FROM LADY CYNTHIA, WHO HAS A WAY OF FINDING OUT ABOUT POTENTIALLY LUCRATIVE OPPORTUNITIES.
RECENTLY WE WERE TASKED WITH MEETING A CHINESE NATIONAL WHO WAS IN POSSESSION OF AN ITEM OF SOME VALUE. BUT IT WASN'T EASY TO FIND HIM.
"THE LAST FIVE YEARS MIGHT HAVE BEEN ALL SUNSHINE AND DAFFODILS FOR CHAIRMAN MAO AND THE PARTY FAITHFUL, BUT NOT EVERYONE HAS HAD SUCH A GOOD TIME WITH IT.
"THOUSANDS OF PEOPLE HAVE FLED SOUTH TO ESCAPE PERSECUTION, AND MOST OF THEM END UP HERE."
THERE ARE ENTIRE COMMUNITIES OF SQUATTERS IN AND AROUND THE CITY, WITH MORE ARRIVING EVERY DAY.
I WENT TO ONE OF THE SETTLEMENTS WITH TWO OF MY ASSOCIATES, THOMAS RHYME AND MARGERY DAW--
THOSE AREN'T YOUR REAL NAMES, SURELY.
ANYWAY, WE WENT OUT TO KOWLOON WALLED CITY TO MEET THE MAN.

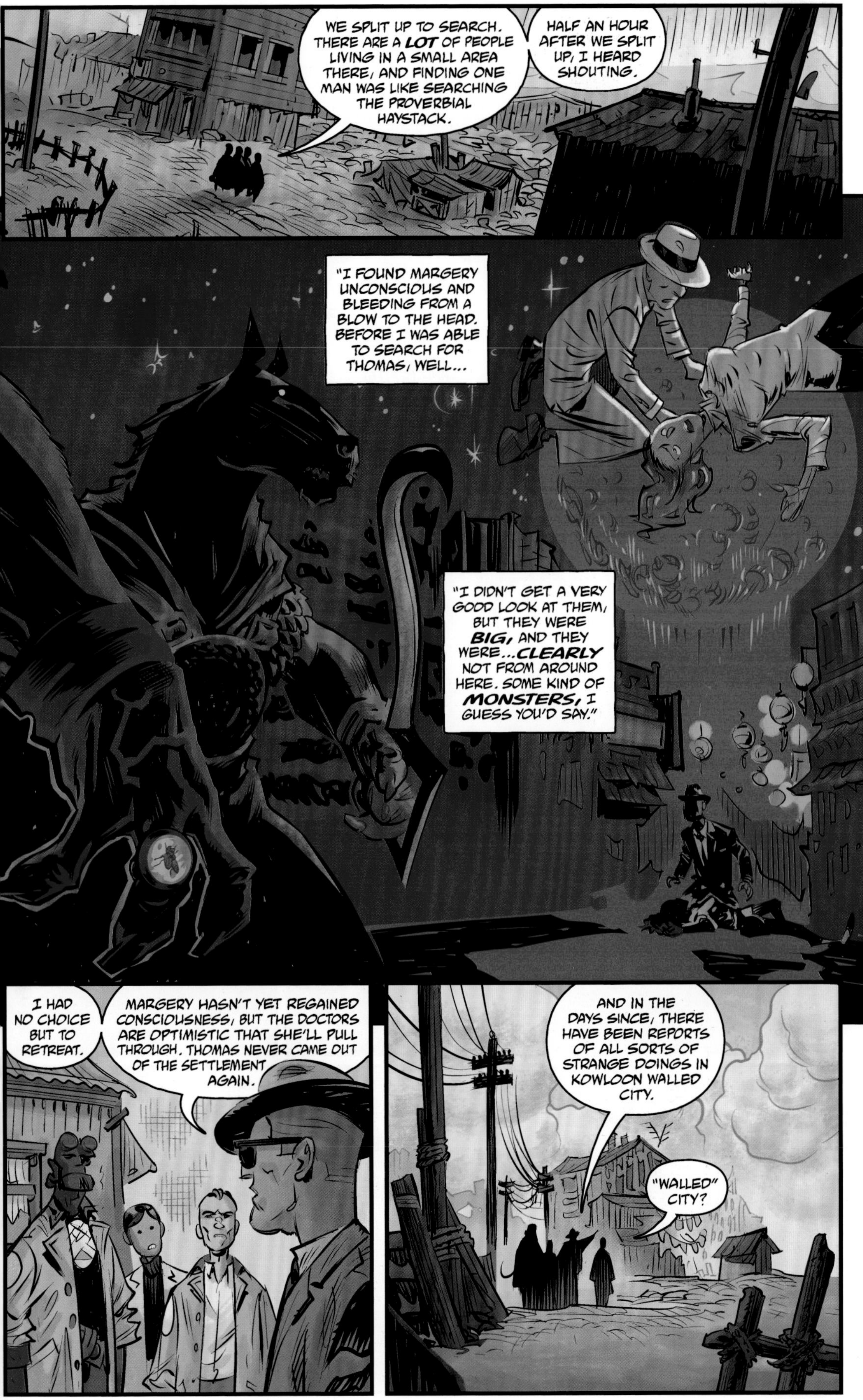

WE SPLIT UP TO SEARCH. THERE ARE A **LOT** OF PEOPLE LIVING IN A SMALL AREA THERE, AND FINDING ONE MAN WAS LIKE SEARCHING THE PROVERBIAL HAYSTACK.
HALF AN HOUR AFTER WE SPLIT UP, I HEARD SHOUTING.
"I FOUND MARGERY UNCONSCIOUS AND BLEEDING FROM A BLOW TO THE HEAD. BEFORE I WAS ABLE TO SEARCH FOR THOMAS, WELL...
"I DIDN'T GET A VERY GOOD LOOK AT THEM, BUT THEY WERE ***BIG,*** AND THEY WERE...***CLEARLY*** NOT FROM AROUND HERE. SOME KIND OF ***MONSTERS,*** I GUESS YOU'D SAY."
I HAD NO CHOICE BUT TO RETREAT.
MARGERY HASN'T YET REGAINED CONSCIOUSNESS, BUT THE DOCTORS ARE OPTIMISTIC THAT SHE'LL PULL THROUGH. THOMAS NEVER CAME OUT OF THE SETTLEMENT AGAIN.
AND IN THE DAYS SINCE, THERE HAVE BEEN REPORTS OF ALL SORTS OF STRANGE DOINGS IN KOWLOON WALLED CITY.
"WALLED" CITY?

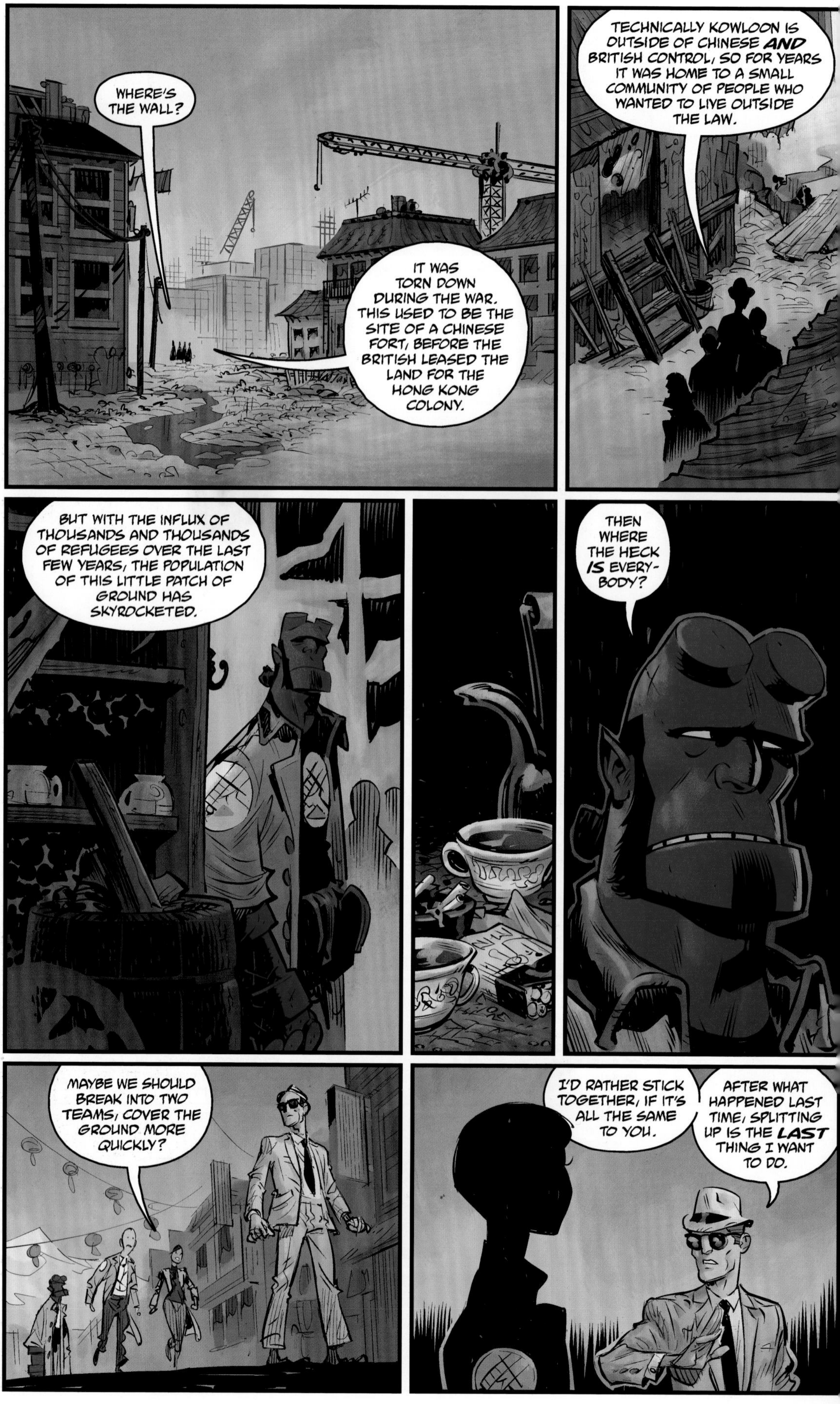
WHERE'S THE WALL?
IT WAS TORN DOWN DURING THE WAR. THIS USED TO BE THE SITE OF A CHINESE FORT, BEFORE THE BRITISH LEASED THE LAND FOR THE HONG KONG COLONY.
TECHNICALLY KOWLOON IS OUTSIDE OF CHINESE AND BRITISH CONTROL, SO FOR YEARS IT WAS HOME TO A SMALL COMMUNITY OF PEOPLE WHO WANTED TO LIVE OUTSIDE THE LAW.
BUT WITH THE INFLUX OF THOUSANDS AND THOUSANDS OF REFUGEES OVER THE LAST FEW YEARS, THE POPULATION OF THIS LITTLE PATCH OF GROUND HAS SKYROCKETED.
THEN WHERE THE HECK IS EVERY-BODY?
MAYBE WE SHOULD BREAK INTO TWO TEAMS, COVER THE GROUND MORE QUICKLY?
I'D RATHER STICK TOGETHER, IF IT'S ALL THE SAME TO YOU.
AFTER WHAT HAPPENED LAST TIME, SPLITTING UP IS THE LAST THING I WANT TO DO.

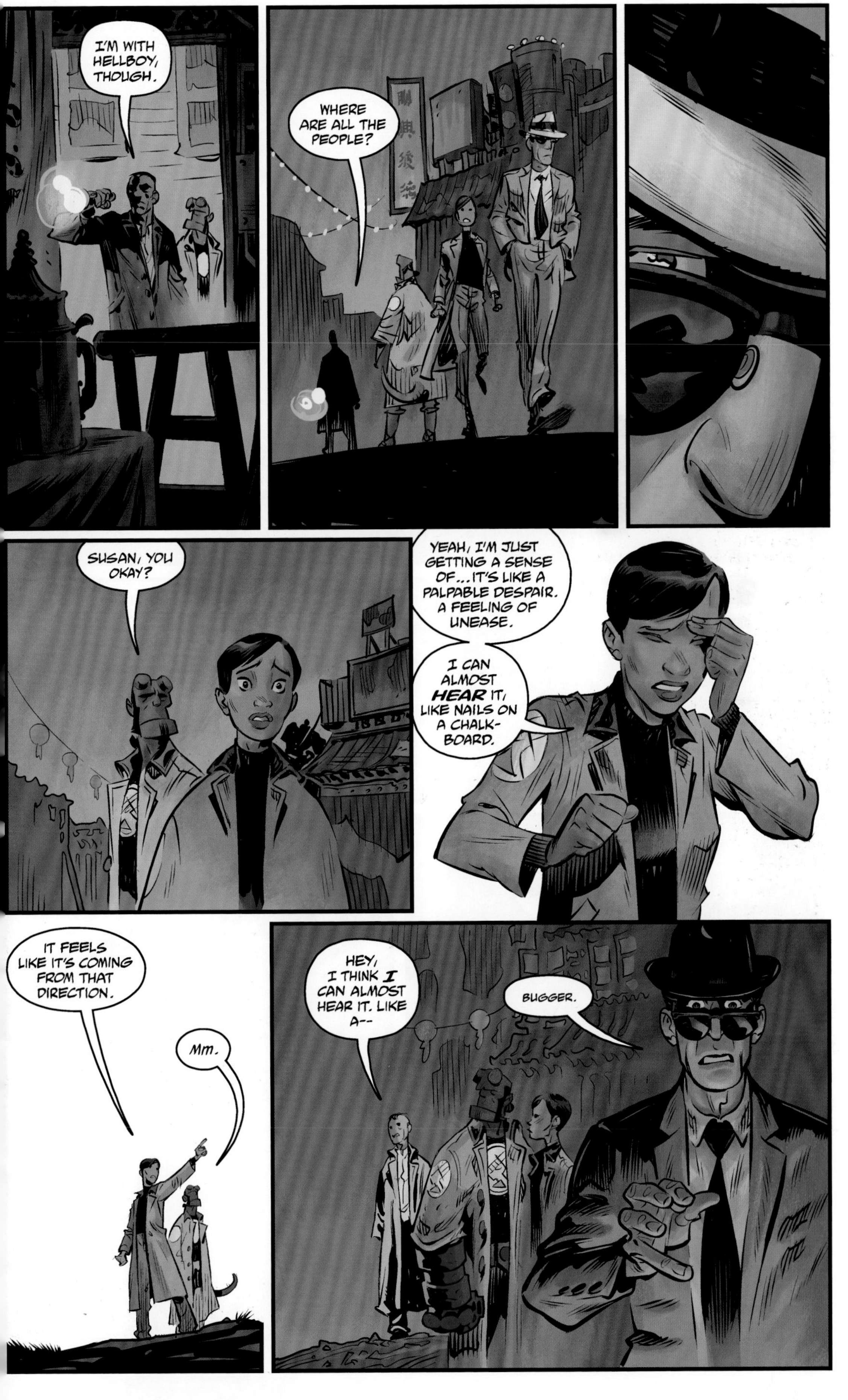
I'M WITH HELLBOY, THOUGH.
WHERE ARE ALL THE PEOPLE?
SUSAN, YOU OKAY?
YEAH, I'M JUST GETTING A SENSE OF... IT'S LIKE A PALPABLE DESPAIR. A FEELING OF UNEASE.
I CAN ALMOST **HEAR** IT, LIKE NAILS ON A CHALK-BOARD.
IT FEELS LIKE IT'S COMING FROM THAT DIRECTION.
Mm.
HEY, I THINK *I* CAN ALMOST HEAR IT. LIKE A--
BUGGER.

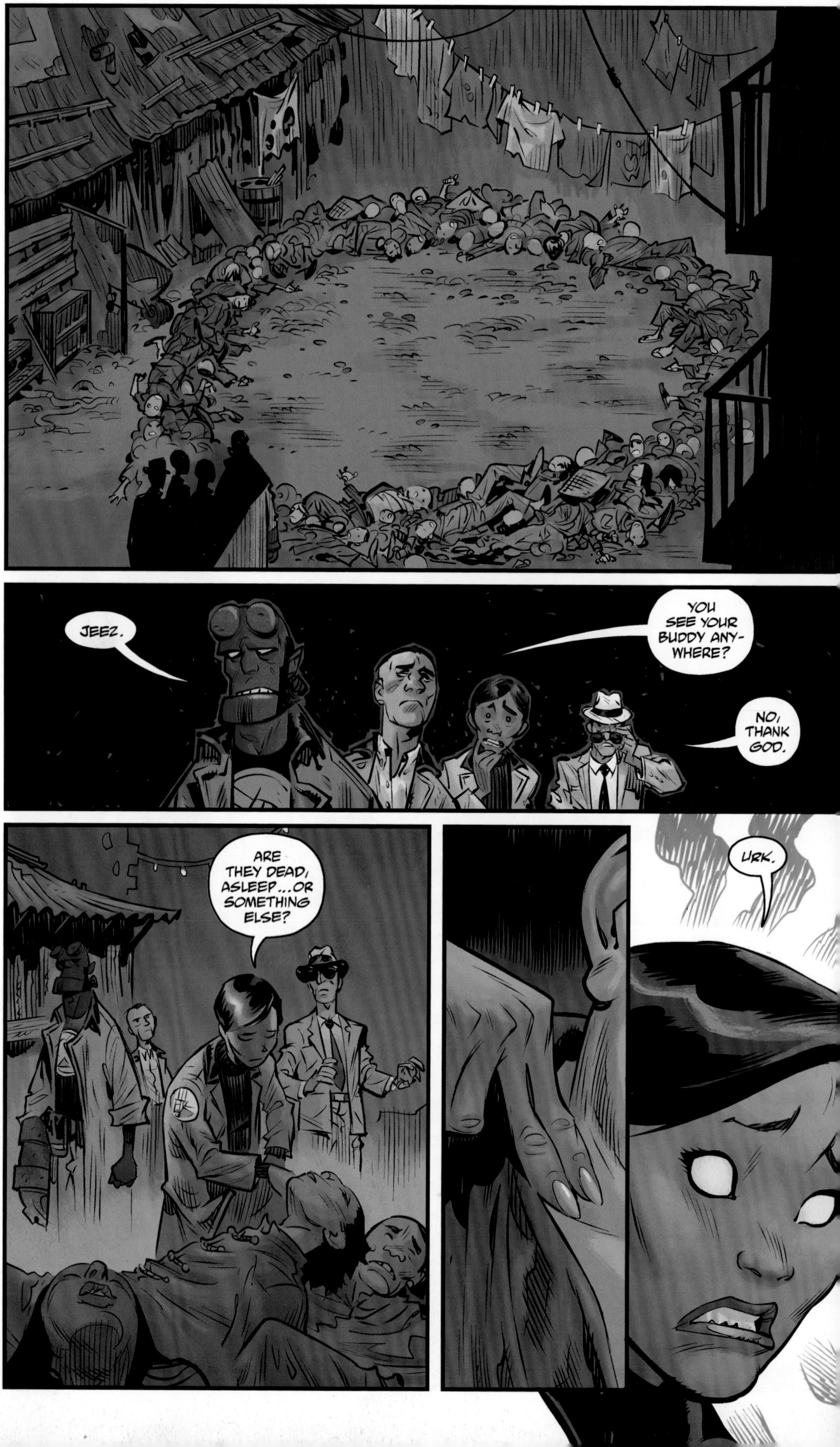
JEEZ.
YOU SEE YOUR BUDDY ANY-WHERE?
NO, THANK GOD.
ARE THEY DEAD, ASLEEP...OR SOMETHING ELSE?
URK.

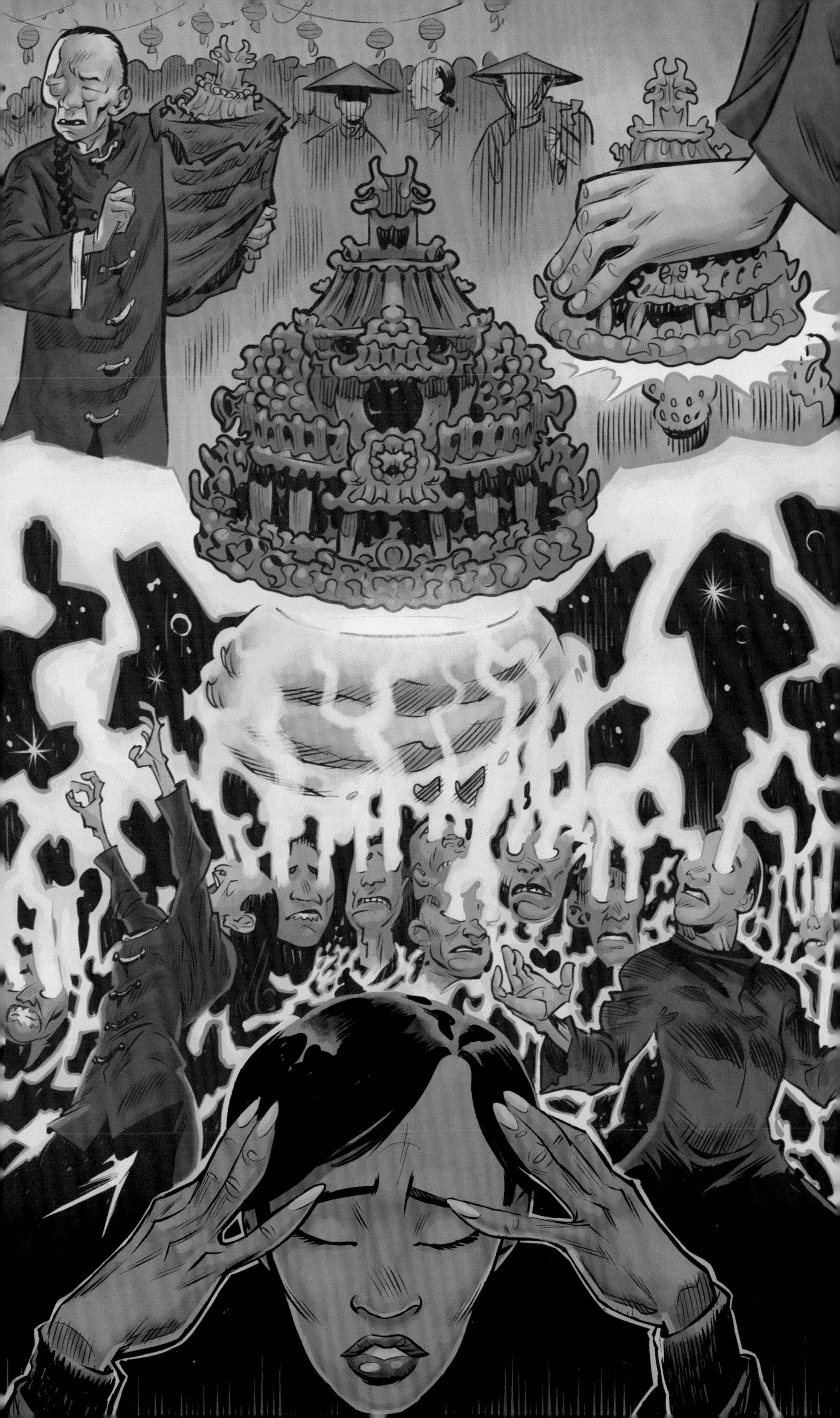

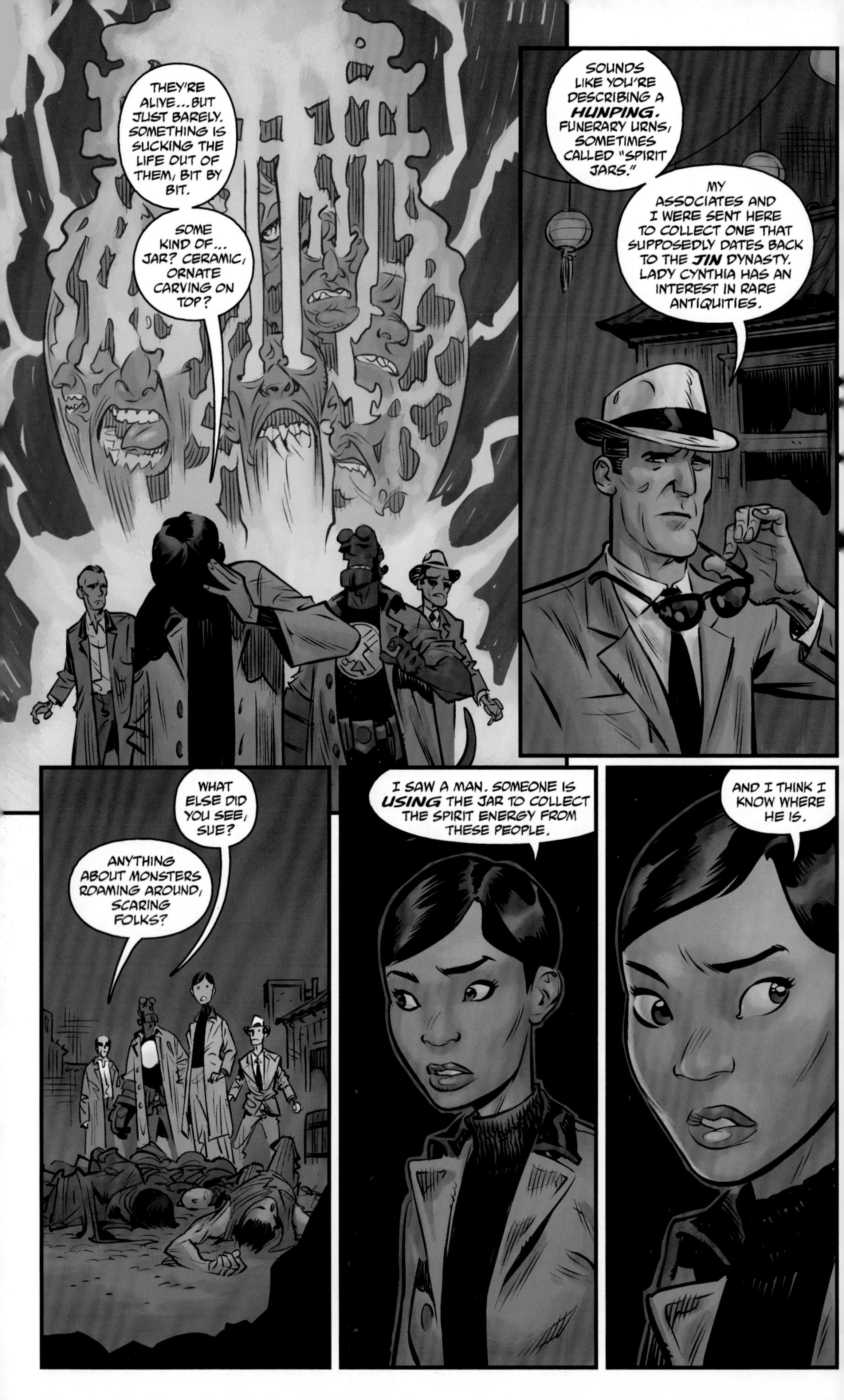

THEY'RE ALIVE... BUT JUST BARELY. SOMETHING IS SUCKING THE LIFE OUT OF THEM, BIT BY BIT.
SOME KIND OF... JAR? CERAMIC, ORNATE CARVING ON TOP?
SOUNDS LIKE YOU'RE DESCRIBING A **HUNPING.** FUNERARY URNS, SOMETIMES CALLED "SPIRIT JARS."
MY ASSOCIATES AND I WERE SENT HERE TO COLLECT ONE THAT SUPPOSEDLY DATES BACK TO THE **JIN** DYNASTY. LADY CYNTHIA HAS AN INTEREST IN RARE ANTIQUITIES.
WHAT ELSE DID YOU SEE, SUE?
ANYTHING ABOUT MONSTERS ROAMING AROUND, SCARING FOLKS?
I SAW A MAN. SOMEONE IS ***USING*** THE JAR TO COLLECT THE SPIRIT ENERGY FROM THESE PEOPLE.
AND I THINK I KNOW WHERE HE IS.

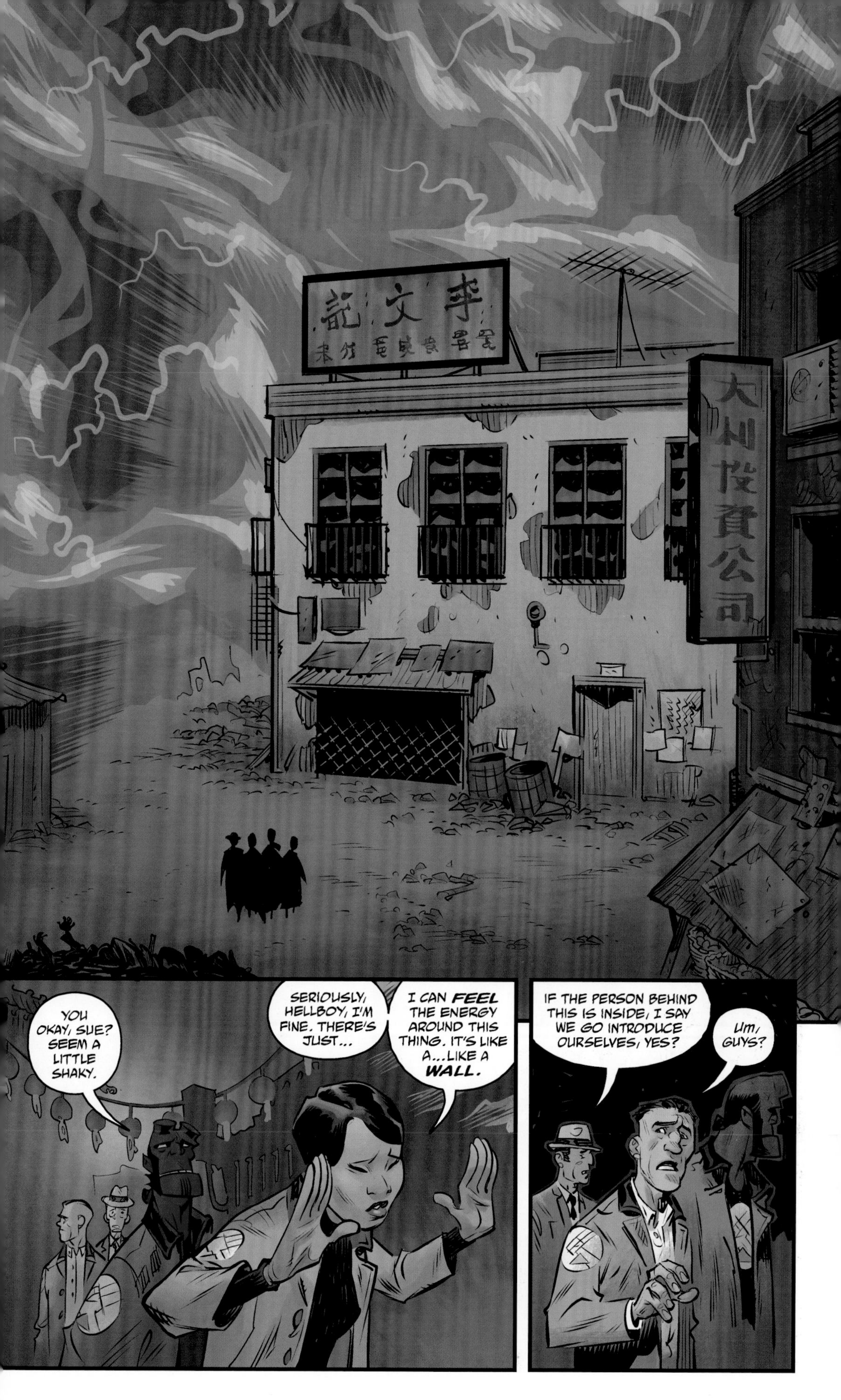
YOU OKAY, SUE? SEEM A LITTLE SHAKY.
SERIOUSLY, HELLBOY, I'M FINE. THERE'S JUST...
I CAN FEEL THE ENERGY AROUND THIS THING. IT'S LIKE A...LIKE A WALL.
IF THE PERSON BEHIND THIS IS INSIDE, I SAY WE GO INTRODUCE OURSELVES, YES?
UM, GUYS?

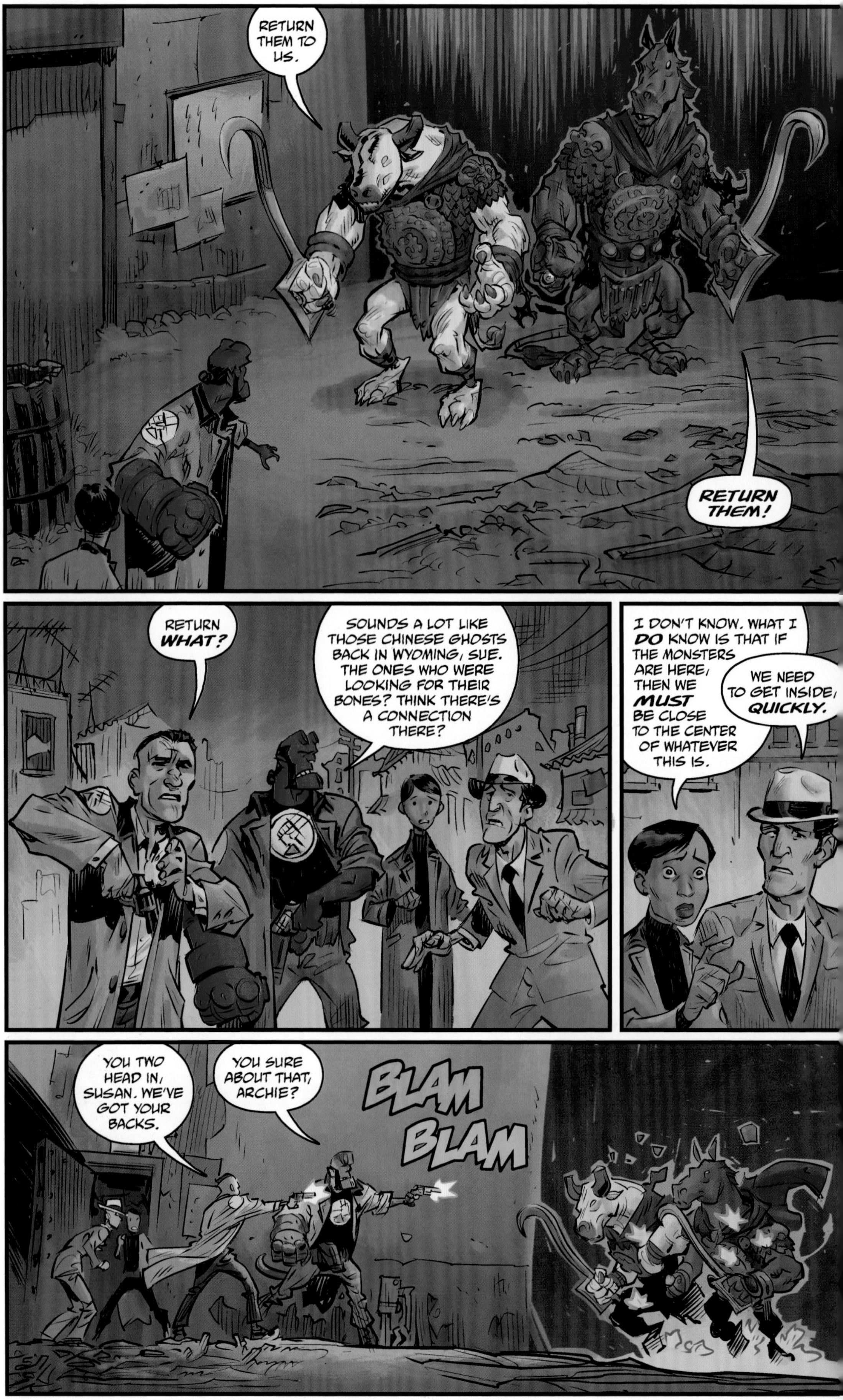
RETURN THEM TO US.
RETURN THEM!
RETURN WHAT?
SOUNDS A LOT LIKE THOSE CHINESE GHOSTS BACK IN WYOMING, SUE. THE ONES WHO WERE LOOKING FOR THEIR BONES? THINK THERE'S A CONNECTION THERE?
I DON'T KNOW. WHAT I DO KNOW IS THAT IF THE MONSTERS ARE HERE, THEN WE MUST BE CLOSE TO THE CENTER OF WHATEVER THIS IS.
WE NEED TO GET INSIDE, QUICKLY.
YOU TWO HEAD IN, SUSAN. WE'VE GOT YOUR BACKS.
YOU SURE ABOUT THAT, ARCHIE?
BLAM
BLAM

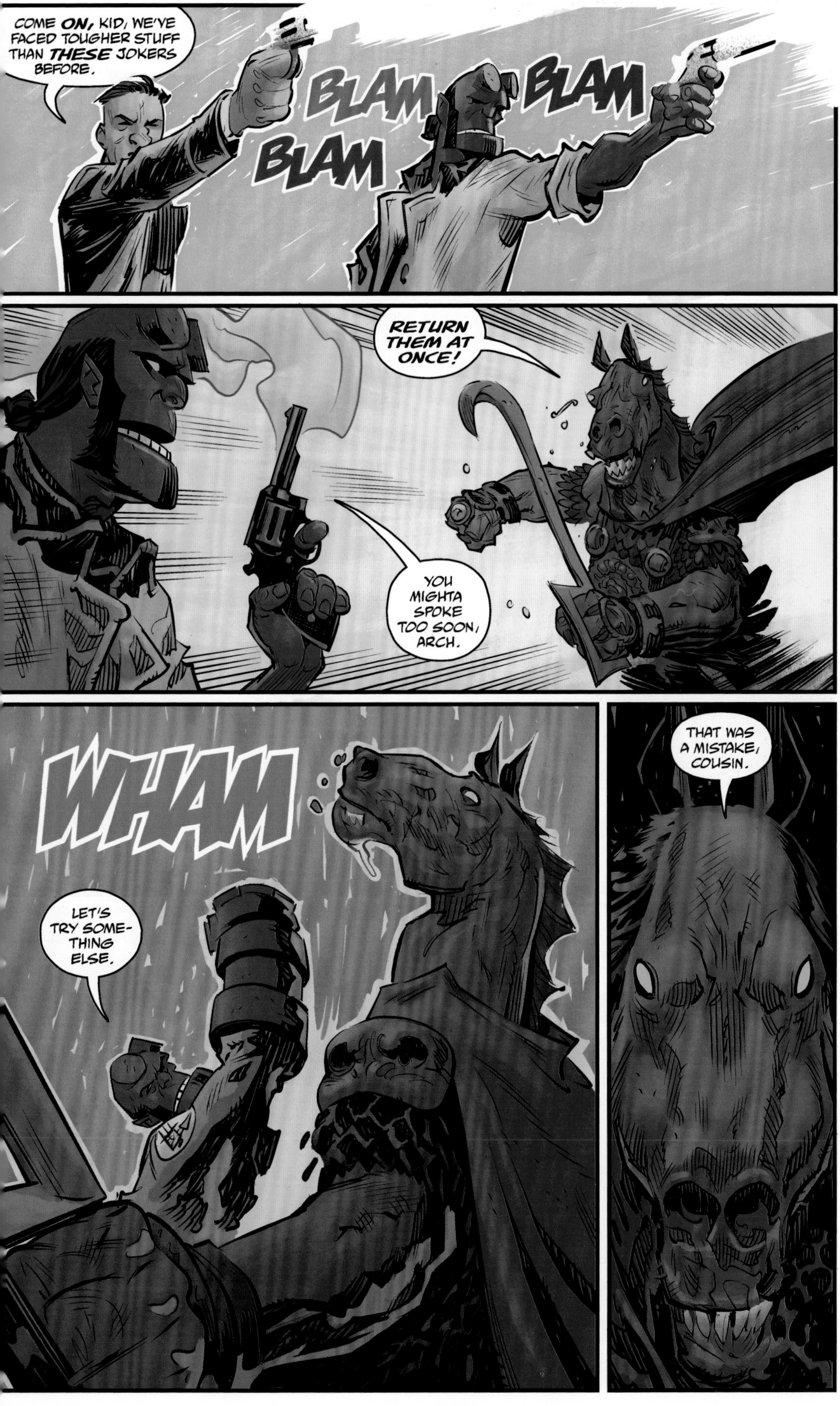
COME **ON,** KID, WE'VE FACED TOUGHER STUFF THAN ***THESE*** JOKERS BEFORE.
BLAM
BLAM
BLAM
RETURN THEM AT ONCE!
YOU MIGHTA SPOKE TOO SOON, ARCH.
WHAM
LET'S TRY SOME-THING ELSE.
THAT WAS A MISTAKE, COUSIN.

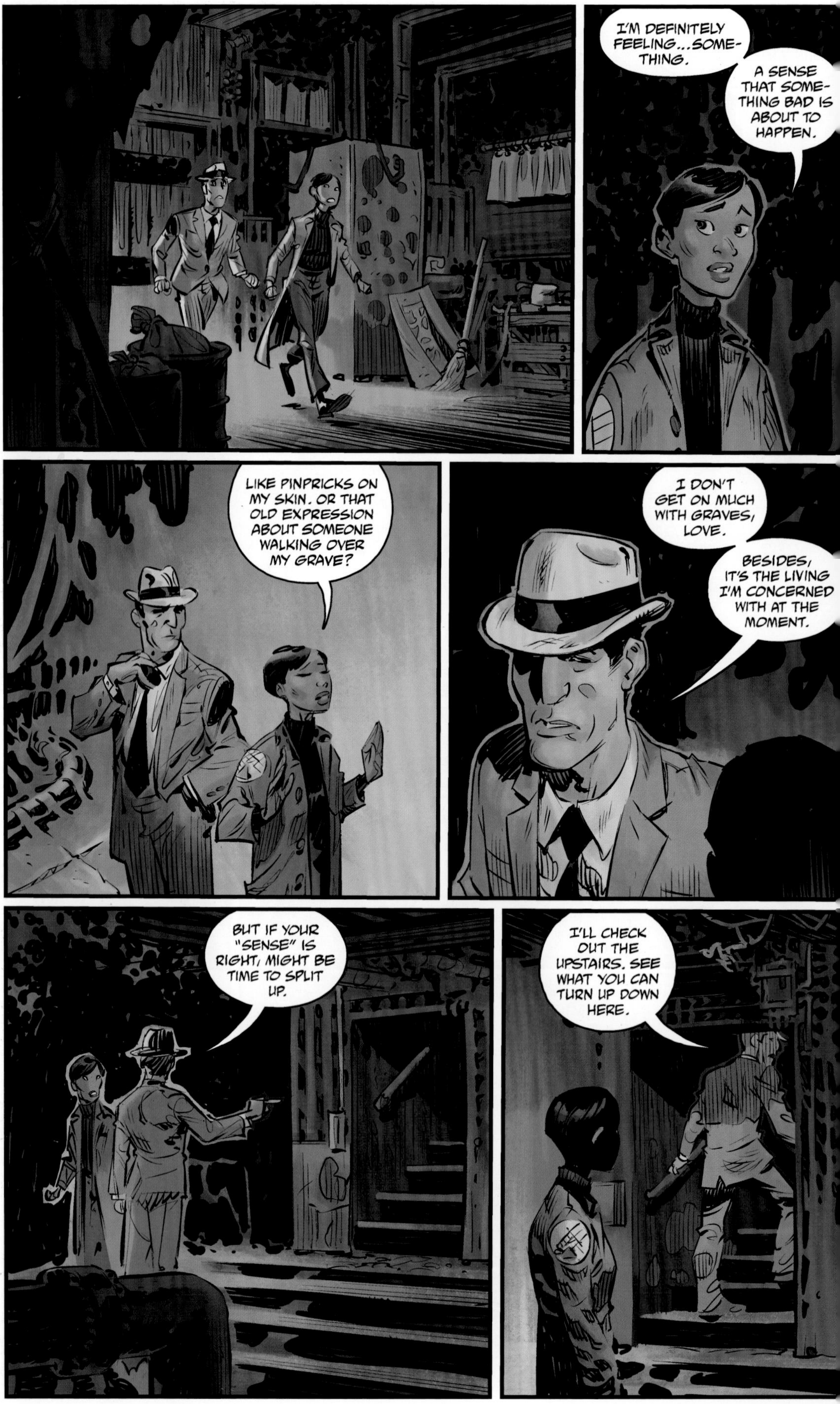
I'M DEFINITELY FEELING...SOME-THING.
A SENSE THAT SOME-THING BAD IS ABOUT TO HAPPEN.
LIKE PINPRICKS ON MY SKIN. OR THAT OLD EXPRESSION ABOUT SOMEONE WALKING OVER MY GRAVE?
I DON'T GET ON MUCH WITH GRAVES, LOVE.
BESIDES, IT'S THE LIVING I'M CONCERNED WITH AT THE MOMENT.
BUT IF YOUR "SENSE" IS RIGHT, MIGHT BE TIME TO SPLIT UP.
I'LL CHECK OUT THE UPSTAIRS. SEE WHAT YOU CAN TURN UP DOWN HERE.

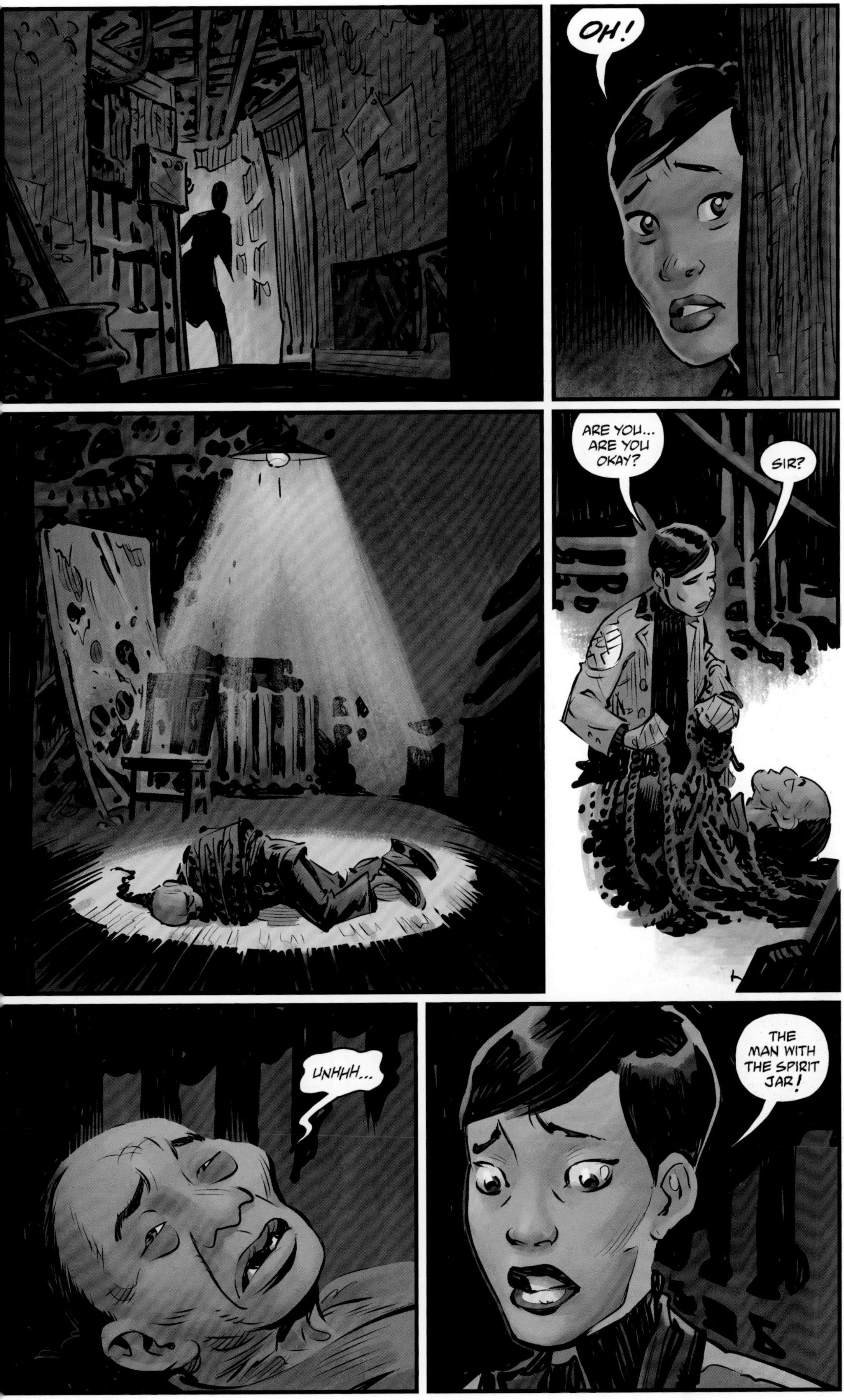
OH!
ARE YOU... ARE YOU OKAY?
SIR?
UNHHH...
THE MAN WITH THE SPIRIT JAR!

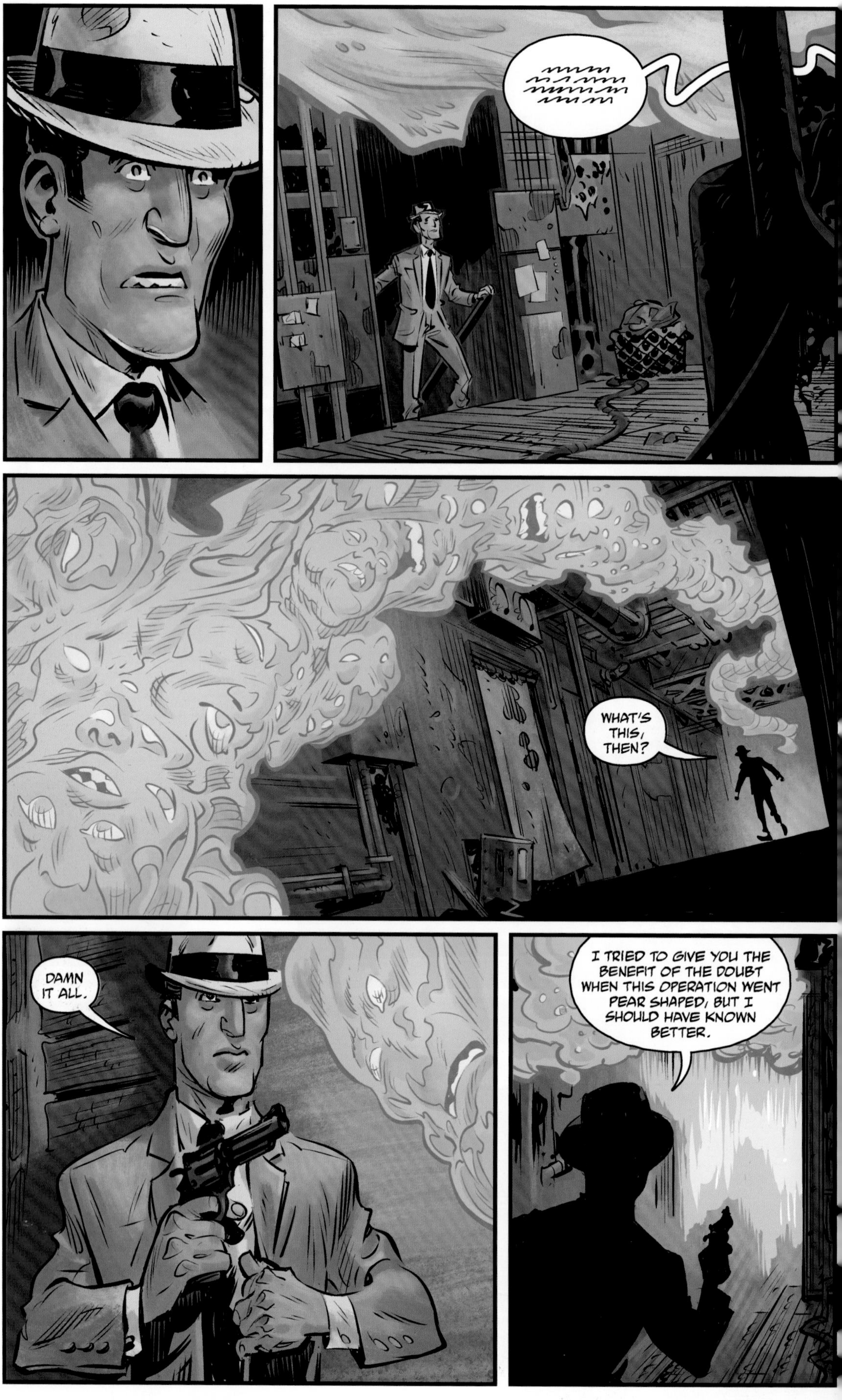
WHAT'S THIS, THEN?
DAMN IT ALL.
I TRIED TO GIVE YOU THE BENEFIT OF THE DOUBT WHEN THIS OPERATION WENT PEAR SHAPED, BUT I SHOULD HAVE KNOWN BETTER.

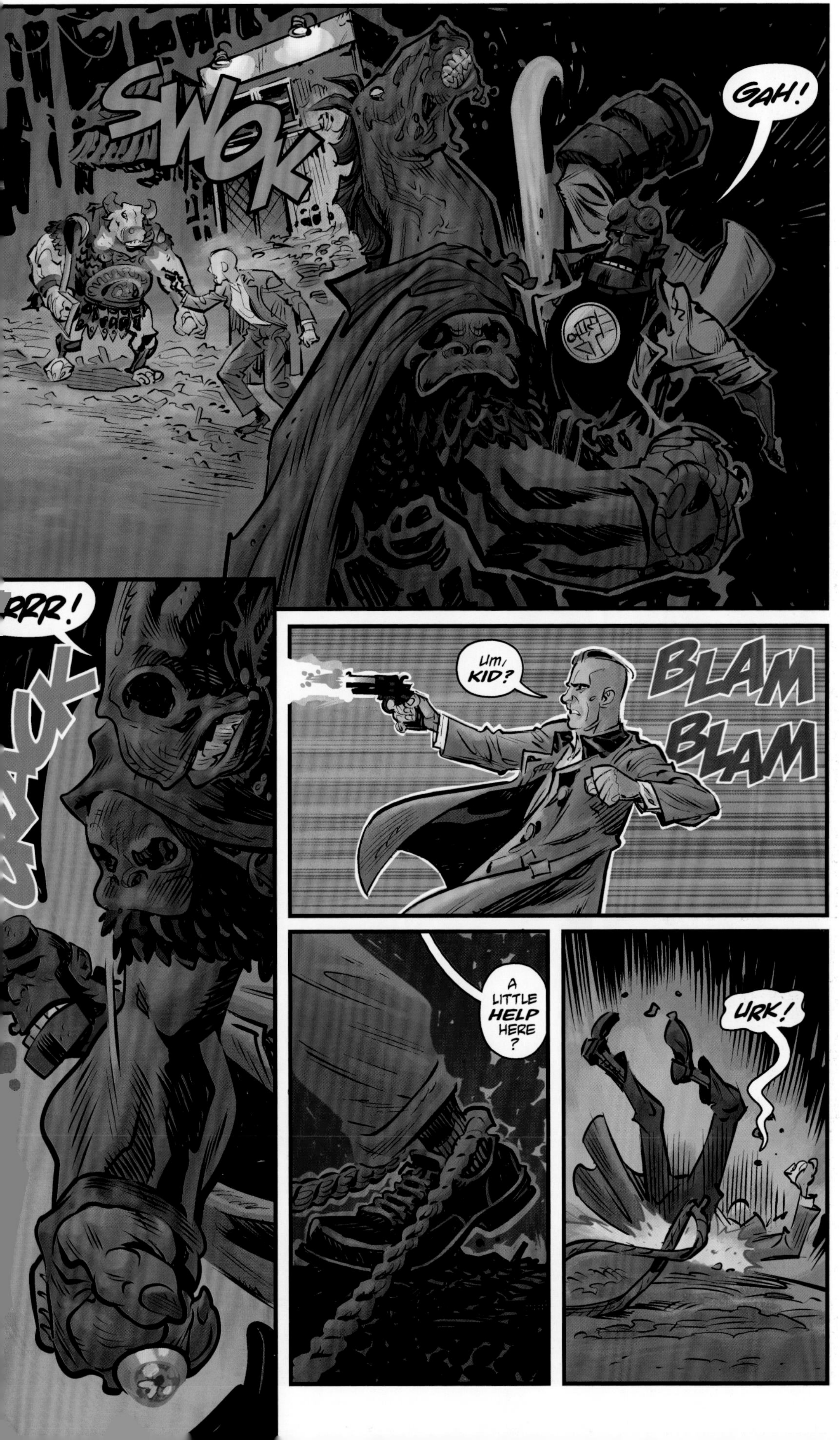
SWOK
GAH!
RRR!
UM, KID?
BLAM
BLAM
A LITTLE HELP HERE?
URK!

RETURN THEM!

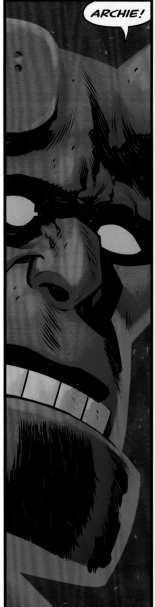

ARCHIE!

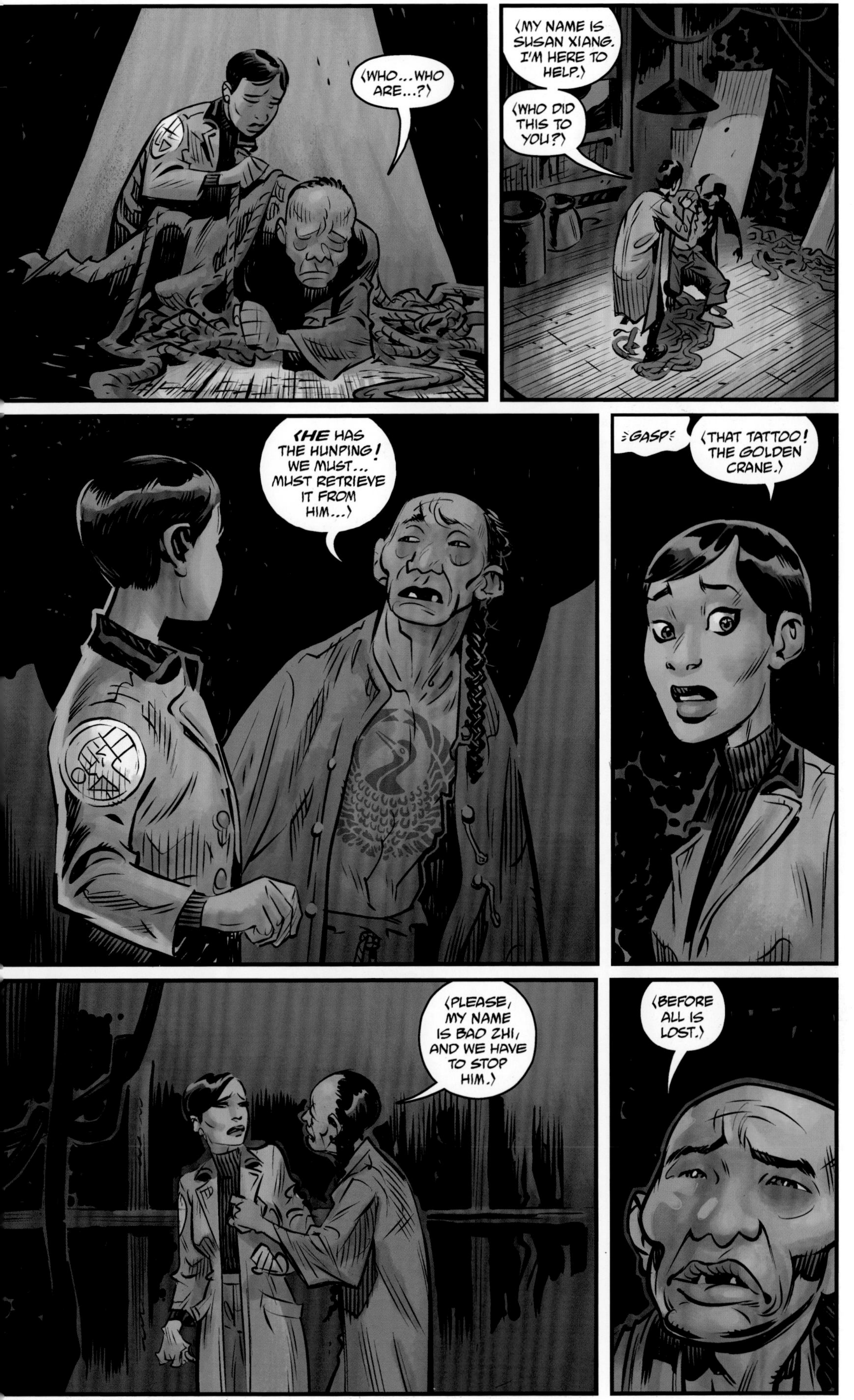

⟨WHO...WHO ARE...?⟩
⟨MY NAME IS SUSAN XIANG. I'M HERE TO HELP.⟩
⟨WHO DID THIS TO YOU?⟩
⟨HE HAS THE HUNPING! WE MUST... MUST RETRIEVE IT FROM HIM...⟩
GASP
⟨THAT TATTOO! THE GOLDEN CRANE.⟩
⟨PLEASE, MY NAME IS BAO ZHI, AND WE HAVE TO STOP HIM.⟩
⟨BEFORE ALL IS LOST.⟩

TRANSLATED FROM CANTONESE⟩

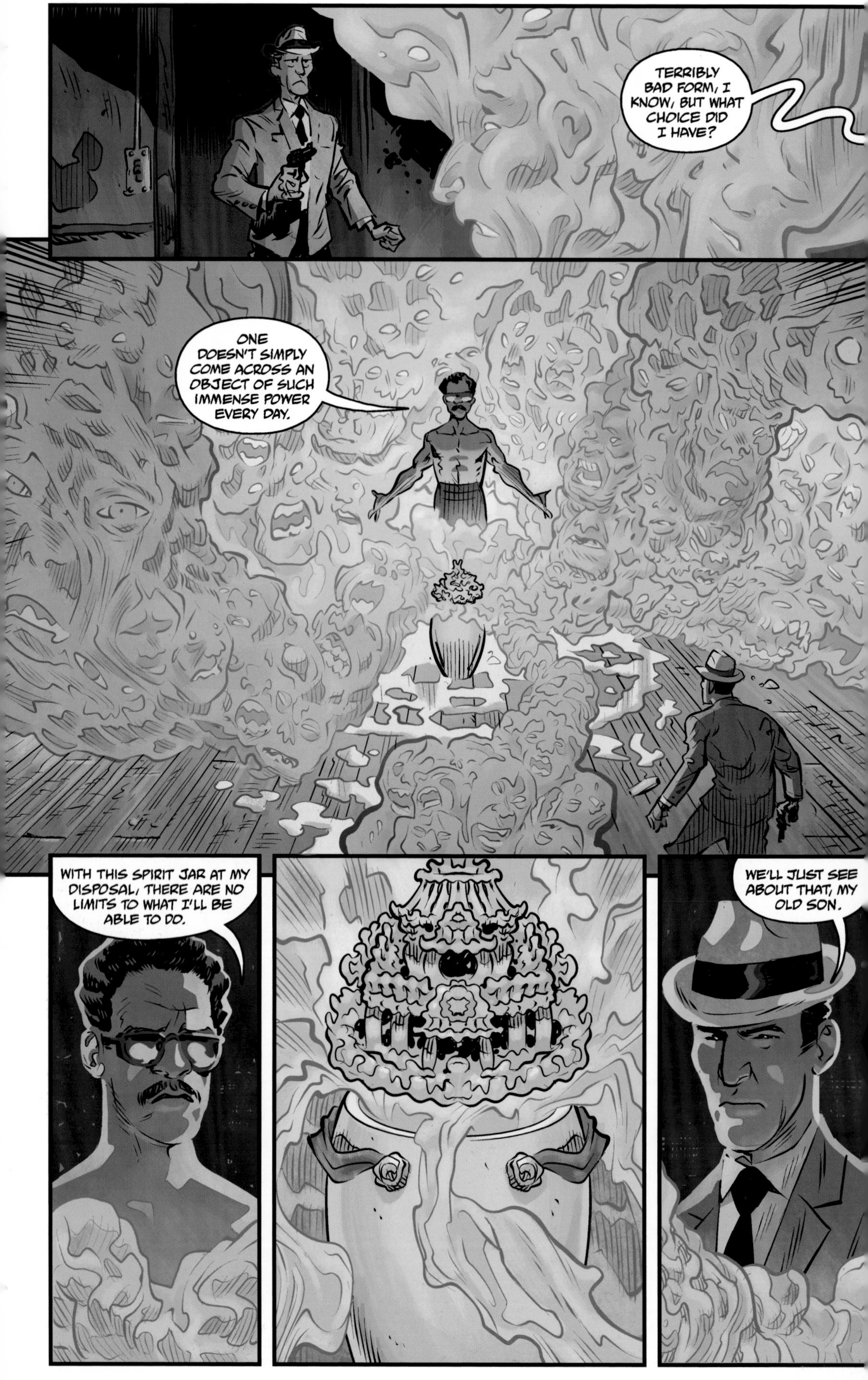
TERRIBLY BAD FORM, I KNOW, BUT WHAT CHOICE DID I HAVE?
ONE DOESN'T SIMPLY COME ACROSS AN OBJECT OF SUCH IMMENSE POWER EVERY DAY.
WITH THIS SPIRIT JAR AT MY DISPOSAL, THERE ARE NO LIMITS TO WHAT I'LL BE ABLE TO DO.
WE'LL JUST SEE ABOUT THAT, MY OLD SON.

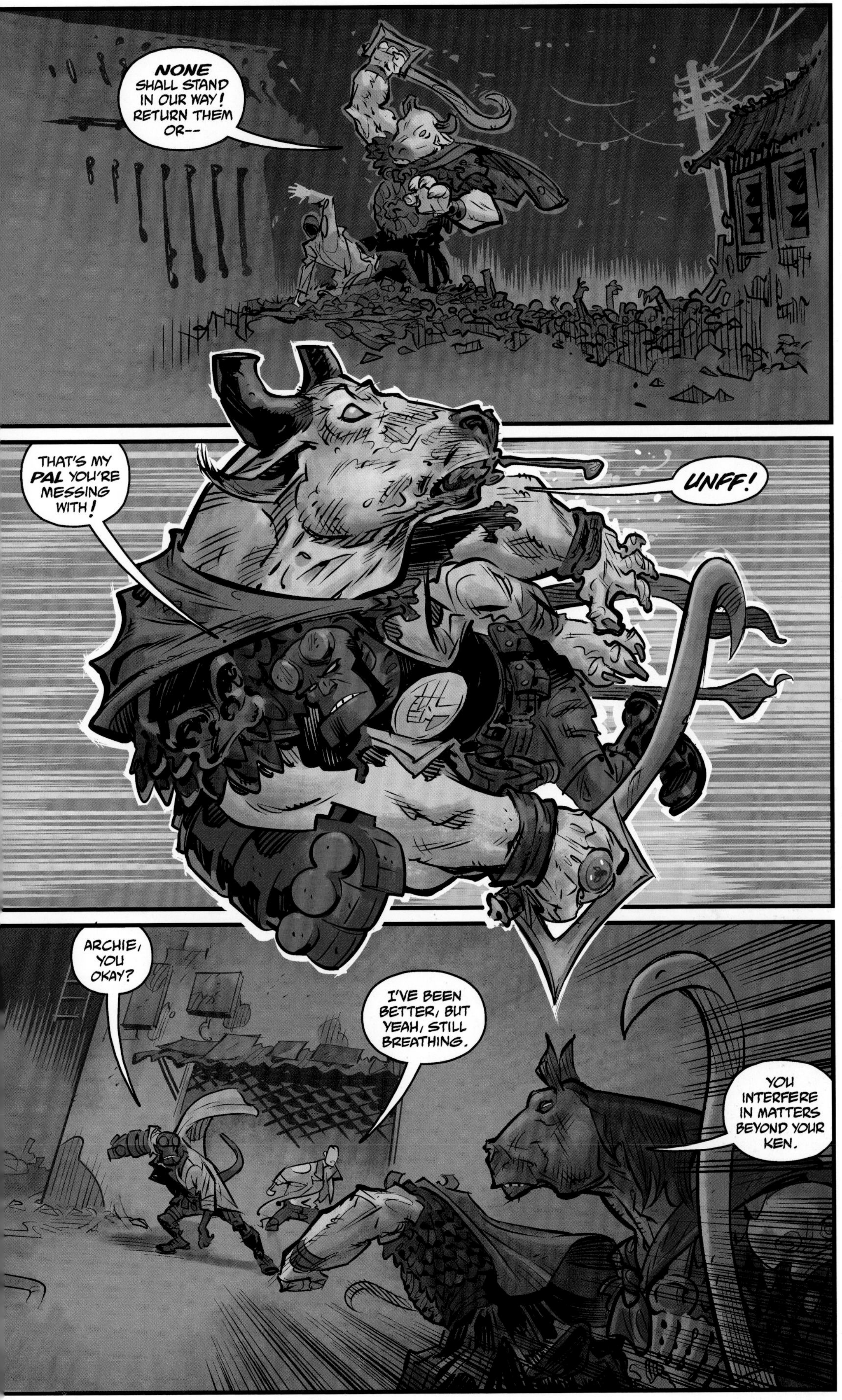
NONE SHALL STAND IN OUR WAY! RETURN THEM OR--
THAT'S MY PAL YOU'RE MESSING WITH!
UNFF!
ARCHIE, YOU OKAY?
I'VE BEEN BETTER, BUT YEAH, STILL BREATHING.
YOU INTERFERE IN MATTERS BEYOND YOUR KEN.

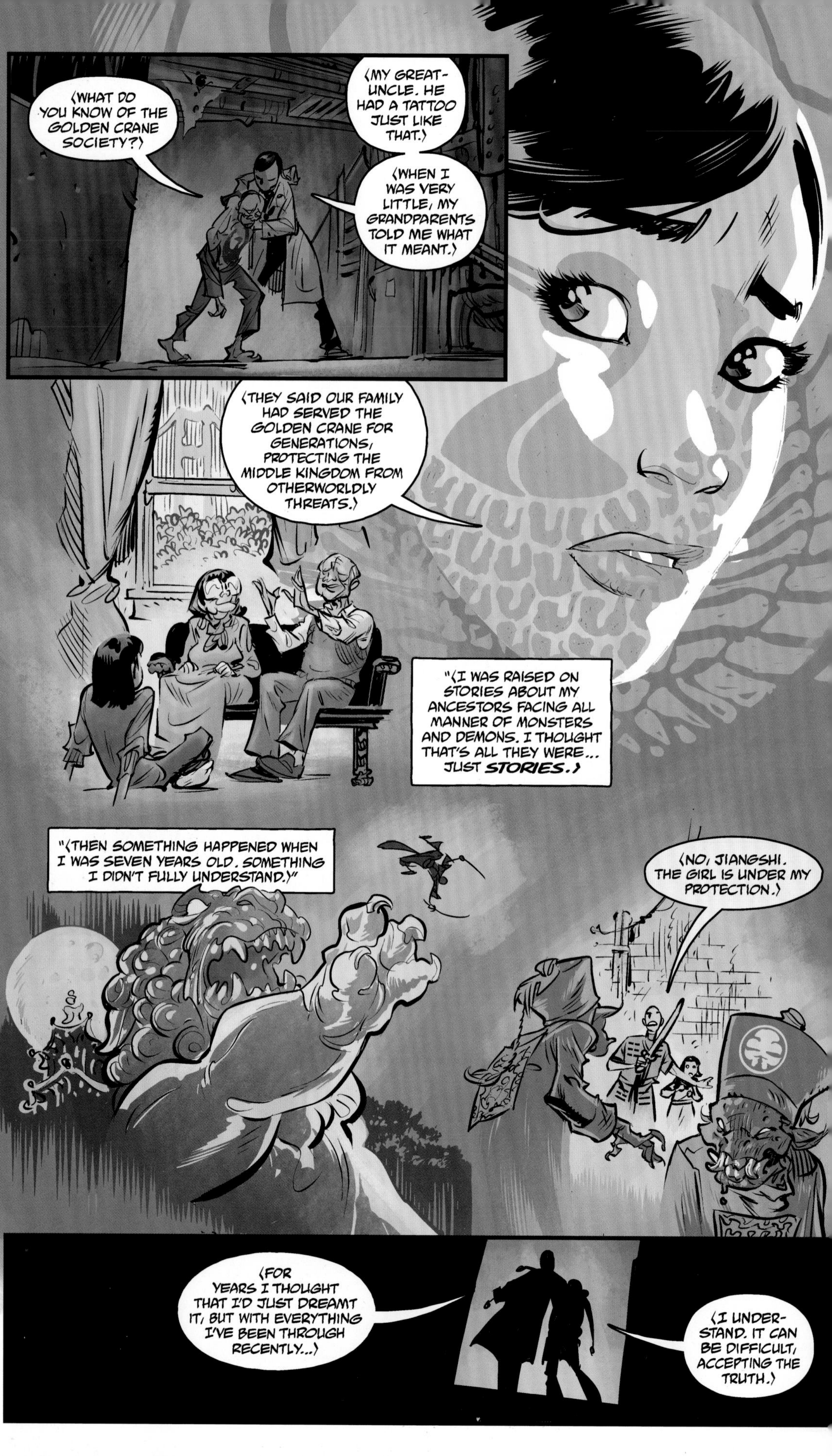
⟨WHAT DO YOU KNOW OF THE GOLDEN CRANE SOCIETY?⟩
⟨MY GREAT-UNCLE. HE HAD A TATTOO JUST LIKE THAT.⟩
⟨WHEN I WAS VERY LITTLE, MY GRANDPARENTS TOLD ME WHAT IT MEANT.⟩
⟨THEY SAID OUR FAMILY HAD SERVED THE GOLDEN CRANE FOR GENERATIONS, PROTECTING THE MIDDLE KINGDOM FROM OTHERWORLDLY THREATS.⟩
"⟨I WAS RAISED ON STORIES ABOUT MY ANCESTORS FACING ALL MANNER OF MONSTERS AND DEMONS. I THOUGHT THAT'S ALL THEY WERE... JUST STORIES.⟩
"⟨THEN SOMETHING HAPPENED WHEN I WAS SEVEN YEARS OLD. SOMETHING I DIDN'T FULLY UNDERSTAND.⟩"
⟨NO, JIANGSHI. THE GIRL IS UNDER MY PROTECTION.⟩
⟨FOR YEARS I THOUGHT THAT I'D JUST DREAMT IT, BUT WITH EVERYTHING I'VE BEEN THROUGH RECENTLY...⟩
⟨I UNDERSTAND. IT CAN BE DIFFICULT, ACCEPTING THE TRUTH.⟩

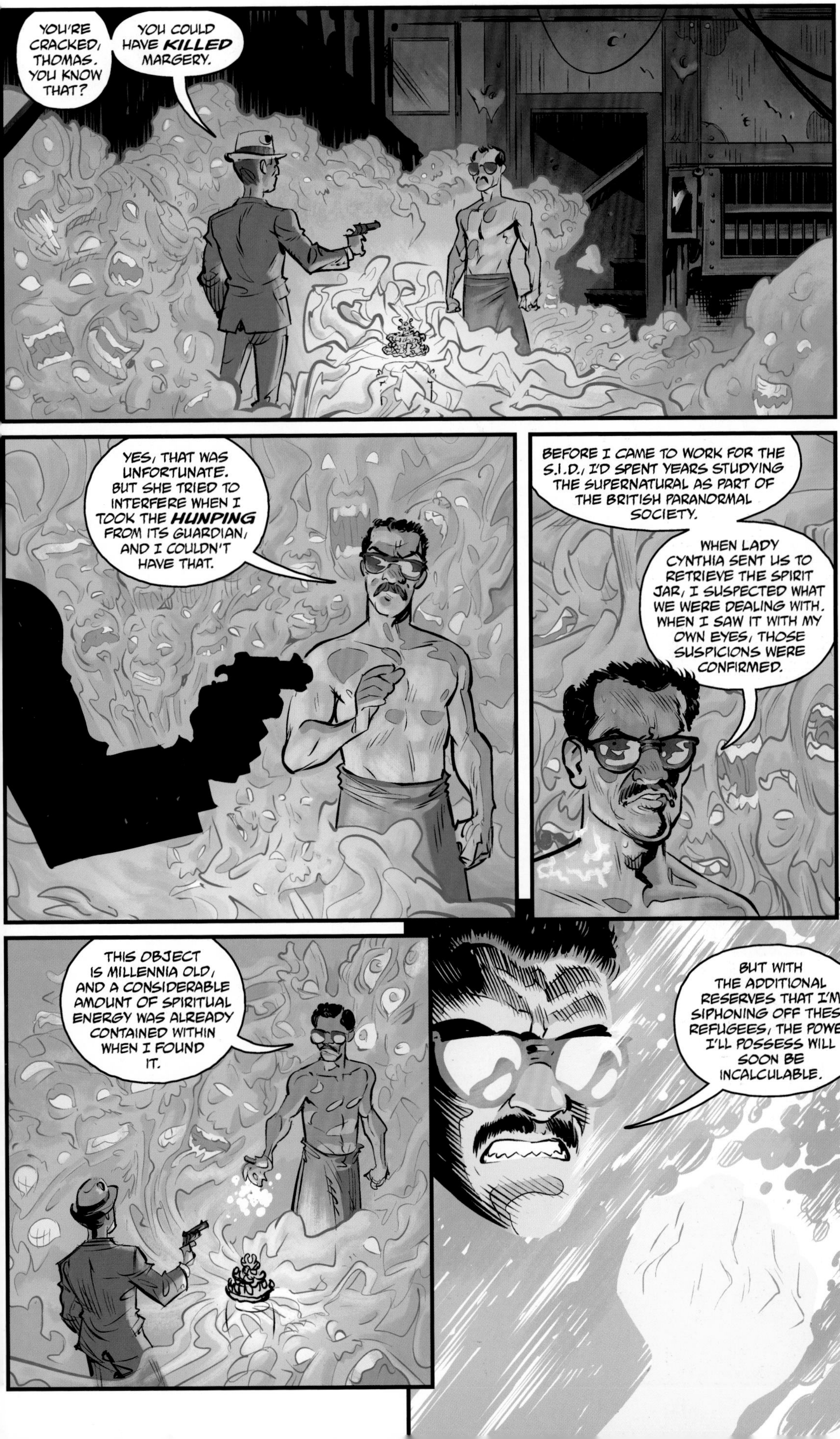

YOU'RE CRACKED, THOMAS. YOU KNOW THAT?
YOU COULD HAVE KILLED MARGERY.
YES, THAT WAS UNFORTUNATE. BUT SHE TRIED TO INTERFERE WHEN I TOOK THE HUNPING FROM ITS GUARDIAN, AND I COULDN'T HAVE THAT.
BEFORE I CAME TO WORK FOR THE S.I.D., I'D SPENT YEARS STUDYING THE SUPERNATURAL AS PART OF THE BRITISH PARANORMAL SOCIETY.
WHEN LADY CYNTHIA SENT US TO RETRIEVE THE SPIRIT JAR, I SUSPECTED WHAT WE WERE DEALING WITH. WHEN I SAW IT WITH MY OWN EYES, THOSE SUSPICIONS WERE CONFIRMED.
THIS OBJECT IS MILLENNIA OLD, AND A CONSIDERABLE AMOUNT OF SPIRITUAL ENERGY WAS ALREADY CONTAINED WITHIN WHEN I FOUND IT.
BUT WITH THE ADDITIONAL RESERVES THAT I'M SIPHONING OFF THESE REFUGEES, THE POWER I'LL POSSESS WILL SOON BE INCALCULABLE.

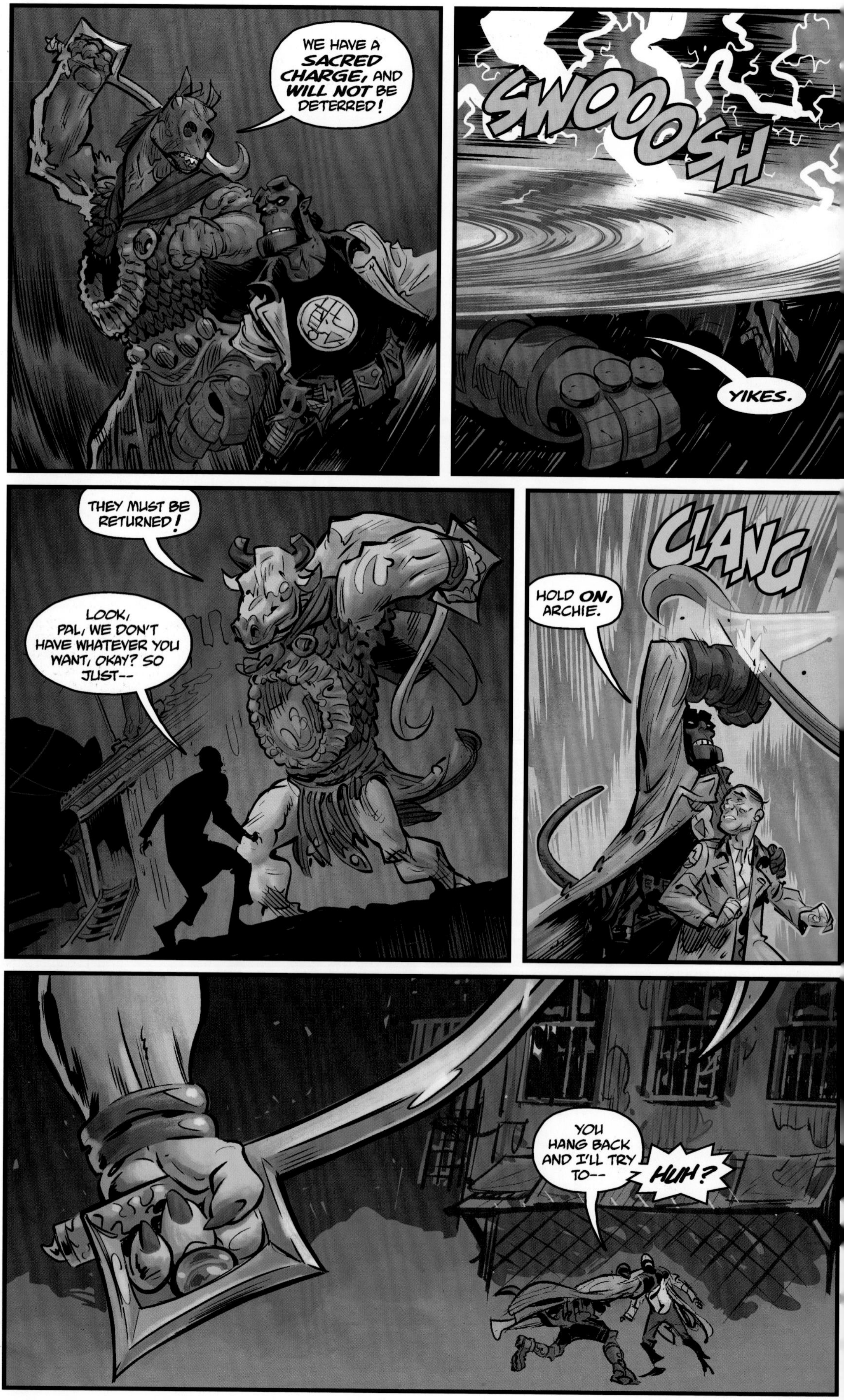
WE HAVE A SACRED CHARGE, AND WILL NOT BE DETERRED!
SWOOOSH
YIKES.
THEY MUST BE RETURNED!
LOOK, PAL, WE DON'T HAVE WHATEVER YOU WANT, OKAY? SO JUST--
CLANG
HOLD ON, ARCHIE.
YOU HANG BACK AND I'LL TRY TO--
HUH?

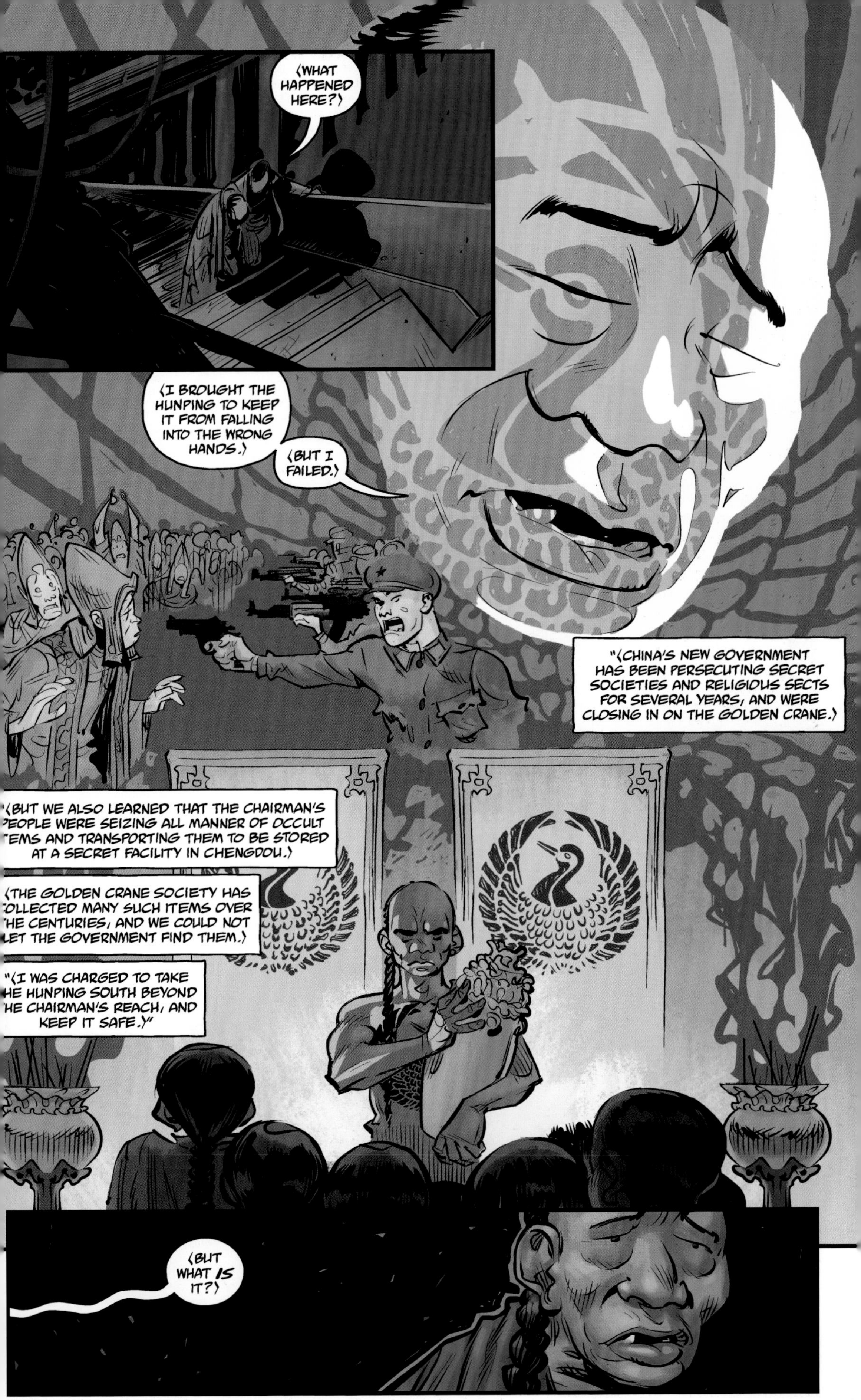

⟨WHAT HAPPENED HERE?⟩
⟨I BROUGHT THE HUNPING TO KEEP IT FROM FALLING INTO THE WRONG HANDS.⟩
⟨BUT I FAILED.⟩
"⟨CHINA'S NEW GOVERNMENT HAS BEEN PERSECUTING SECRET SOCIETIES AND RELIGIOUS SECTS FOR SEVERAL YEARS, AND WERE CLOSING IN ON THE GOLDEN CRANE.⟩
⟨BUT WE ALSO LEARNED THAT THE CHAIRMAN'S PEOPLE WERE SEIZING ALL MANNER OF OCCULT ITEMS AND TRANSPORTING THEM TO BE STORED AT A SECRET FACILITY IN CHENGDOU.⟩
⟨THE GOLDEN CRANE SOCIETY HAS COLLECTED MANY SUCH ITEMS OVER THE CENTURIES, AND WE COULD NOT LET THE GOVERNMENT FIND THEM.⟩
"⟨I WAS CHARGED TO TAKE THE HUNPING SOUTH BEYOND THE CHAIRMAN'S REACH, AND KEEP IT SAFE.⟩"
⟨BUT WHAT *IS* IT?⟩

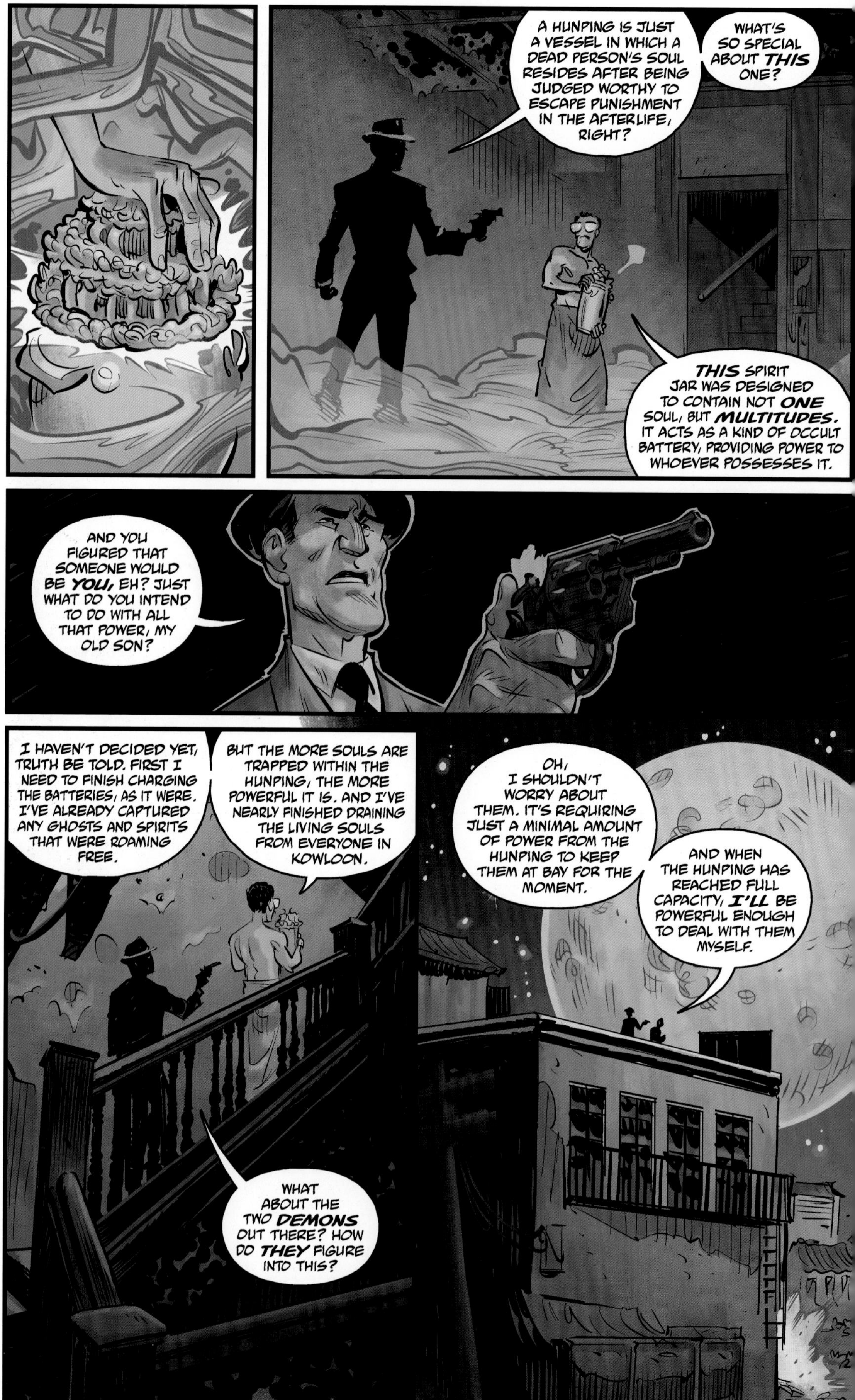
A HUNPING IS JUST A VESSEL IN WHICH A DEAD PERSON'S SOUL RESIDES AFTER BEING JUDGED WORTHY TO ESCAPE PUNISHMENT IN THE AFTERLIFE, RIGHT?
WHAT'S SO SPECIAL ABOUT THIS ONE?
THIS SPIRIT JAR WAS DESIGNED TO CONTAIN NOT ONE SOUL, BUT MULTITUDES. IT ACTS AS A KIND OF OCCULT BATTERY, PROVIDING POWER TO WHOEVER POSSESSES IT.
AND YOU FIGURED THAT SOMEONE WOULD BE YOU, EH? JUST WHAT DO YOU INTEND TO DO WITH ALL THAT POWER, MY OLD SON?
I HAVEN'T DECIDED YET, TRUTH BE TOLD. FIRST I NEED TO FINISH CHARGING THE BATTERIES, AS IT WERE. I'VE ALREADY CAPTURED ANY GHOSTS AND SPIRITS THAT WERE ROAMING FREE.
BUT THE MORE SOULS ARE TRAPPED WITHIN THE HUNPING, THE MORE POWERFUL IT IS. AND I'VE NEARLY FINISHED DRAINING THE LIVING SOULS FROM EVERYONE IN KOWLOON.
WHAT ABOUT THE TWO DEMONS OUT THERE? HOW DO THEY FIGURE INTO THIS?
OH, I SHOULDN'T WORRY ABOUT THEM. IT'S REQUIRING JUST A MINIMAL AMOUNT OF POWER FROM THE HUNPING TO KEEP THEM AT BAY FOR THE MOMENT.
AND WHEN THE HUNPING HAS REACHED FULL CAPACITY, I'LL BE POWERFUL ENOUGH TO DEAL WITH THEM MYSELF.

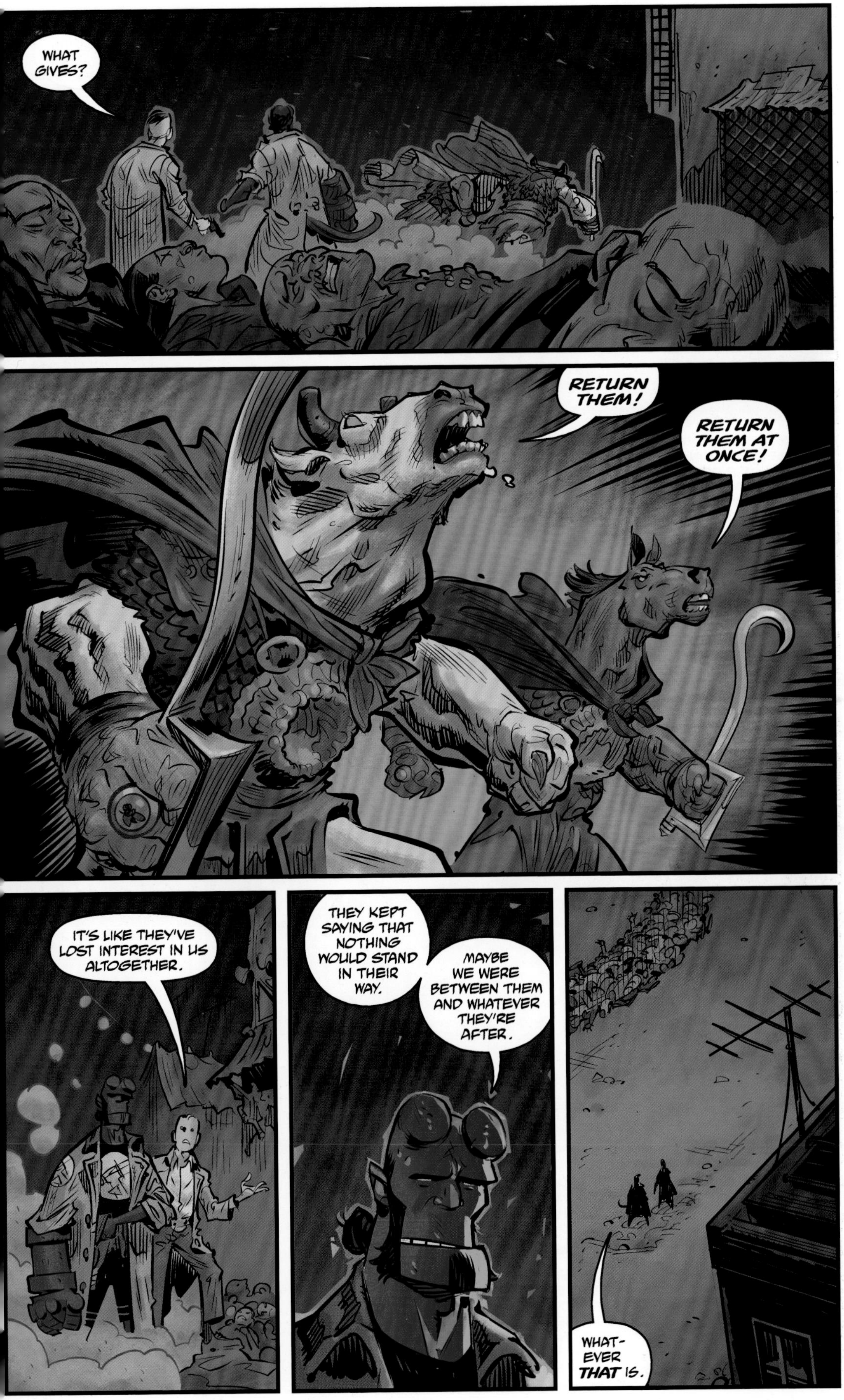
WHAT GIVES?
RETURN THEM!
RETURN THEM AT ONCE!
IT'S LIKE THEY'VE LOST INTEREST IN US ALTOGETHER.
THEY KEPT SAYING THAT NOTHING WOULD STAND IN THEIR WAY.
MAYBE WE WERE BETWEEN THEM AND WHATEVER THEY'RE AFTER.
WHAT-EVER THAT IS.

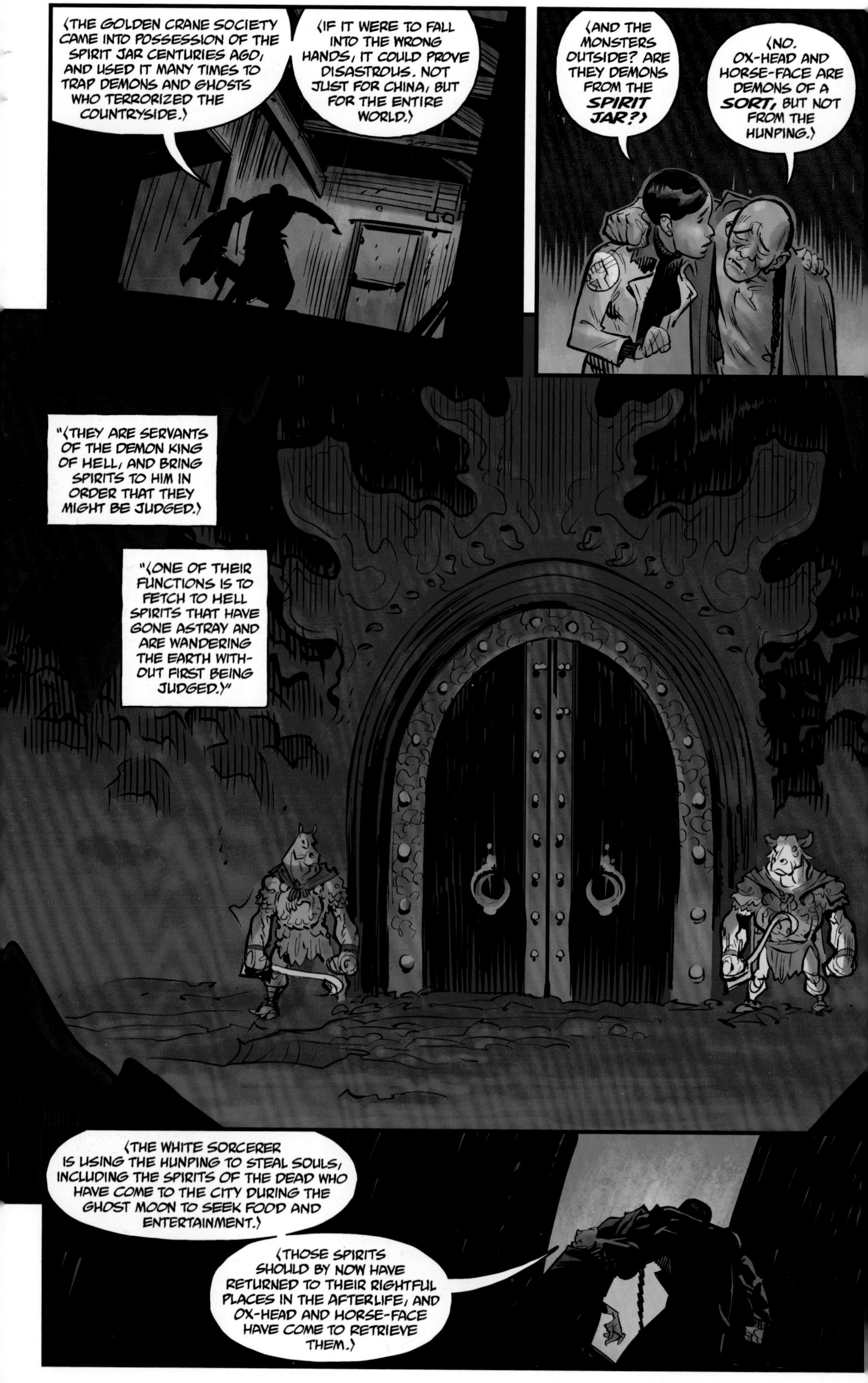
⟨THE GOLDEN CRANE SOCIETY CAME INTO POSSESSION OF THE SPIRIT JAR CENTURIES AGO, AND USED IT MANY TIMES TO TRAP DEMONS AND GHOSTS WHO TERRORIZED THE COUNTRYSIDE.⟩
⟨IF IT WERE TO FALL INTO THE WRONG HANDS, IT COULD PROVE DISASTROUS. NOT JUST FOR CHINA, BUT FOR THE ENTIRE WORLD.⟩
⟨AND THE MONSTERS OUTSIDE? ARE THEY DEMONS FROM THE **SPIRIT JAR?**⟩
⟨NO. OX-HEAD AND HORSE-FACE ARE DEMONS OF A **SORT,** BUT NOT FROM THE HUNPING.⟩
"⟨THEY ARE SERVANTS OF THE DEMON KING OF HELL, AND BRING SPIRITS TO HIM IN ORDER THAT THEY MIGHT BE JUDGED.⟩
"⟨ONE OF THEIR FUNCTIONS IS TO FETCH TO HELL SPIRITS THAT HAVE GONE ASTRAY AND ARE WANDERING THE EARTH WITHOUT FIRST BEING JUDGED.⟩"
⟨THE WHITE SORCERER IS USING THE HUNPING TO STEAL SOULS, INCLUDING THE SPIRITS OF THE DEAD WHO HAVE COME TO THE CITY DURING THE GHOST MOON TO SEEK FOOD AND ENTERTAINMENT.⟩
⟨THOSE SPIRITS SHOULD BY NOW HAVE RETURNED TO THEIR RIGHTFUL PLACES IN THE AFTERLIFE, AND OX-HEAD AND HORSE-FACE HAVE COME TO RETRIEVE THEM.⟩

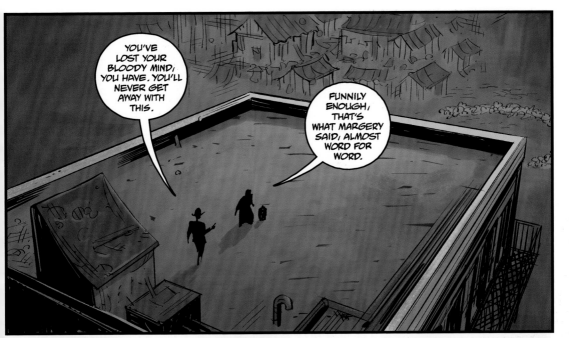

YOU'VE LOST YOUR BLOODY MIND, YOU HAVE. YOU'LL NEVER GET AWAY WITH THIS.

FUNNILY ENOUGH, THAT'S WHAT MARGERY SAID, ALMOST WORD FOR WORD.

SHE WAS YOUR *PARTNER*, THOMAS. WE'RE SUPPOSED TO WATCH OUT FOR EACH OTHER!

WE GET ENOUGH *STICK* FROM THE REDS WITHOUT HAVING TO WORRY ABOUT BEING STABBED IN THE BACK BY OUR OWN SIDE.

THE REDS. THE YANKS. THE BLOODY IRISH REPUBLICANS. YOU ALL THINK TOO SMALL!

YOU HAVE SEEN SUCH WONDROUS SIGHTS, AND YET UNDERSTOOD *NOTHING*. ONLY *I* HAVE THE VISION AND THE WILL TO DO WHAT MUST BE DONE.

BUT I'LL MAKE YOU THE SAME OFFER THAT MARGERY AND THAT OLD CHINESE FOOL REFUSED. PLEDGE TO SERVE ME, AND IN RETURN I WILL SPARE YOUR LIFE AND GRANT YOU--

RIGHT, THEN. THAT'S ENOUGH OF THAT.

BLAM

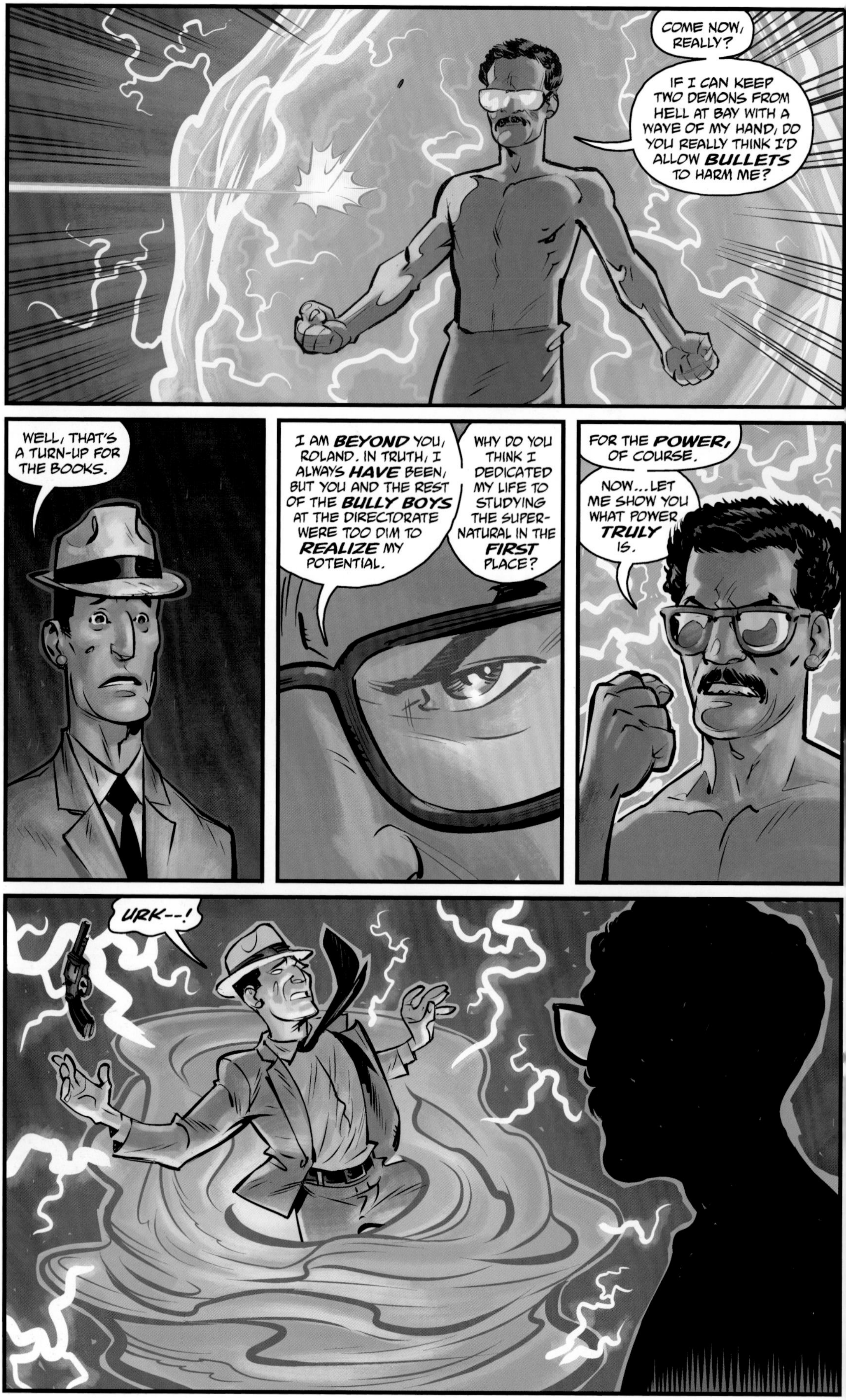
COME NOW, REALLY?
IF I CAN KEEP TWO DEMONS FROM HELL AT BAY WITH A WAVE OF MY HAND, DO YOU REALLY THINK I'D ALLOW BULLETS TO HARM ME?
WELL, THAT'S A TURN-UP FOR THE BOOKS.
I AM BEYOND YOU, ROLAND. IN TRUTH, I ALWAYS HAVE BEEN, BUT YOU AND THE REST OF THE BULLY BOYS AT THE DIRECTORATE WERE TOO DIM TO REALIZE MY POTENTIAL.
WHY DO YOU THINK I DEDICATED MY LIFE TO STUDYING THE SUPER-NATURAL IN THE FIRST PLACE?
FOR THE POWER, OF COURSE.
NOW...LET ME SHOW YOU WHAT POWER TRULY IS.
URK--!

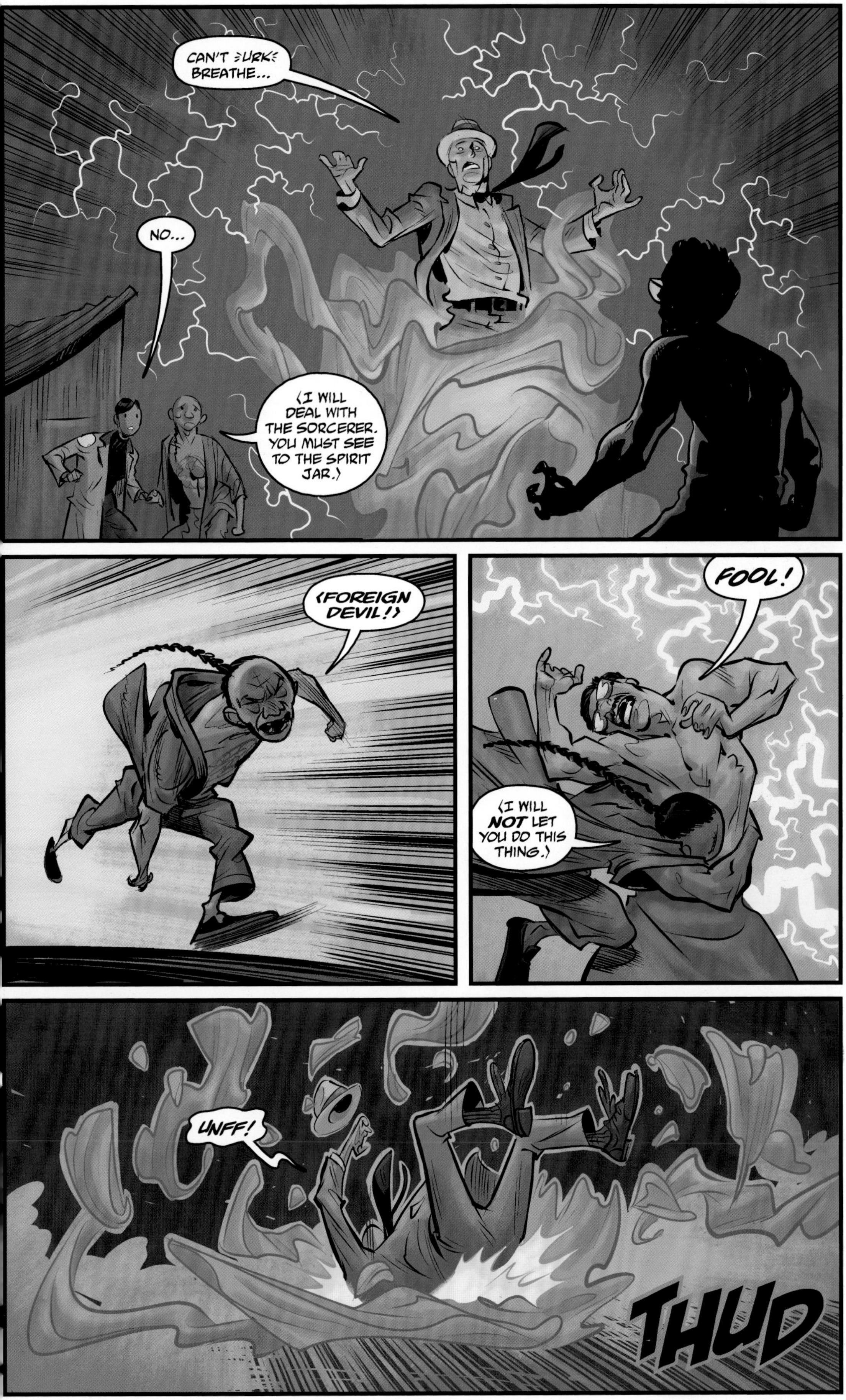

CAN'T ≷URK≶ BREATHE...
NO...
‹I WILL DEAL WITH THE SORCERER. YOU MUST SEE TO THE SPIRIT JAR.›
‹FOREIGN DEVIL!›
FOOL!
‹I WILL **NOT** LET YOU DO THIS THING.›
UNFF!
THUD

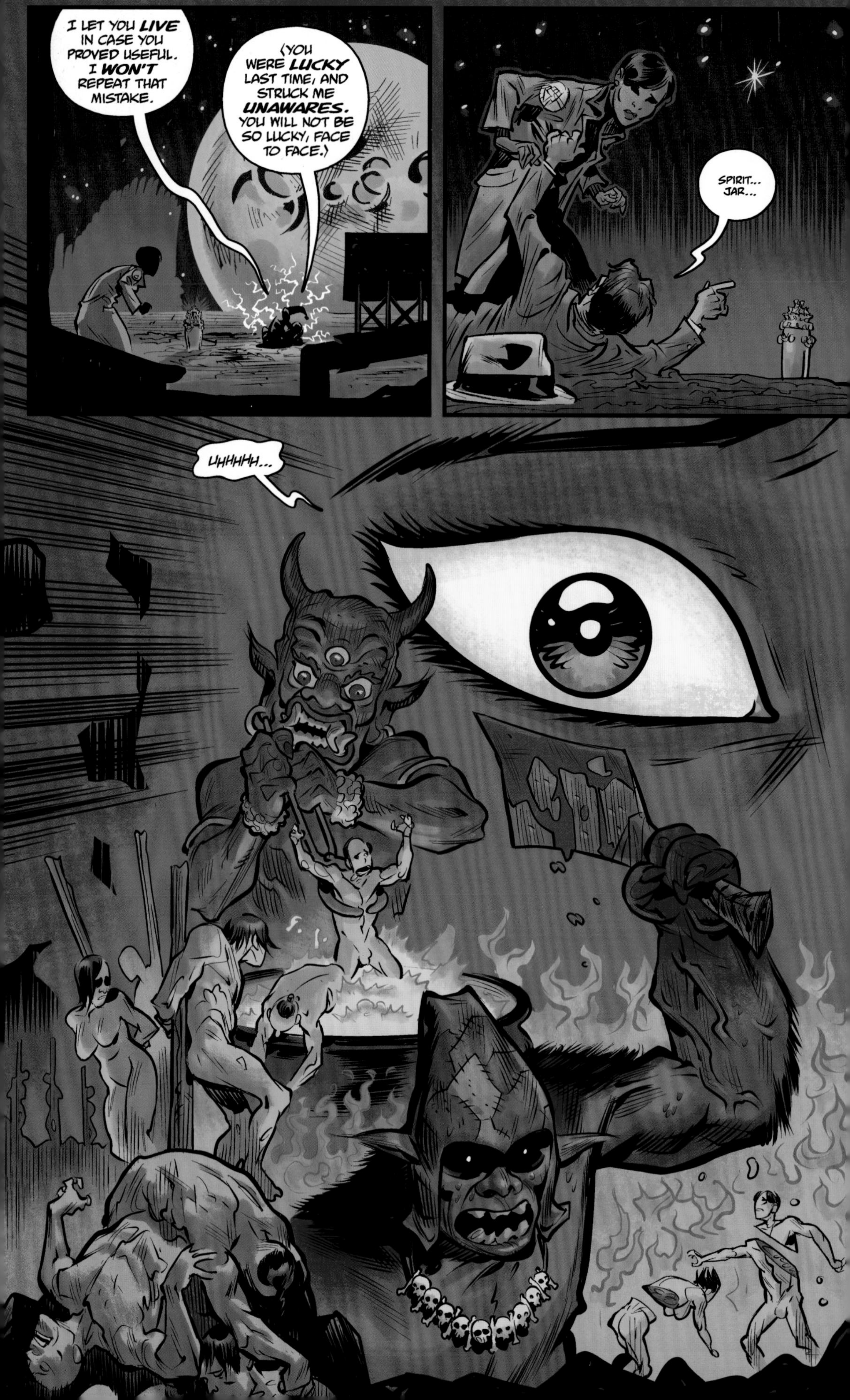
I LET YOU LIVE IN CASE YOU PROVED USEFUL. I WON'T REPEAT THAT MISTAKE.
(YOU WERE LUCKY LAST TIME, AND STRUCK ME UNAWARES. YOU WILL NOT BE SO LUCKY, FACE TO FACE.)
SPIRIT... JAR...
UHHHHH...

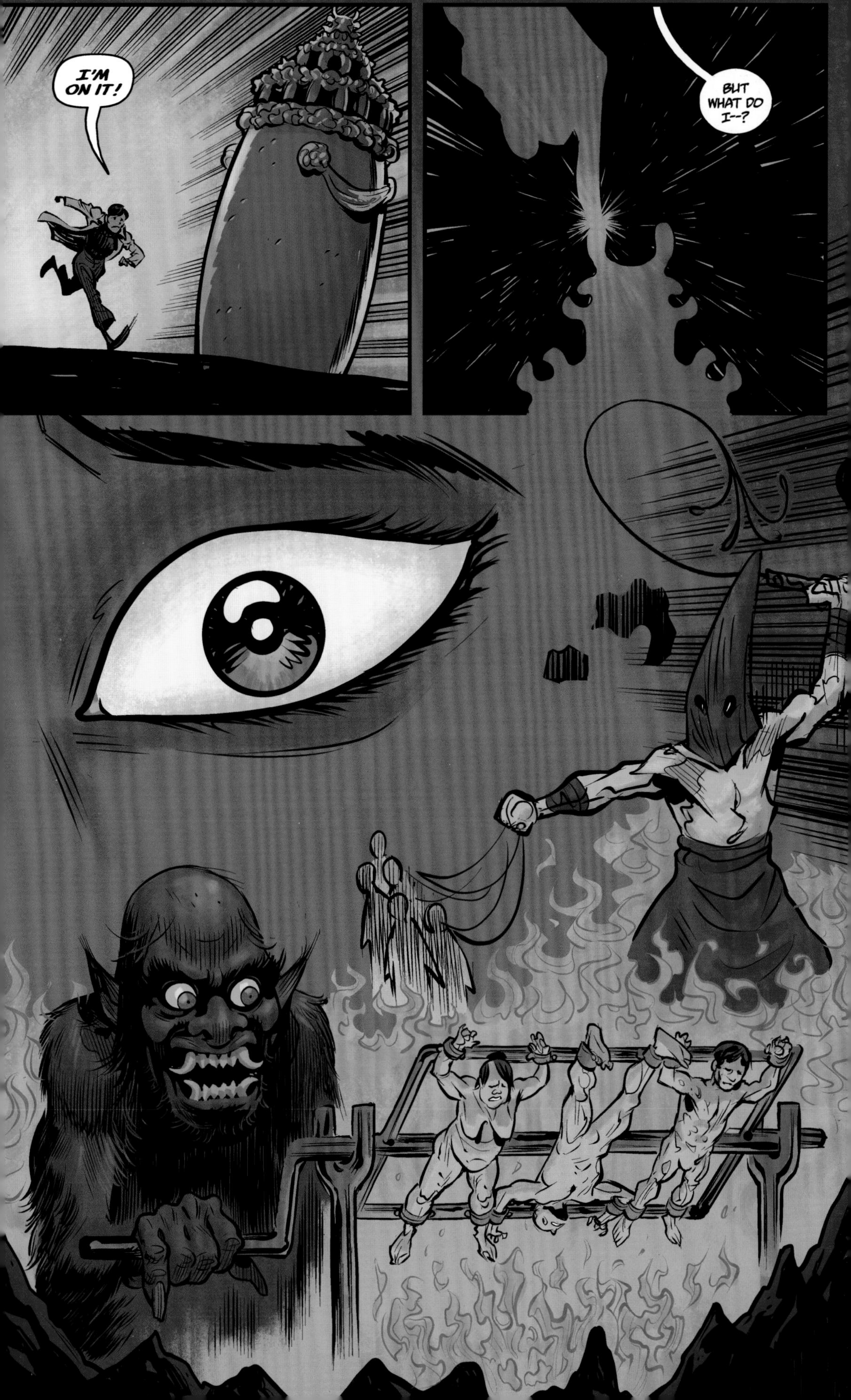
I'M ON IT!
BUT WHAT DO I--?

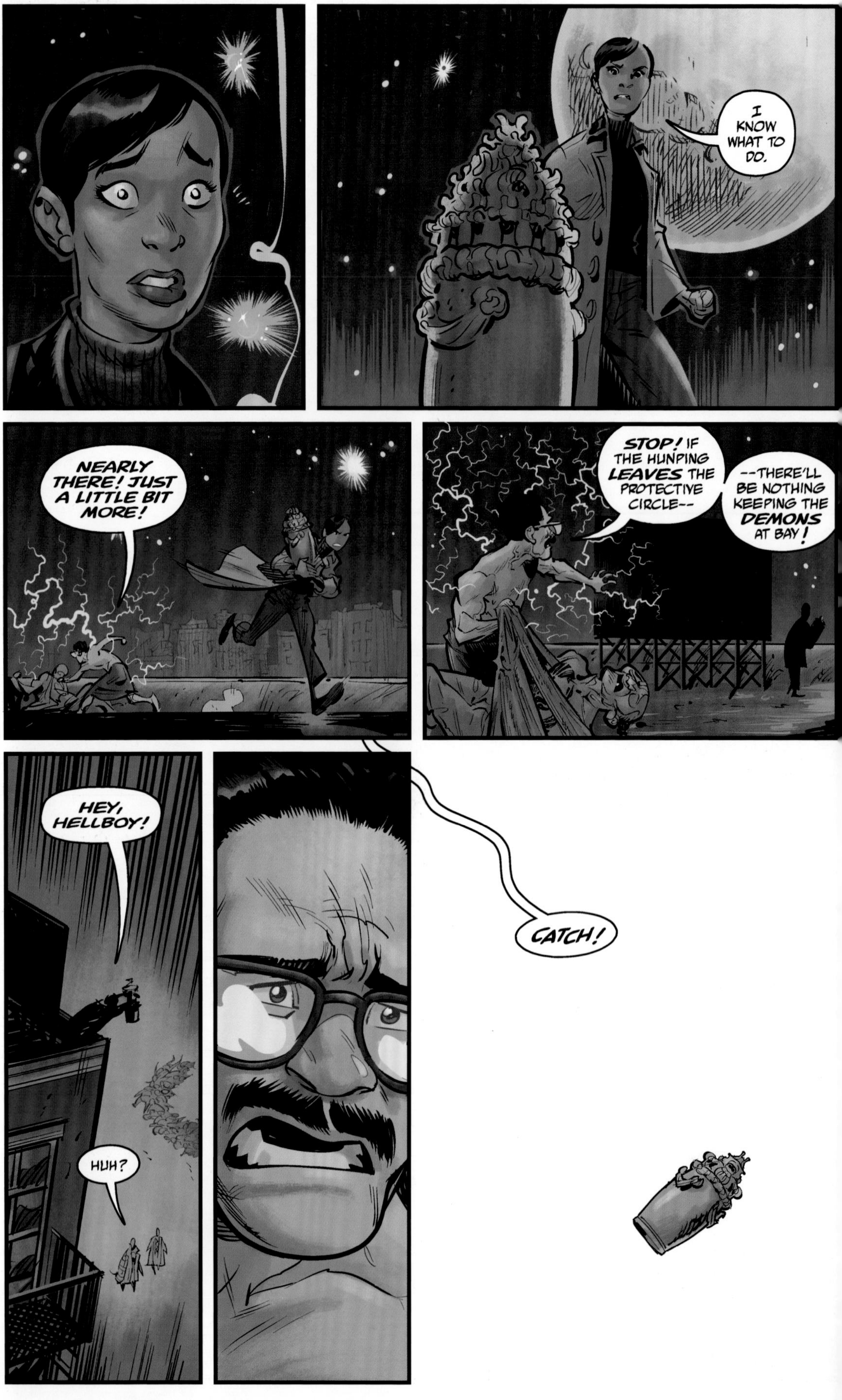
I KNOW WHAT TO DO.
NEARLY THERE! JUST A LITTLE BIT MORE!
STOP! IF THE HUNPING LEAVES THE PROTECTIVE CIRCLE--
--THERE'LL BE NOTHING KEEPING THE DEMONS AT BAY!
HEY, HELLBOY!
HUH?
CATCH!

WHOA! GOT IT.

WHAT'RE YOU SUPPOSED TO DO WITH IT?

SMASH IT!

QUICKLY!

SO WHY'D I HAVE TO--?

NEVER MIND.

DON'T GOTTA TELL ME TWICE.

SMASH

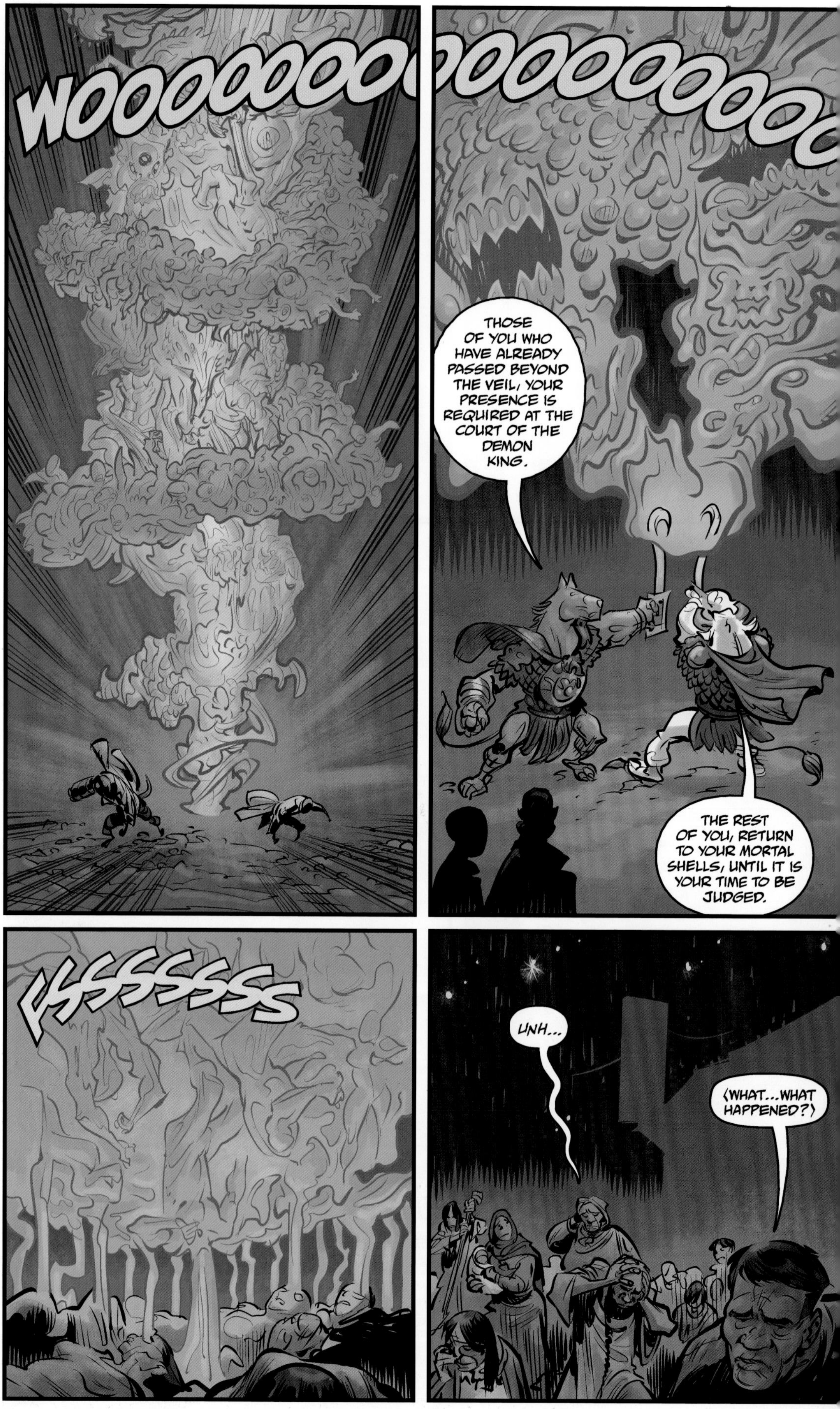
WOOOOOOOOOOOOOOOOOO
THOSE OF YOU WHO HAVE ALREADY PASSED BEYOND THE VEIL, YOUR PRESENCE IS REQUIRED AT THE COURT OF THE DEMON KING.
THE REST OF YOU, RETURN TO YOUR MORTAL SHELLS, UNTIL IT IS YOUR TIME TO BE JUDGED.
HSSSSSSS
UNH...
⟨WHAT...WHAT HAPPENED?⟩

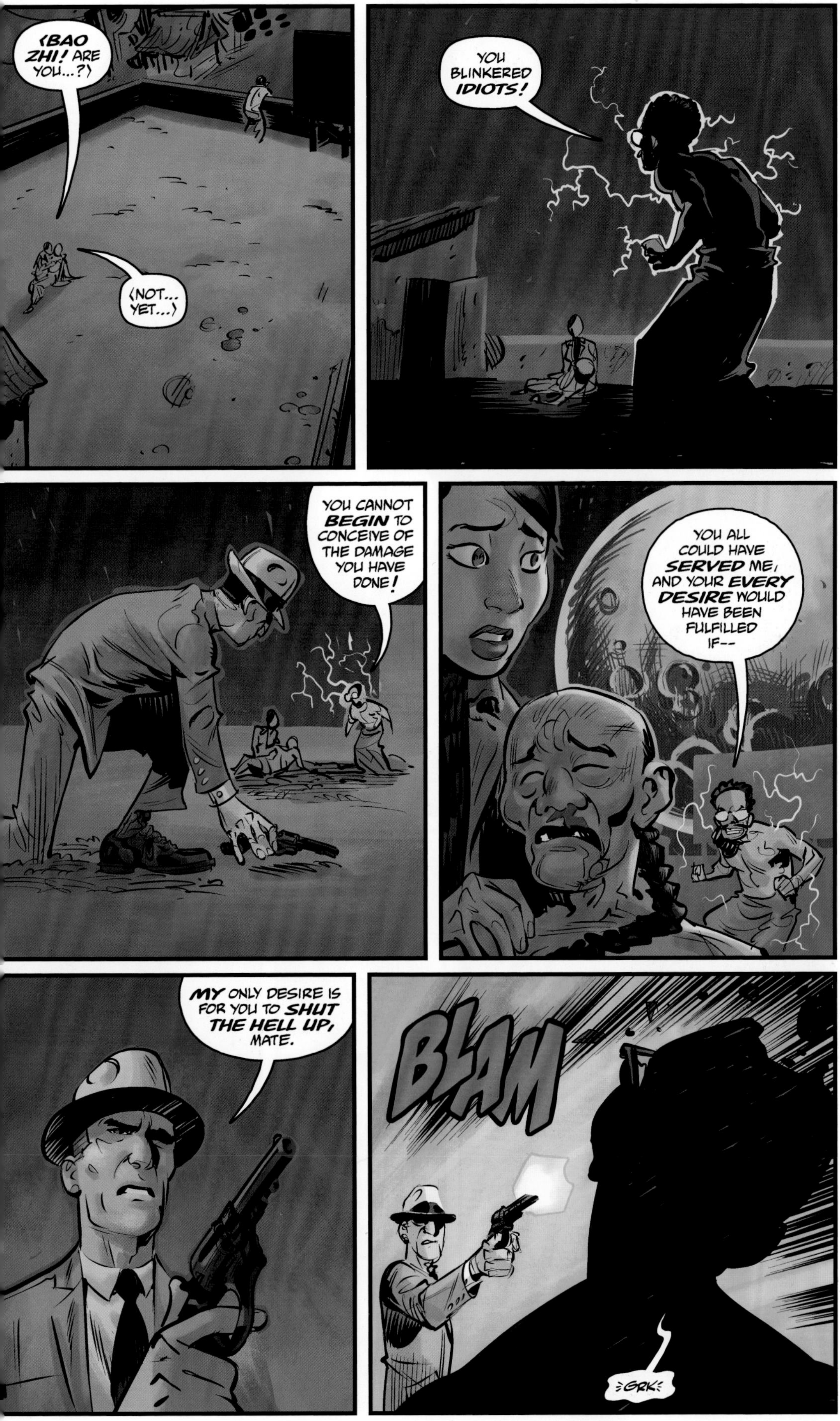

‹BAO ZHI! ARE YOU...?›
‹NOT... YET...›
YOU BLINKERED IDIOTS!
YOU CANNOT BEGIN TO CONCEIVE OF THE DAMAGE YOU HAVE DONE!
YOU ALL COULD HAVE SERVED ME, AND YOUR EVERY DESIRE WOULD HAVE BEEN FULFILLED IF--
MY ONLY DESIRE IS FOR YOU TO SHUT THE HELL UP, MATE.
BLAM
GRK

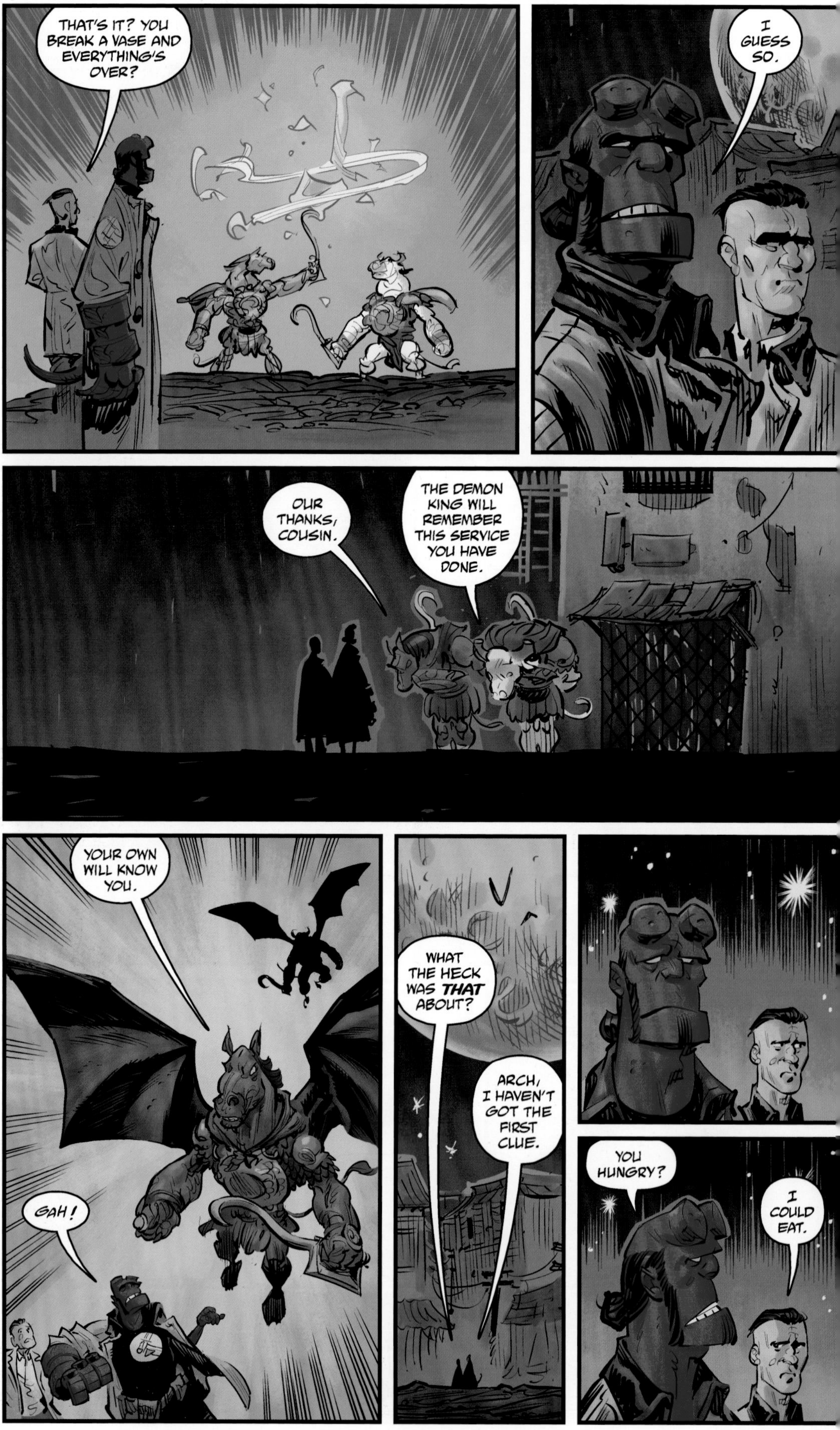
THAT'S IT? YOU BREAK A VASE AND EVERYTHING'S OVER?
I GUESS SO.
OUR THANKS, COUSIN.
THE DEMON KING WILL REMEMBER THIS SERVICE YOU HAVE DONE.
YOUR OWN WILL KNOW YOU.
GAH!
WHAT THE HECK WAS **THAT** ABOUT?
ARCH, I HAVEN'T GOT THE FIRST CLUE.
YOU HUNGRY?
I COULD EAT.

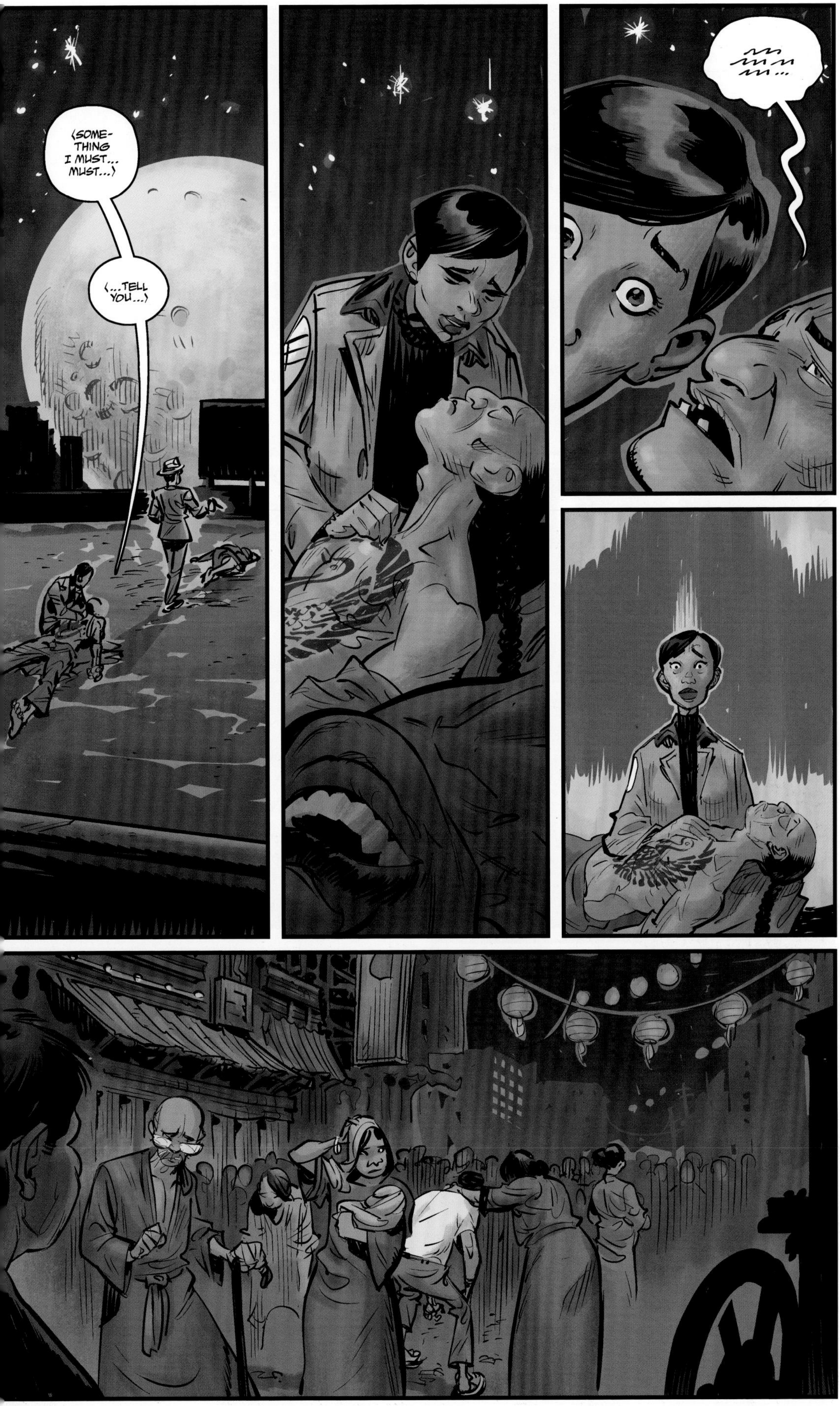

⟨SOME-THING I MUST... MUST...⟩
⟨...TELL YOU...⟩

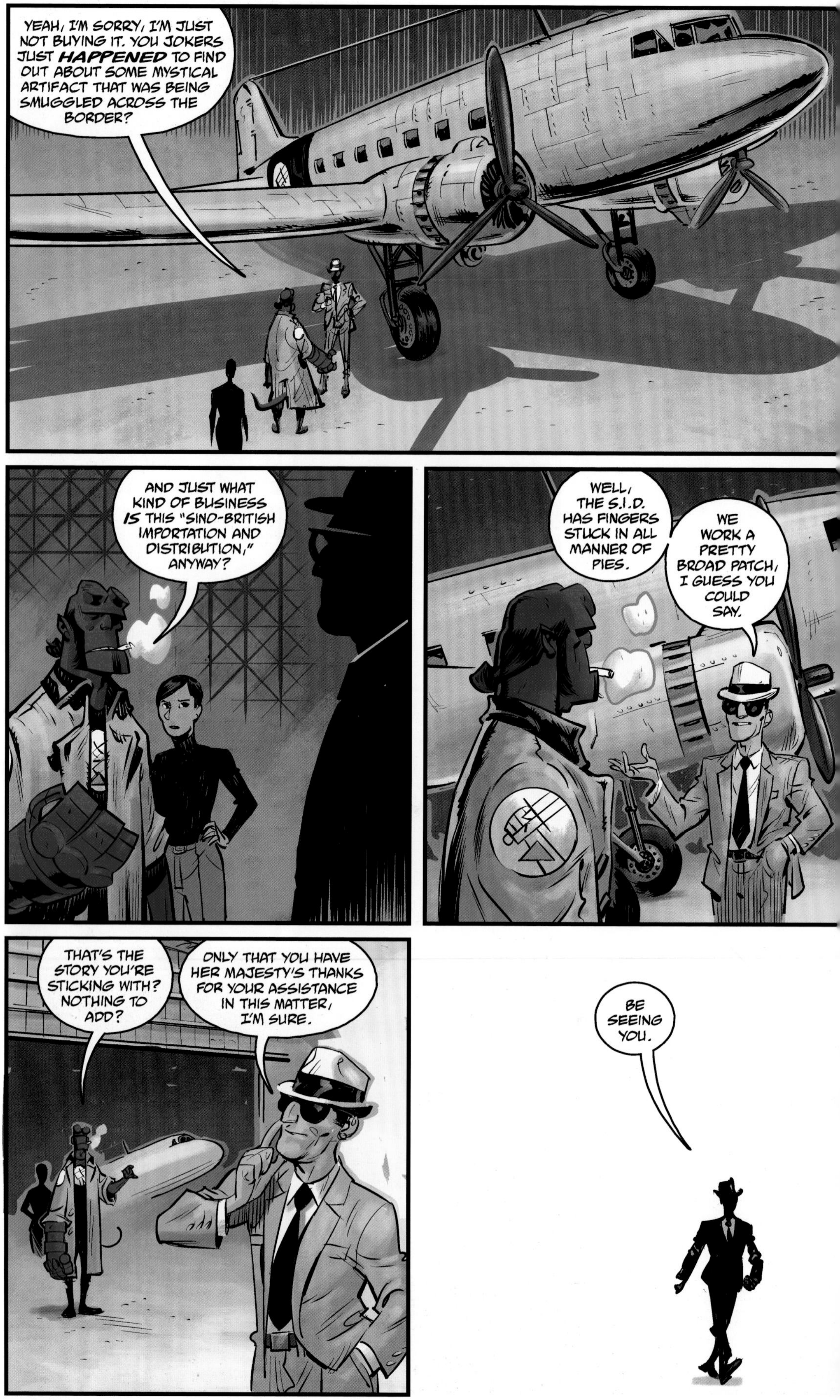
YEAH, I'M SORRY, I'M JUST NOT BUYING IT. YOU JOKERS JUST **HAPPENED** TO FIND OUT ABOUT SOME MYSTICAL ARTIFACT THAT WAS BEING SMUGGLED ACROSS THE BORDER?
AND JUST WHAT KIND OF BUSINESS *IS* THIS "SINO-BRITISH IMPORTATION AND DISTRIBUTION," ANYWAY?
WELL, THE S.I.D. HAS FINGERS STUCK IN ALL MANNER OF PIES.
WE WORK A PRETTY BROAD PATCH, I GUESS YOU COULD SAY.
THAT'S THE STORY YOU'RE STICKING WITH? NOTHING TO ADD?
ONLY THAT YOU HAVE HER MAJESTY'S THANKS FOR YOUR ASSISTANCE IN THIS MATTER, I'M SURE.
BE SEEING YOU.

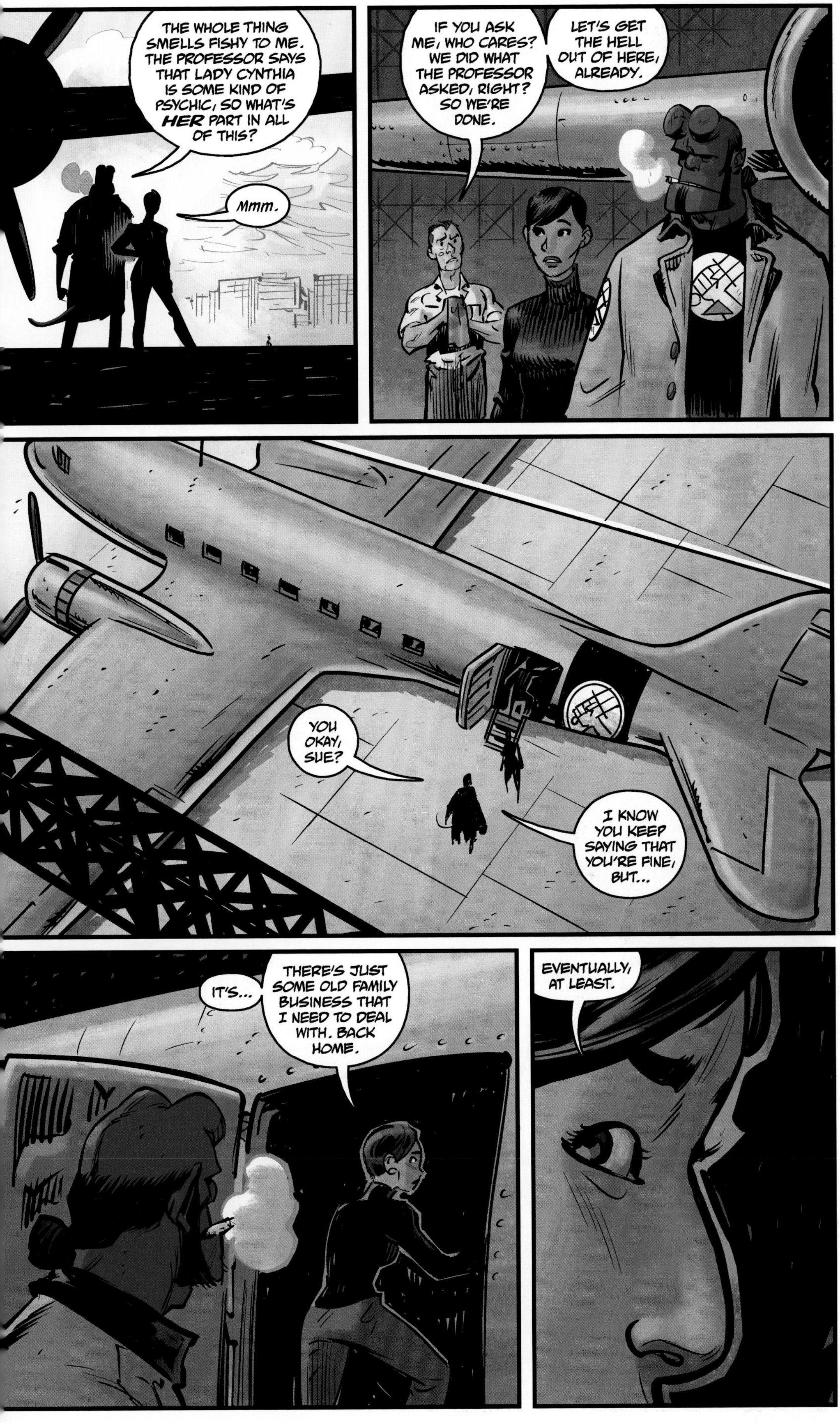
THE WHOLE THING SMELLS FISHY TO ME. THE PROFESSOR SAYS THAT LADY CYNTHIA IS SOME KIND OF PSYCHIC, SO WHAT'S **HER** PART IN ALL OF THIS?
Mmm.
IF YOU ASK ME, WHO CARES? WE DID WHAT THE PROFESSOR ASKED, RIGHT? SO WE'RE DONE.
LET'S GET THE HELL OUT OF HERE, ALREADY.
YOU OKAY, SUE?
I KNOW YOU KEEP SAYING THAT YOU'RE FINE, BUT...
IT'S...
THERE'S JUST SOME OLD FAMILY BUSINESS THAT I NEED TO DEAL WITH. BACK HOME.
EVENTUALLY, AT LEAST.

...AND THEN?

HEADQUARTERS OF THE SPECIAL INTELLIGENCE DIRECTORATE, DISUSED TOWER OF LONDON UNDERGROUND STATION, ENGLAND. SEPTEMBER 1954.

THAT WAS AN END TO IT. THE YANKS WENT BACK HOME, I SAW TO IT THAT AGENT RHYME'S REMAINS WERE SAFELY DISPOSED OF, AND WE CLOSED THE BOOKS ON THE WHOLE MATTER.

BY THE TIME I WAS OUT OF HOSPITAL, AGENT CHILDE HAD COMPLETED THE ENTIRE AFFAIR.

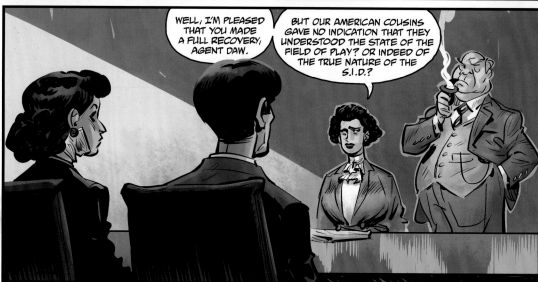

WELL, I'M PLEASED THAT YOU MADE A FULL RECOVERY, AGENT DAW.

BUT OUR AMERICAN COUSINS GAVE NO INDICATION THAT THEY UNDERSTOOD THE STATE OF THE FIELD OF PLAY? OR INDEED OF THE TRUE NATURE OF THE S.I.D.?

NO, LADY CYNTHIA. THEY WERE USEFUL IN A TUSSLE, BUT VIRTUALLY CLUELESS OTHERWISE.

GOOD. BECAUSE THE STAKES ARE ABOUT TO GET EVEN HIGHER. D., IF YOU WOULDN'T MIND?

THESE ARE SURVEILLANCE PHOTOS PROVIDED BY OUR MAN IN COPENHAGEN. LOOKS LIKE THE REDS HAVE LET RAHEL REBANE AND VALENTIN MORAVEC OFF THEIR LEASHES.

WE NEED TO FIND OUT WHAT THEY'RE UP TO, BEFORE IT'S TOO LATE.

THE END

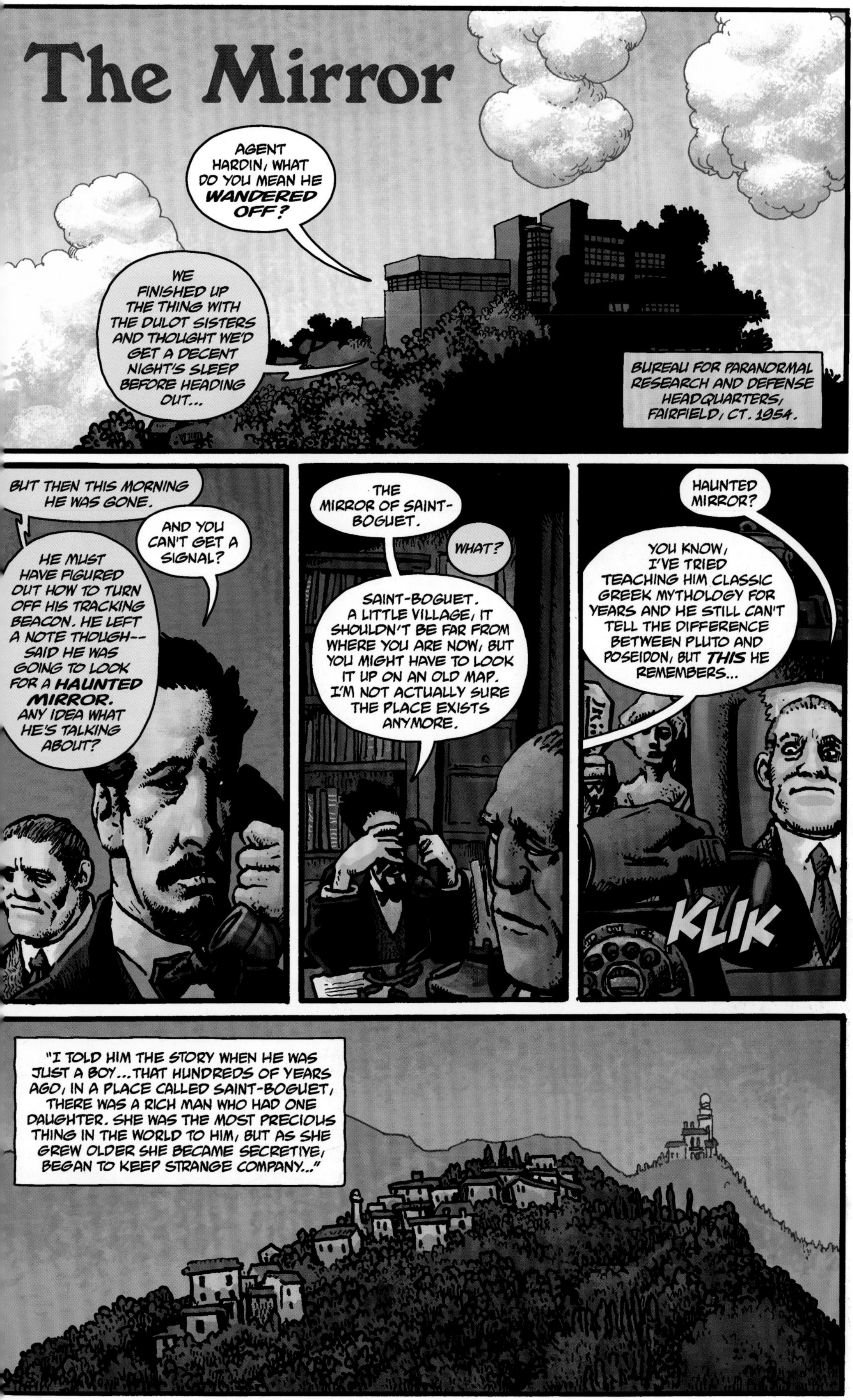
The Mirror
AGENT HARDIN, WHAT DO YOU MEAN HE WANDERED OFF?
WE FINISHED UP THE THING WITH THE DULOT SISTERS AND THOUGHT WE'D GET A DECENT NIGHT'S SLEEP BEFORE HEADING OUT...
BUREAU FOR PARANORMAL RESEARCH AND DEFENSE HEADQUARTERS, FAIRFIELD, CT. 1954.
BUT THEN THIS MORNING HE WAS GONE.
AND YOU CAN'T GET A SIGNAL?
HE MUST HAVE FIGURED OUT HOW TO TURN OFF HIS TRACKING BEACON. HE LEFT A NOTE THOUGH-- SAID HE WAS GOING TO LOOK FOR A HAUNTED MIRROR. ANY IDEA WHAT HE'S TALKING ABOUT?
THE MIRROR OF SAINT-BOGUET.
WHAT?
SAINT-BOGUET. A LITTLE VILLAGE, IT SHOULDN'T BE FAR FROM WHERE YOU ARE NOW, BUT YOU MIGHT HAVE TO LOOK IT UP ON AN OLD MAP. I'M NOT ACTUALLY SURE THE PLACE EXISTS ANYMORE.
HAUNTED MIRROR?
YOU KNOW, I'VE TRIED TEACHING HIM CLASSIC GREEK MYTHOLOGY FOR YEARS AND HE STILL CAN'T TELL THE DIFFERENCE BETWEEN PLUTO AND POSEIDON, BUT THIS HE REMEMBERS...
KLIK
"I TOLD HIM THE STORY WHEN HE WAS JUST A BOY...THAT HUNDREDS OF YEARS AGO, IN A PLACE CALLED SAINT-BOGUET, THERE WAS A RICH MAN WHO HAD ONE DAUGHTER. SHE WAS THE MOST PRECIOUS THING IN THE WORLD TO HIM, BUT AS SHE GREW OLDER SHE BECAME SECRETIVE, BEGAN TO KEEP STRANGE COMPANY..."

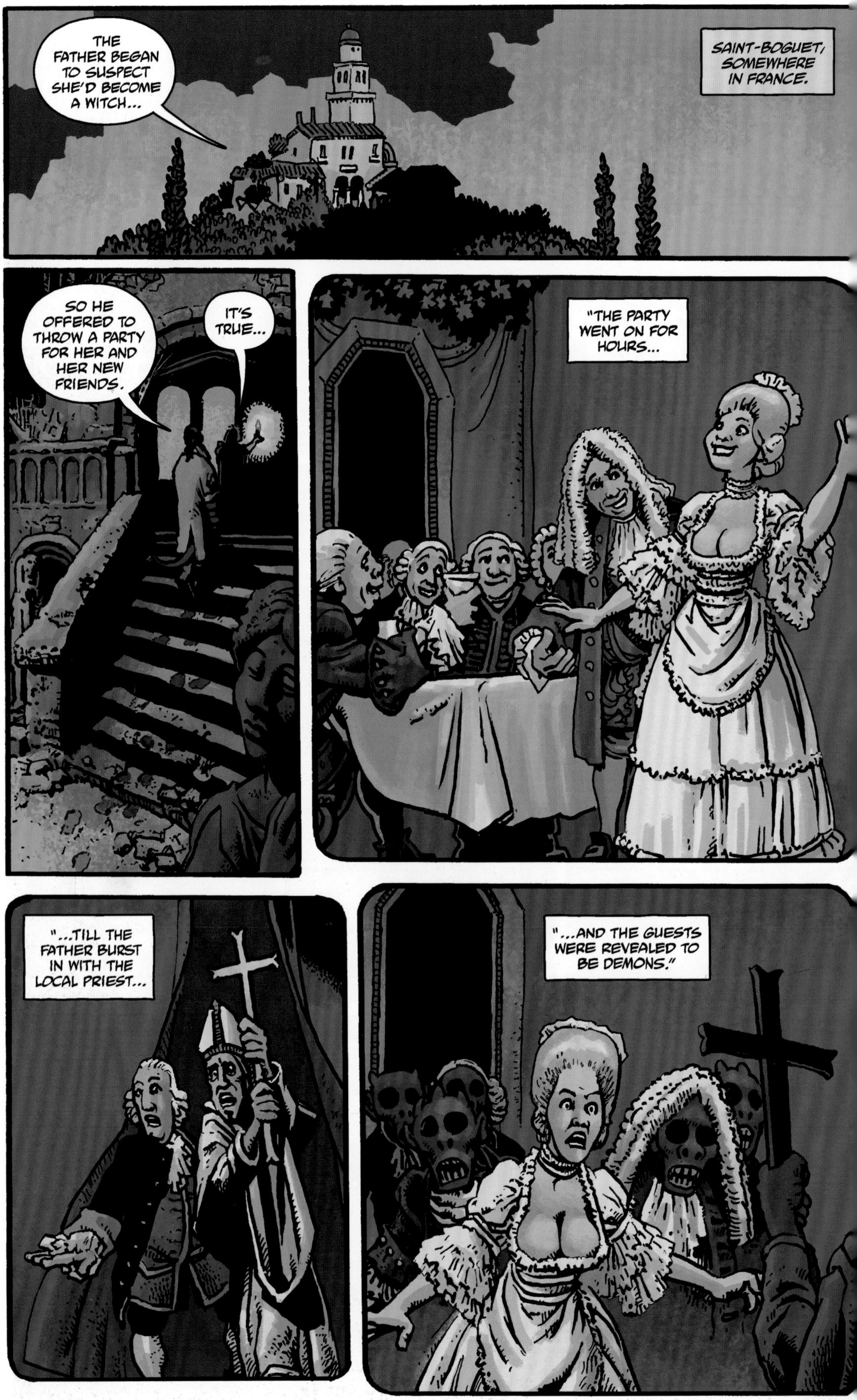
SAINT-BOGUET, SOMEWHERE IN FRANCE.
THE FATHER BEGAN TO SUSPECT SHE'D BECOME A WITCH...
SO HE OFFERED TO THROW A PARTY FOR HER AND HER NEW FRIENDS.
IT'S TRUE...
"THE PARTY WENT ON FOR HOURS...
"...TILL THE FATHER BURST IN WITH THE LOCAL PRIEST...
"...AND THE GUESTS WERE REVEALED TO BE DEMONS."

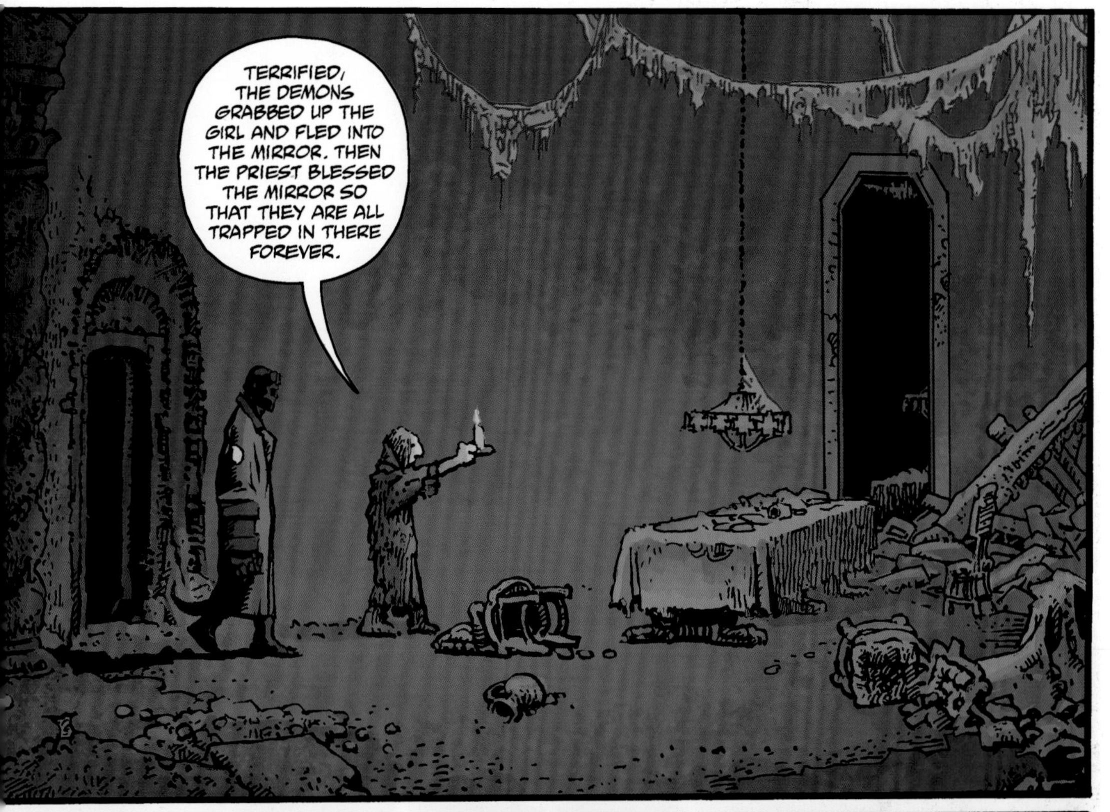
TERRIFIED, THE DEMONS GRABBED UP THE GIRL AND FLED INTO THE MIRROR. THEN THE PRIEST BLESSED THE MIRROR SO THAT THEY ARE ALL TRAPPED IN THERE FOREVER.

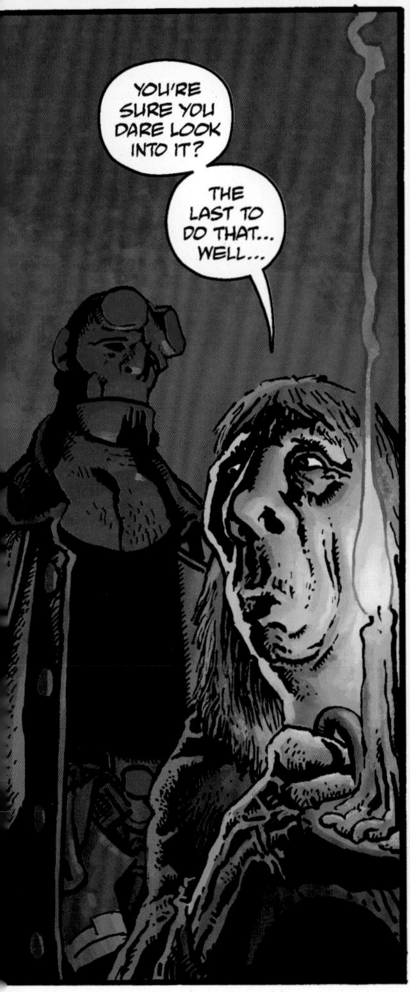
YOU'RE SURE YOU DARE LOOK INTO IT?
THE LAST TO DO THAT... WELL...

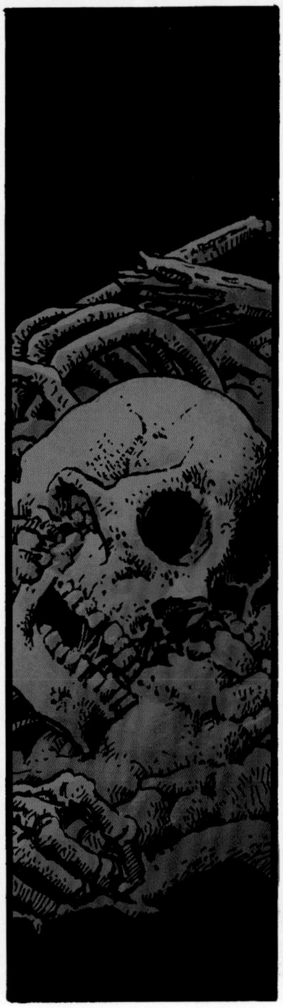

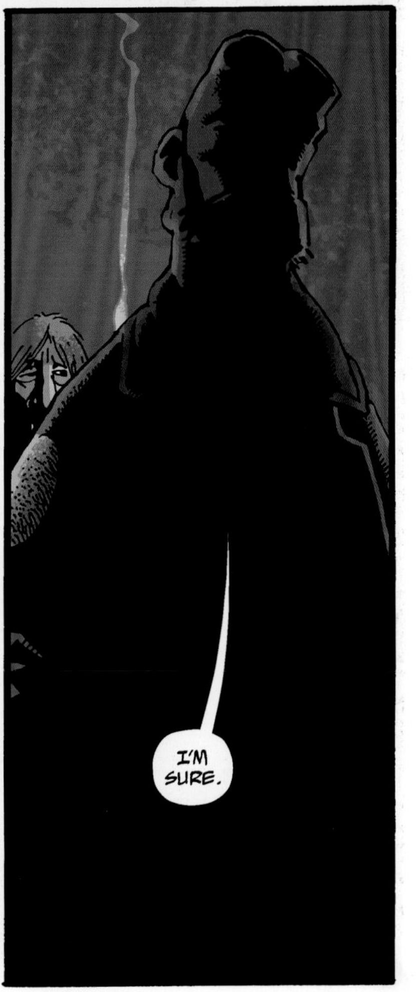
I'M SURE.

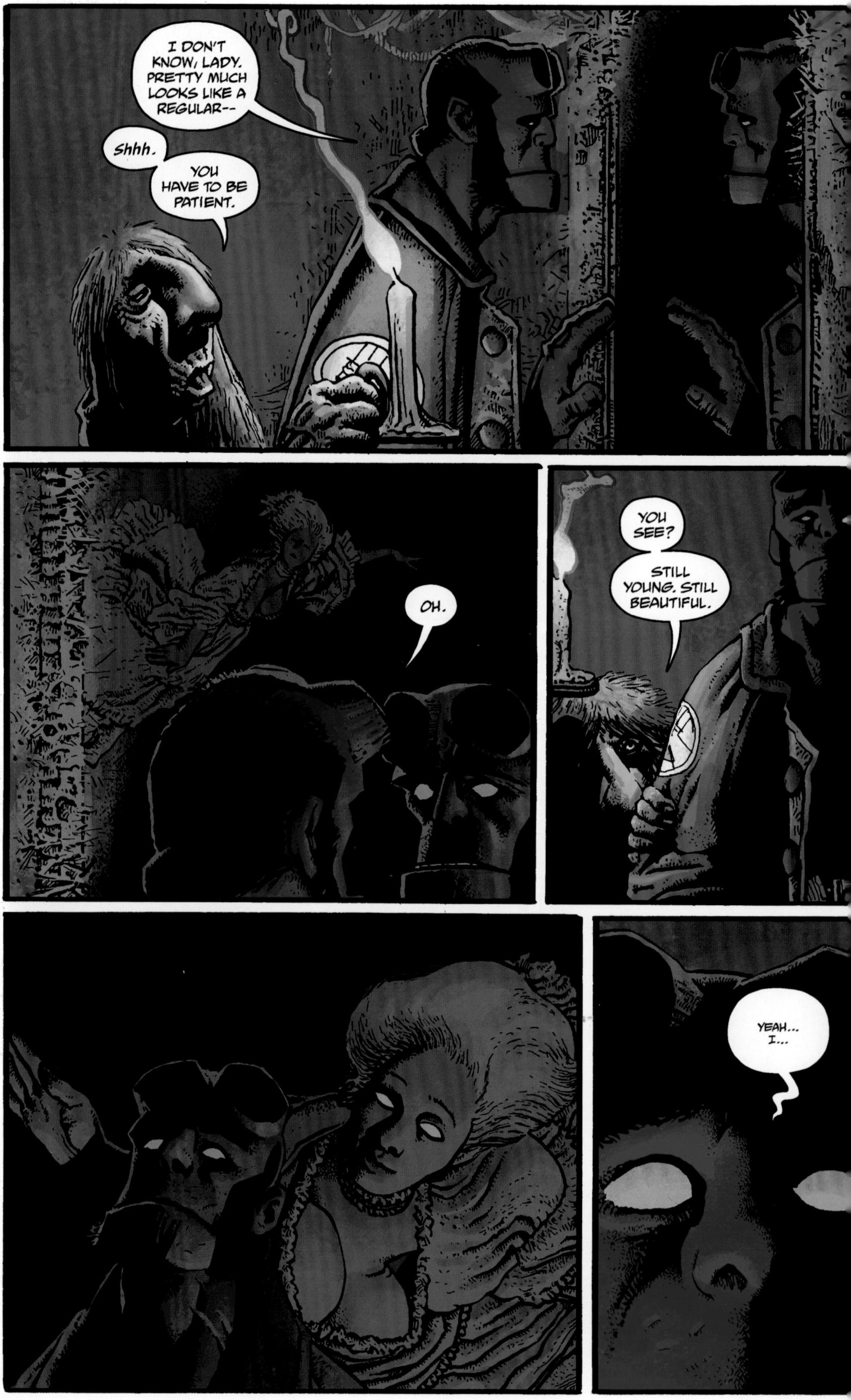
I DON'T KNOW, LADY. PRETTY MUCH LOOKS LIKE A REGULAR--
Shhh.
YOU HAVE TO BE PATIENT.
OH.
YOU SEE?
STILL YOUNG. STILL BEAUTIFUL.
YEAH... I...

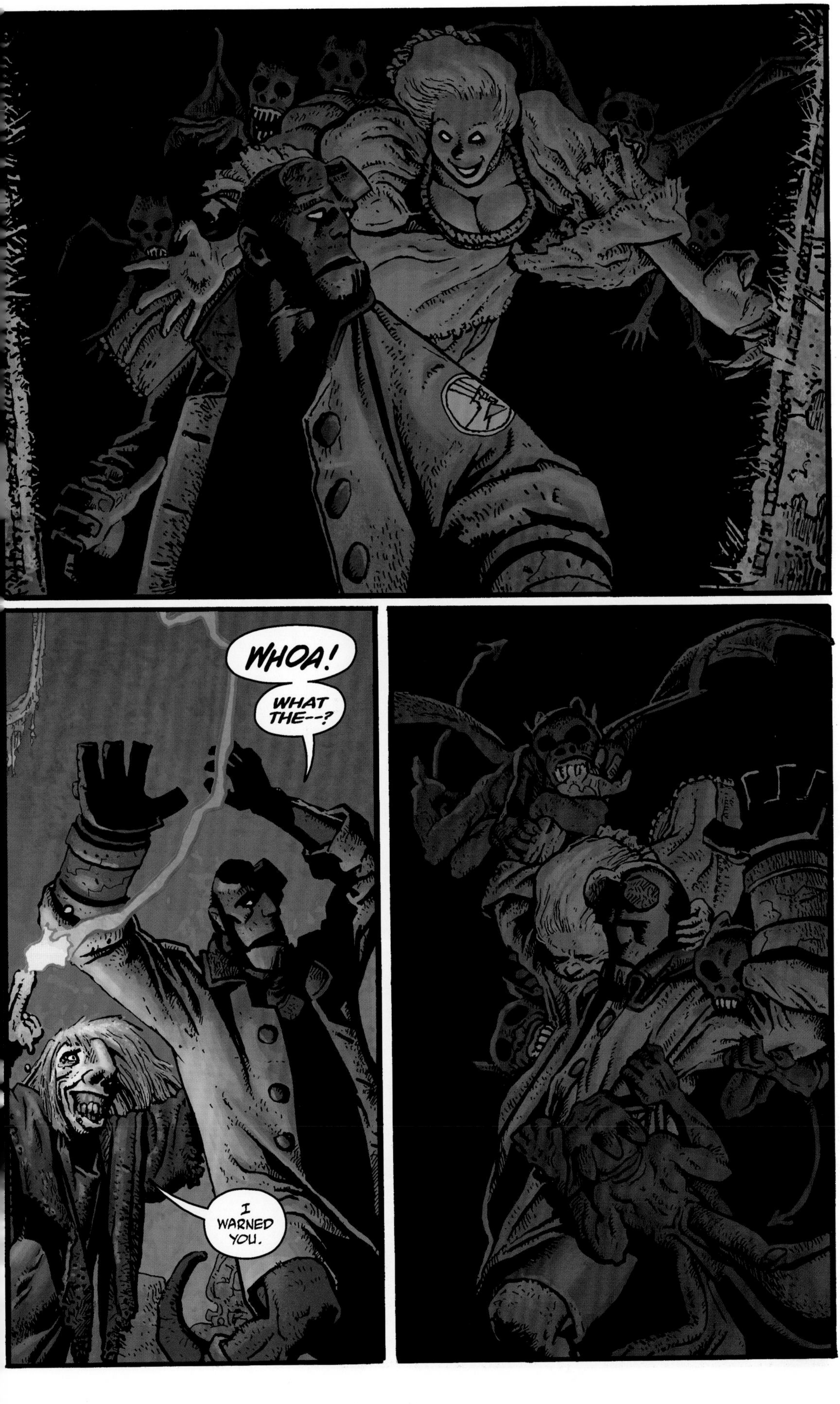
WHOA!
WHAT THE--?
I WARNED YOU.

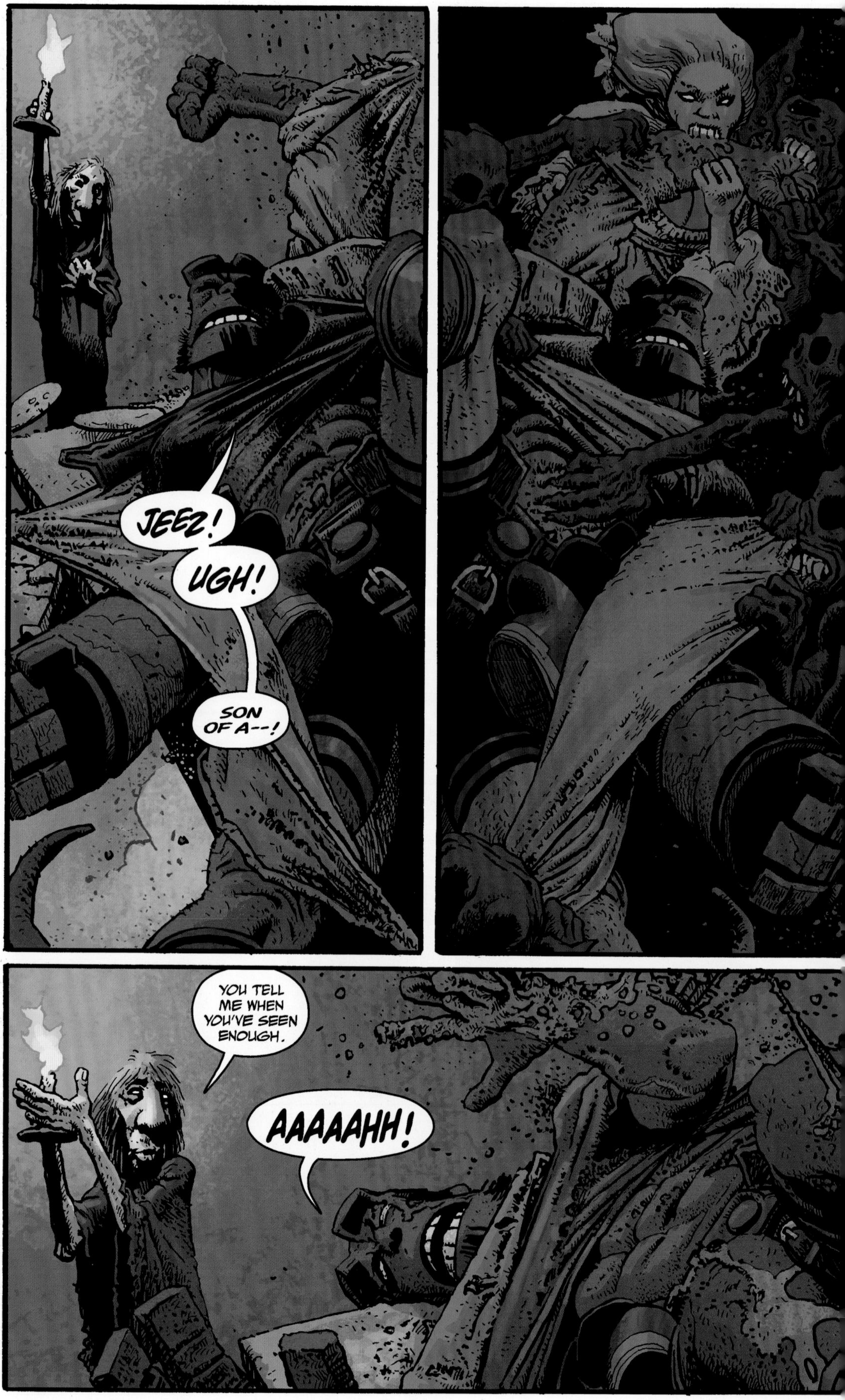
JEEZ!
UGH!
SON OF A--!
YOU TELL ME WHEN YOU'VE SEEN ENOUGH.
AAAAAHH!

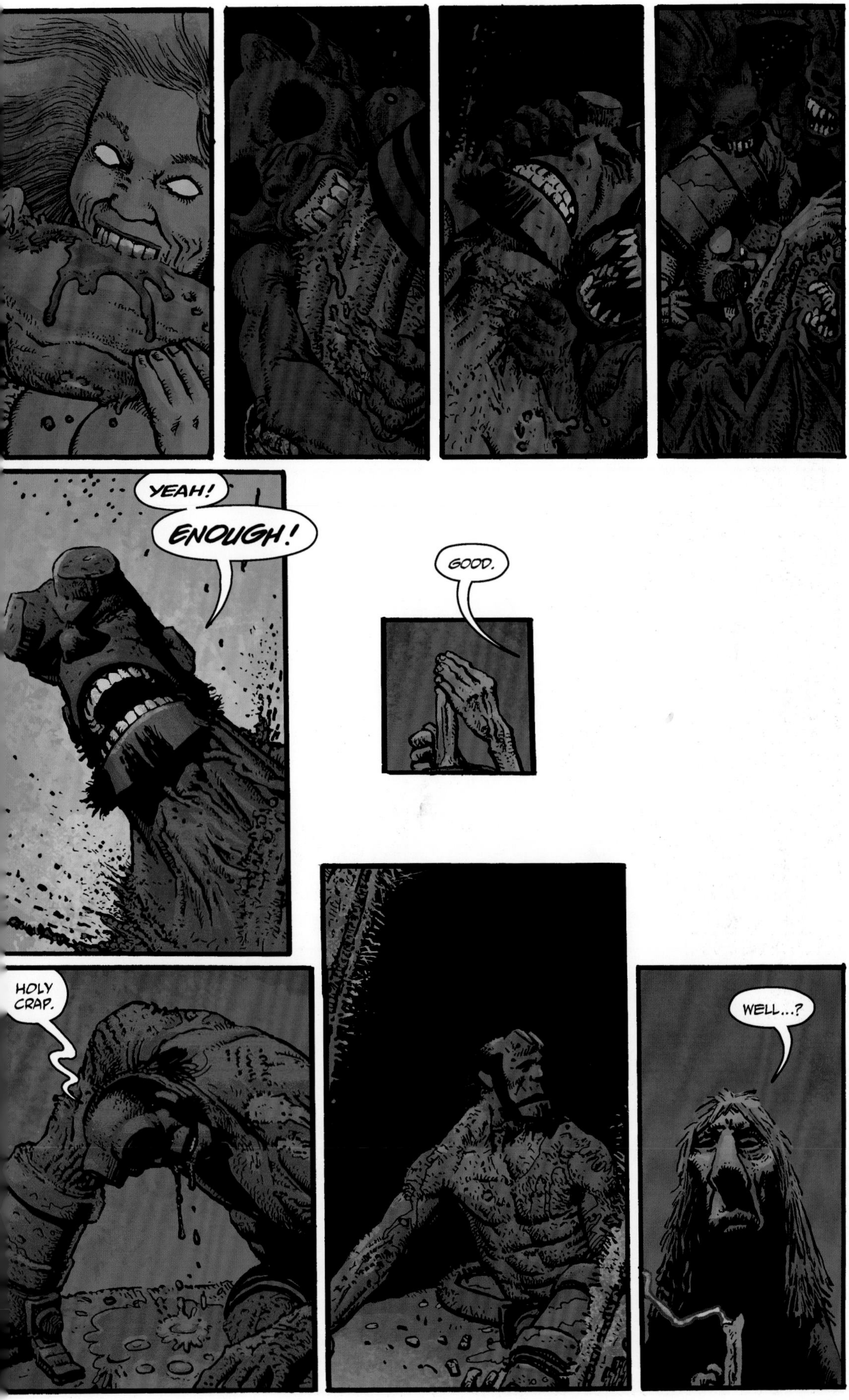
YEAH!
ENOUGH!
GOOD.
HOLY CRAP.
WELL...?

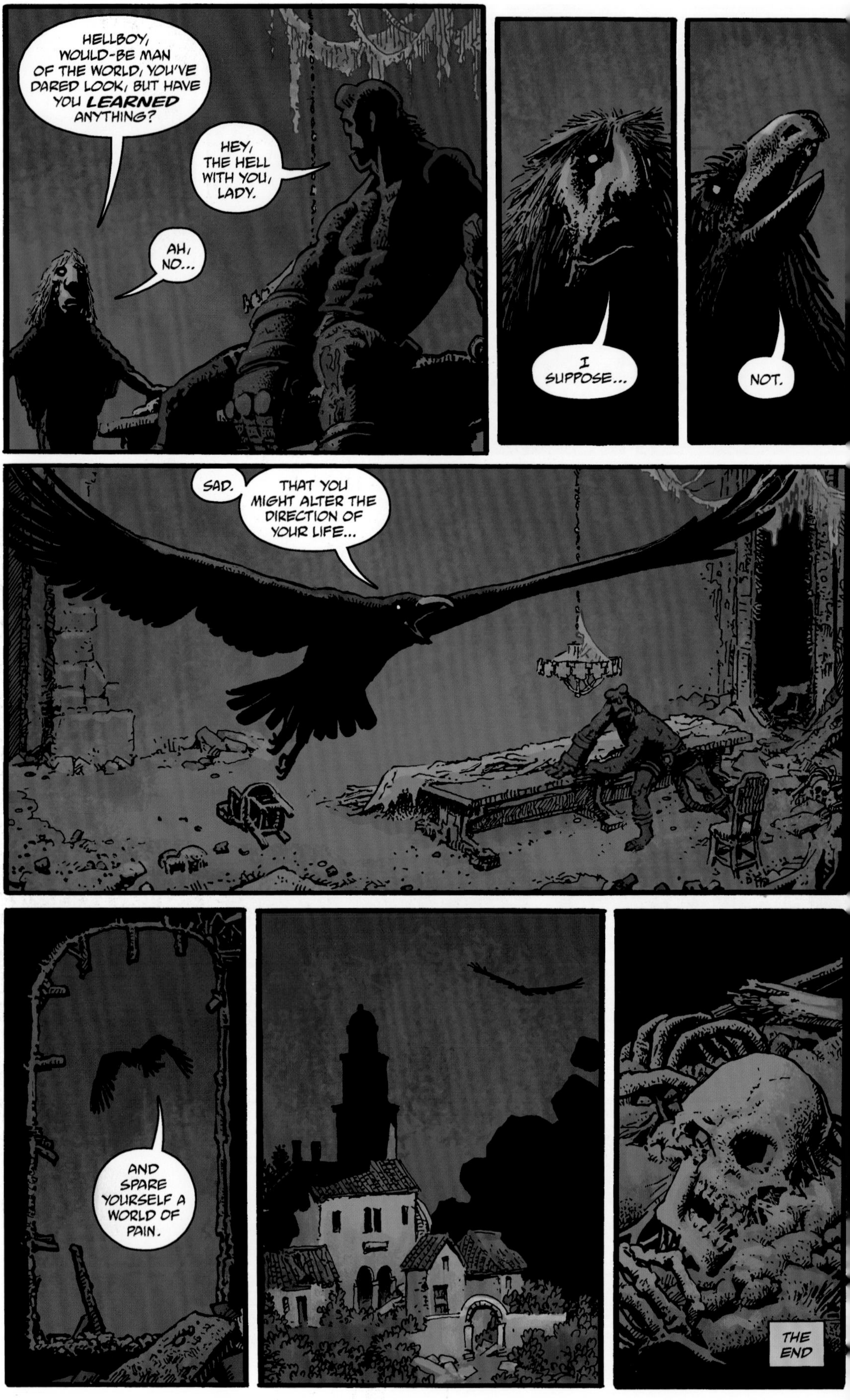
HELLBOY, WOULD-BE MAN OF THE WORLD, YOU'VE DARED LOOK, BUT HAVE YOU LEARNED ANYTHING?
HEY, THE HELL WITH YOU, LADY.
AH, NO...
I SUPPOSE...
NOT.
SAD.
THAT YOU MIGHT ALTER THE DIRECTION OF YOUR LIFE...
AND SPARE YOURSELF A WORLD OF PAIN.
THE END

HELLBOY AND THE B.P.R.D. 1954

SKETCHBOOK

Notes by Scott Allie

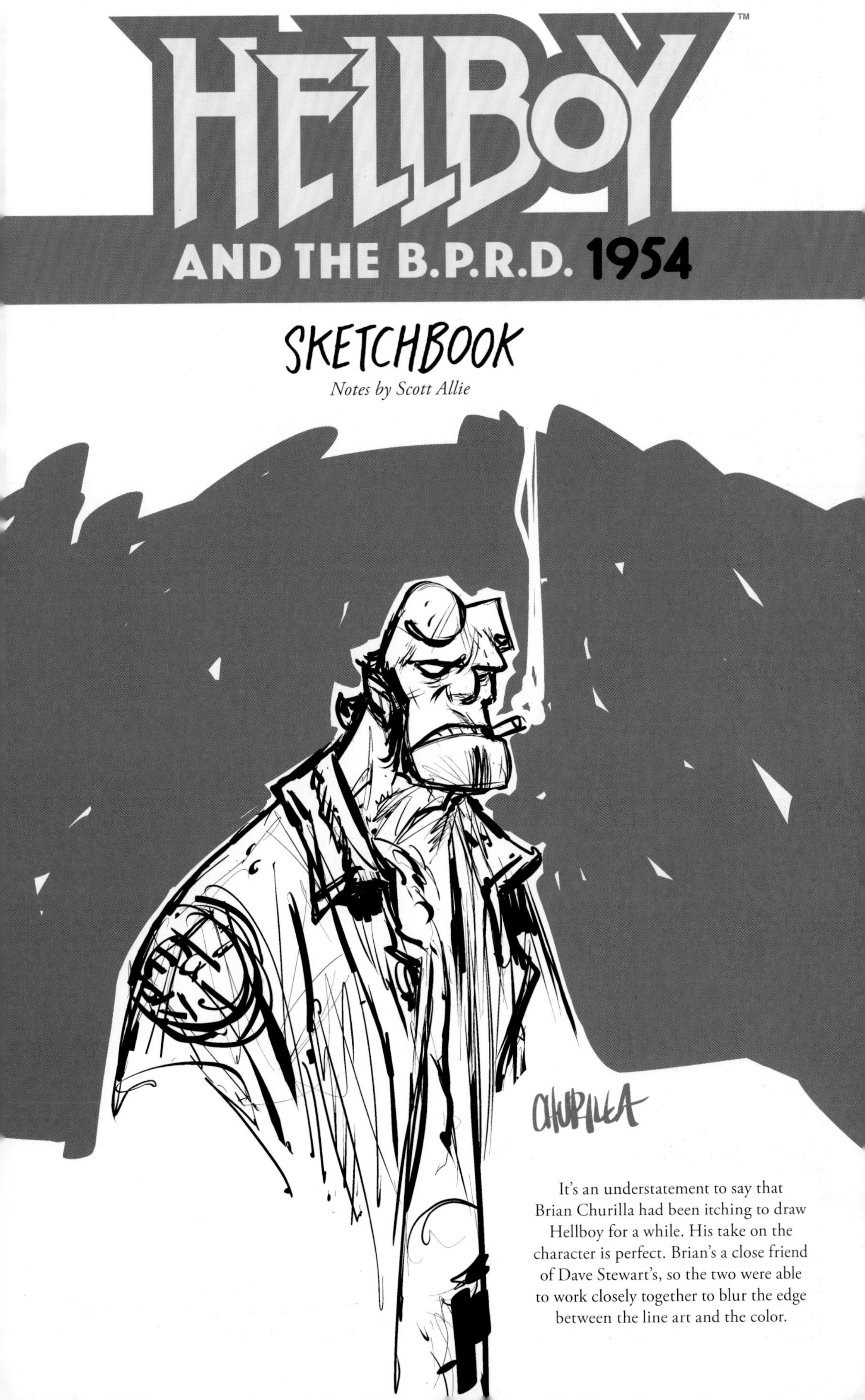

CHURILLA

It's an understatement to say that Brian Churilla had been itching to draw Hellboy for a while. His take on the character is perfect. Brian's a close friend of Dave Stewart's, so the two were able to work closely together to blur the edge between the line art and the color.

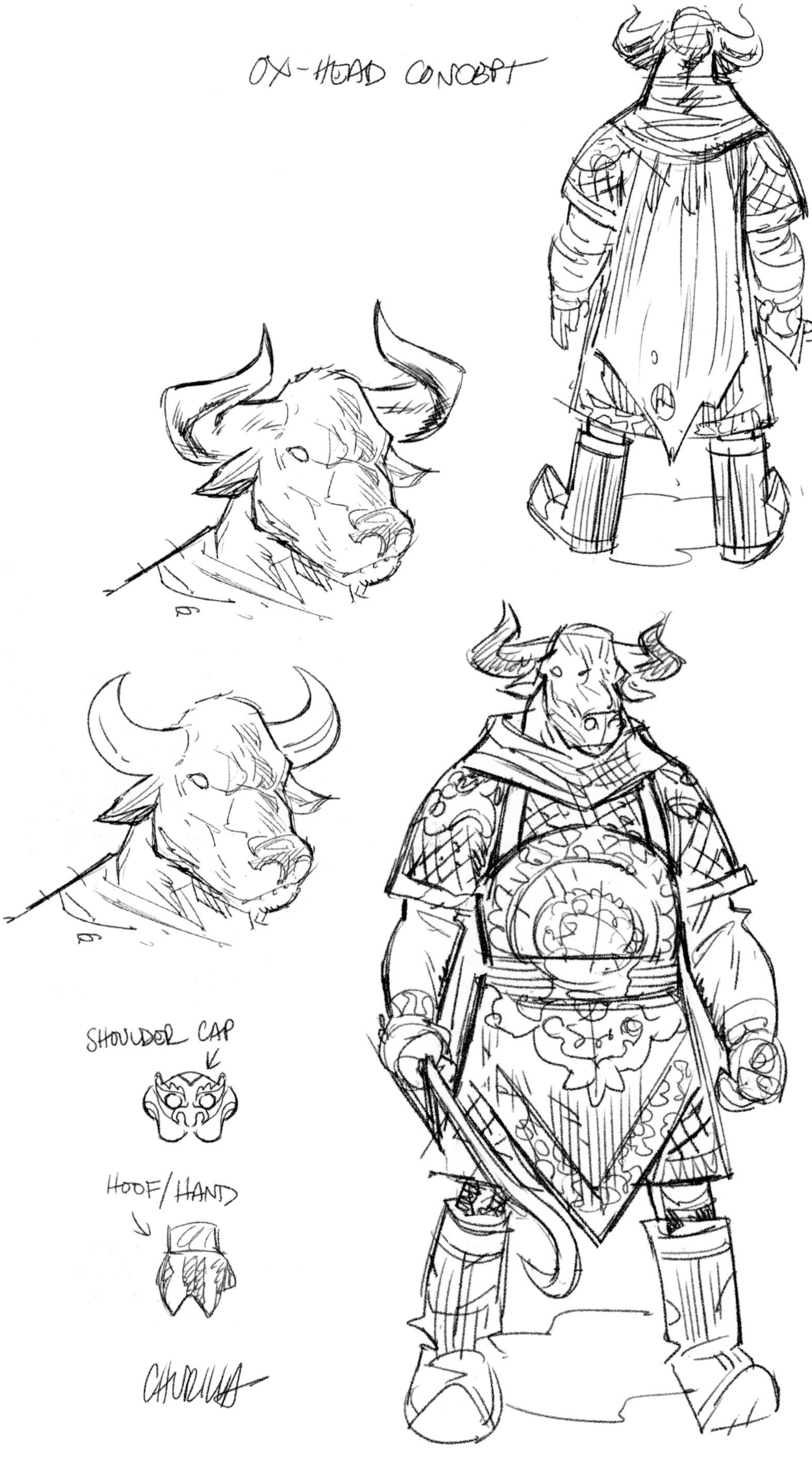
OX-HEAD CONCEPT
SHOULDER CAP
HOOF/HAND

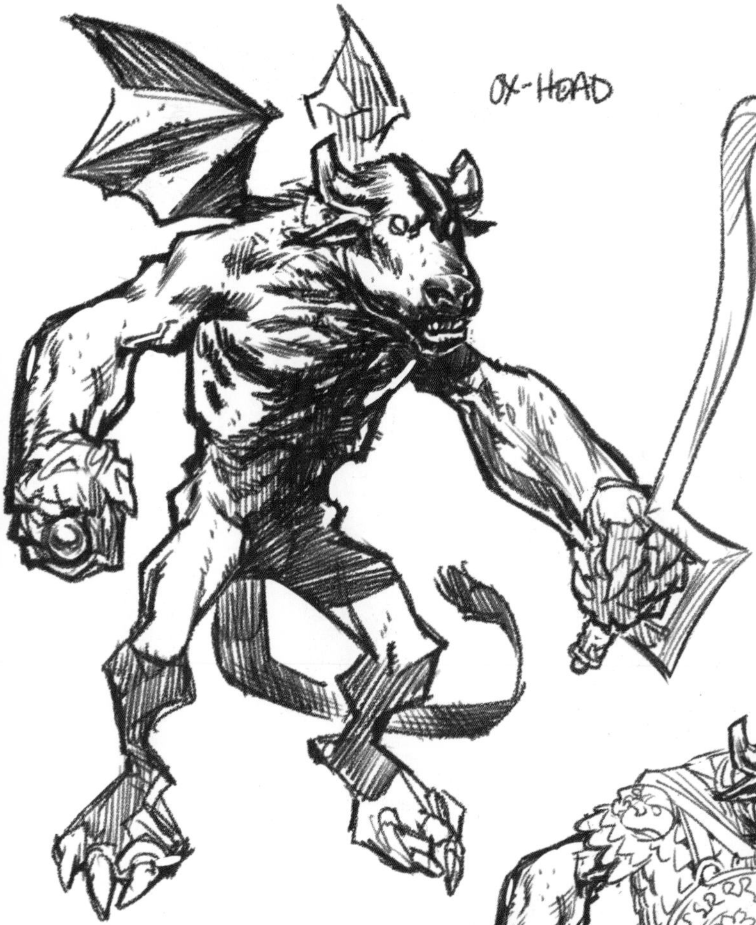

OX-HEAD

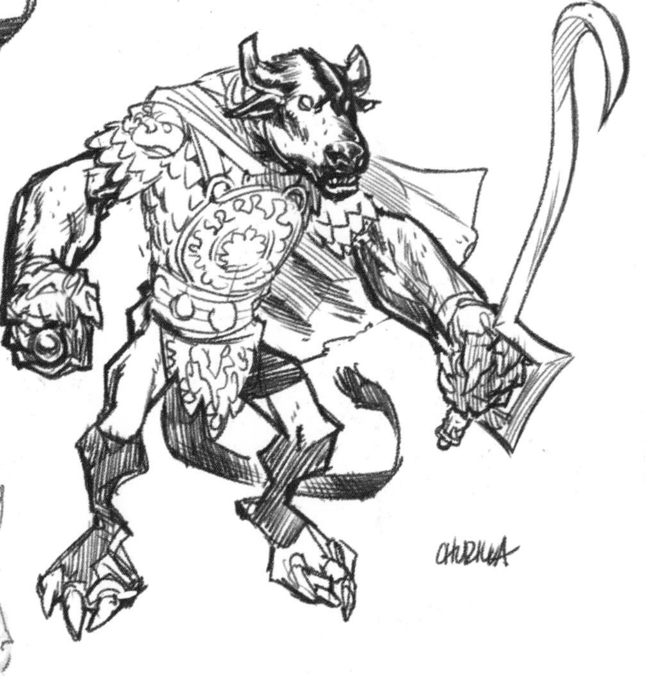

CHURILLA

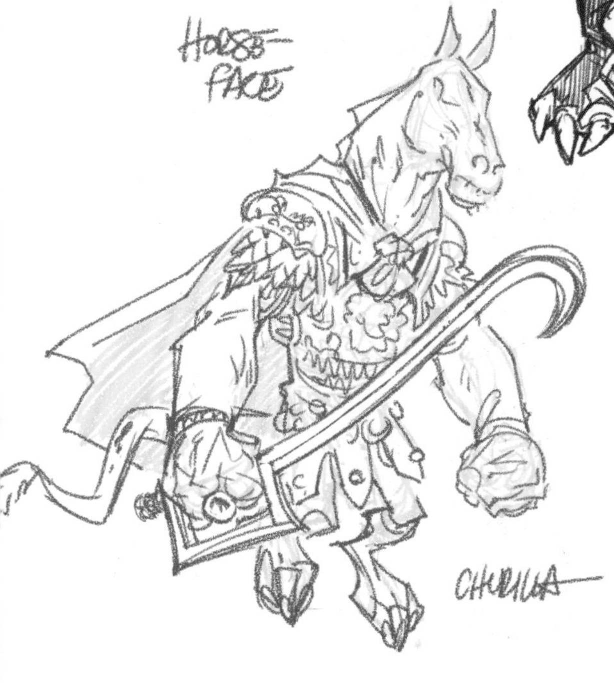

HORSE-FACE
CHURILLA

With Ox-Head and Horse-Face, Chris and Brian blended Chinese mythology with Mignola's version of demons and Hell.

Study of Hellboy.

Facing: Brian did these as decorations for
the inside cover of his individual issues.

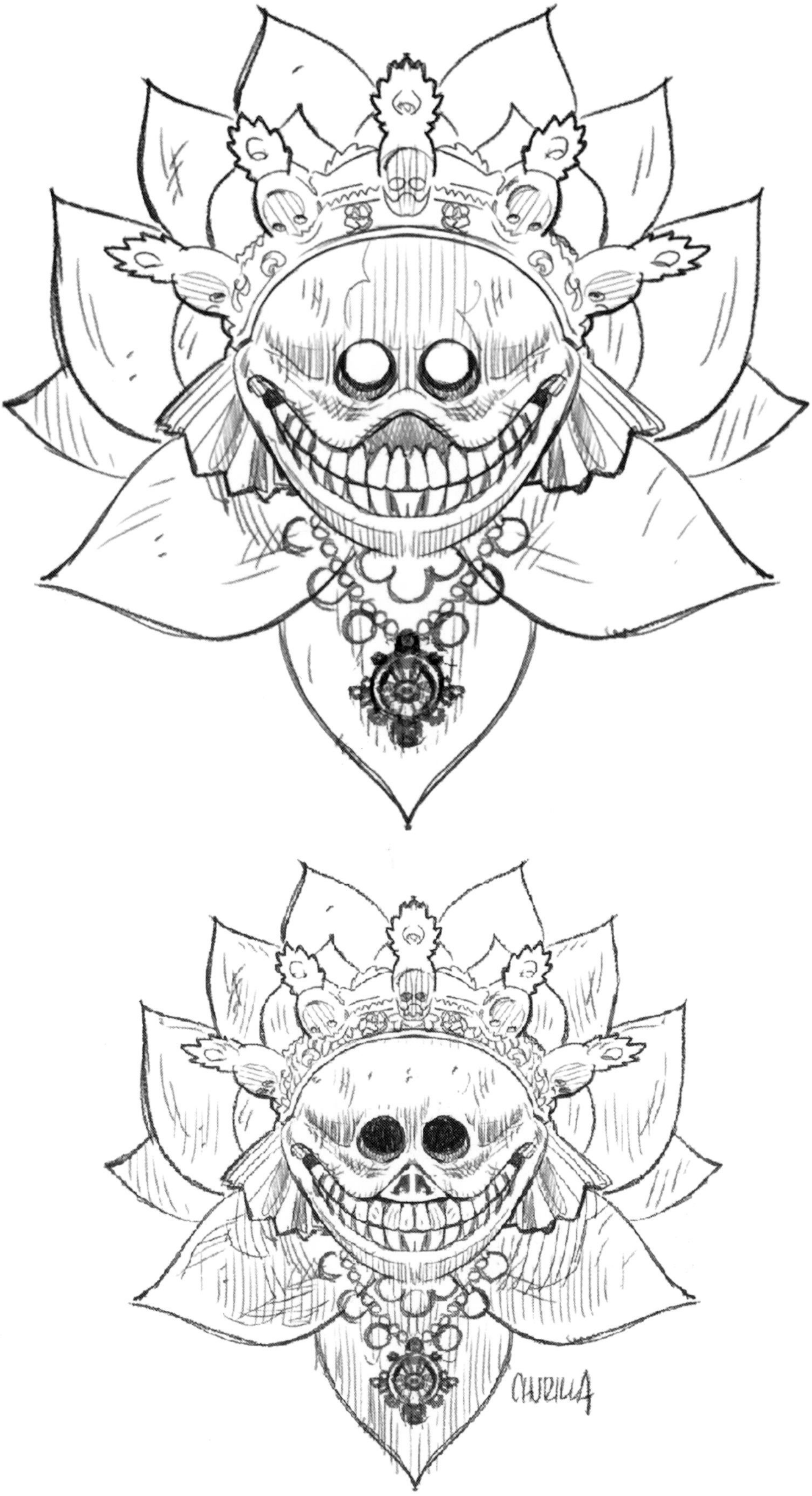
CHURILLA

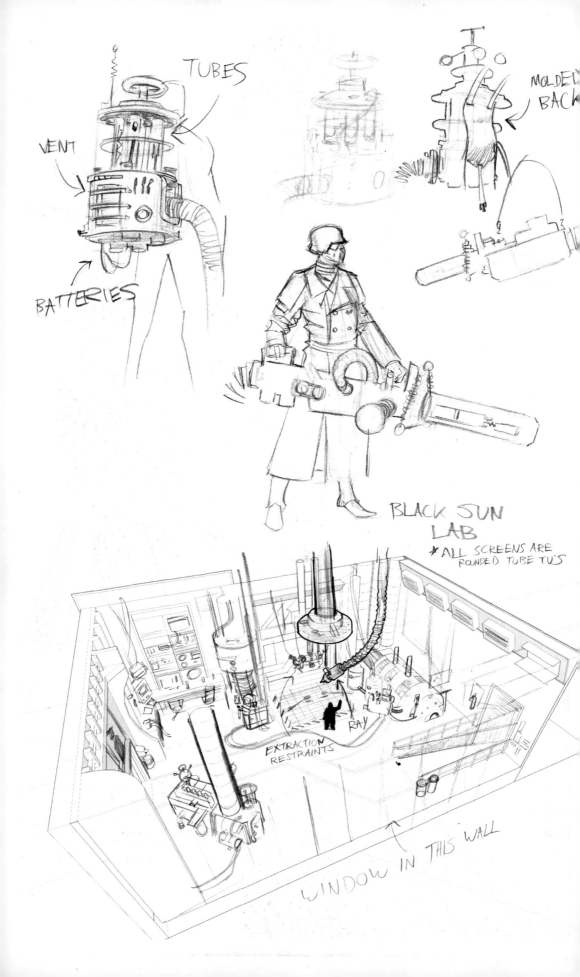

TUBES

VENT

BATTERIES

MOLDED BACK

BLACK SUN LAB

*ALL SCREENS ARE
ROUNDED TUBE TV'S

EXTRACTION
RESTRAINTS

RAY

WINDOW IN THIS WALL

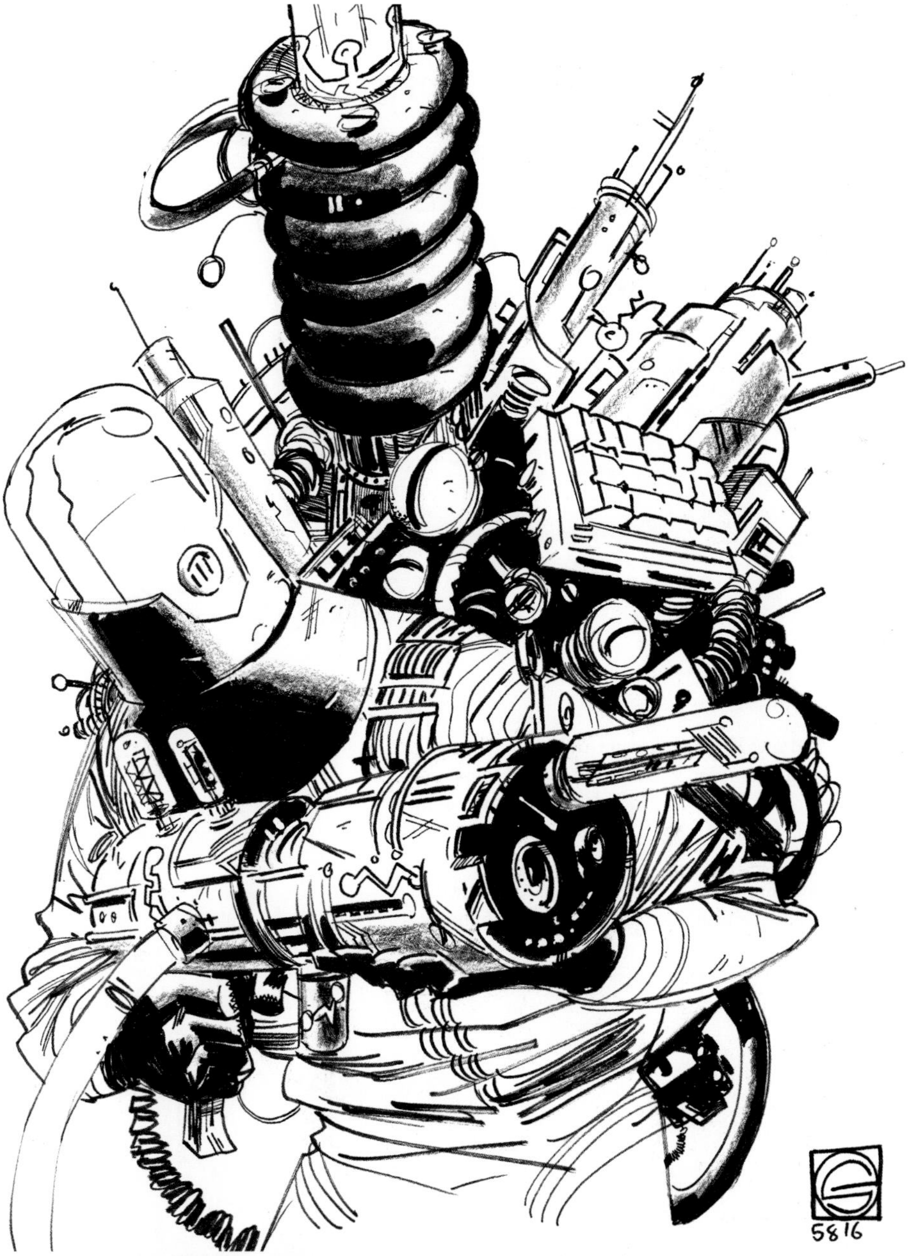

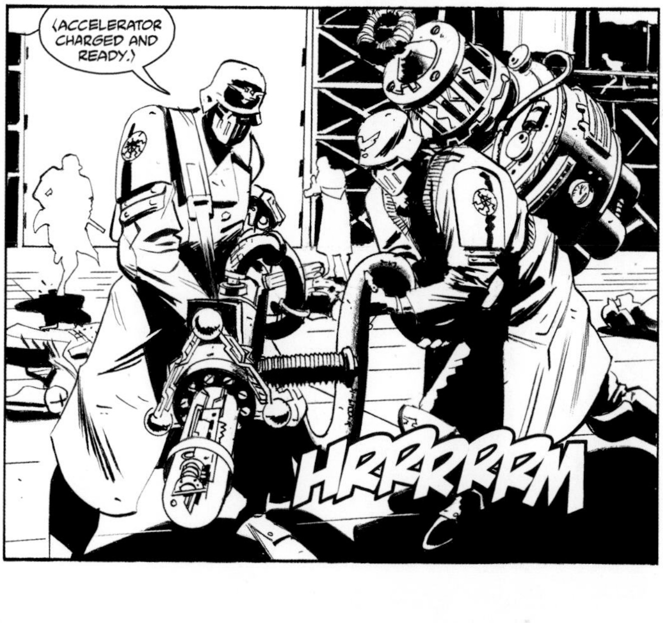

‹ACCELERATOR CHARGED AND READY.›
HRRRRRM

Stephen's designs for Nazi headquarters and hardware (*facing*), reminiscent of some Guy Davis designs from *B.P.R.D. The Dead* (2004), to which Stephen had paid tribute in his Johann Kraus sketch above.

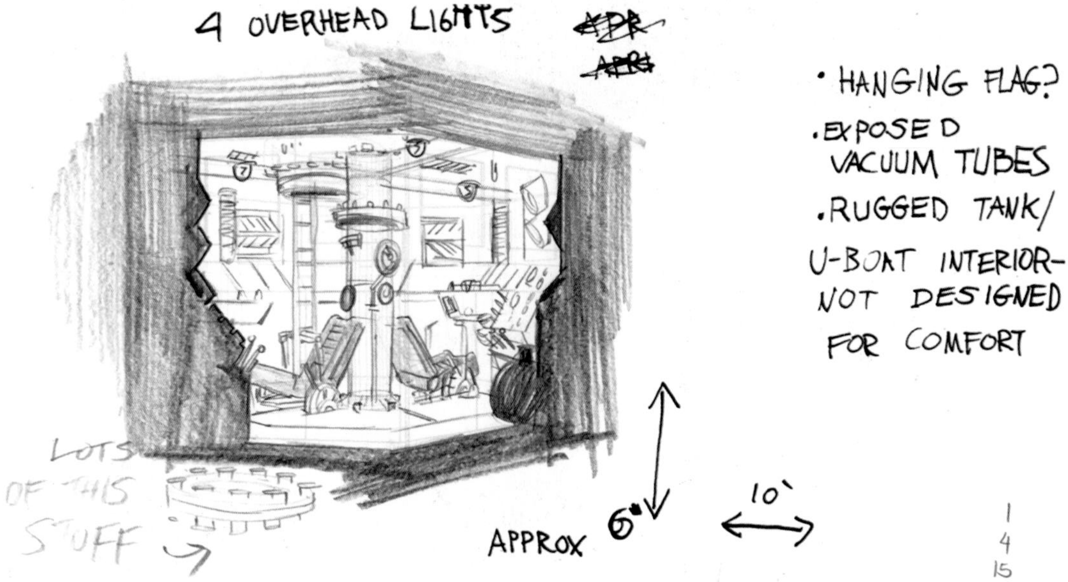
4 OVERHEAD LIGHTS
• HANGING FLAG?
• EXPOSED VACUUM TUBES
• RUGGED TANK/ U-BOAT INTERIOR- NOT DESIGNED FOR COMFORT
LOTS OF THIS STUFF
APPROX 6'
10'
1 4 15

I'd met Stephen Green through his mentor, Sean Murphy, at North Carolina Comicon. It took a little while before we were able to line up a job for him, but after the two parter here Arcudi requested him for a *Lobster Johnson* one-shot. In these designs, Stephen pushed to make the inside of the saucer claustrophobic.

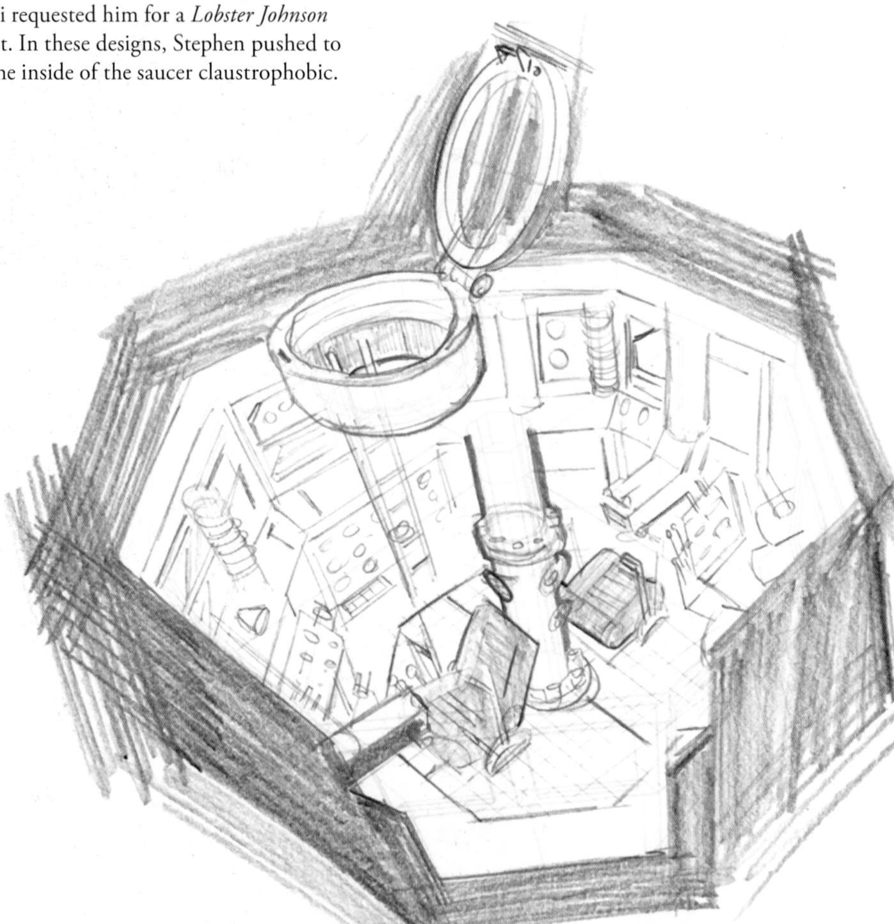

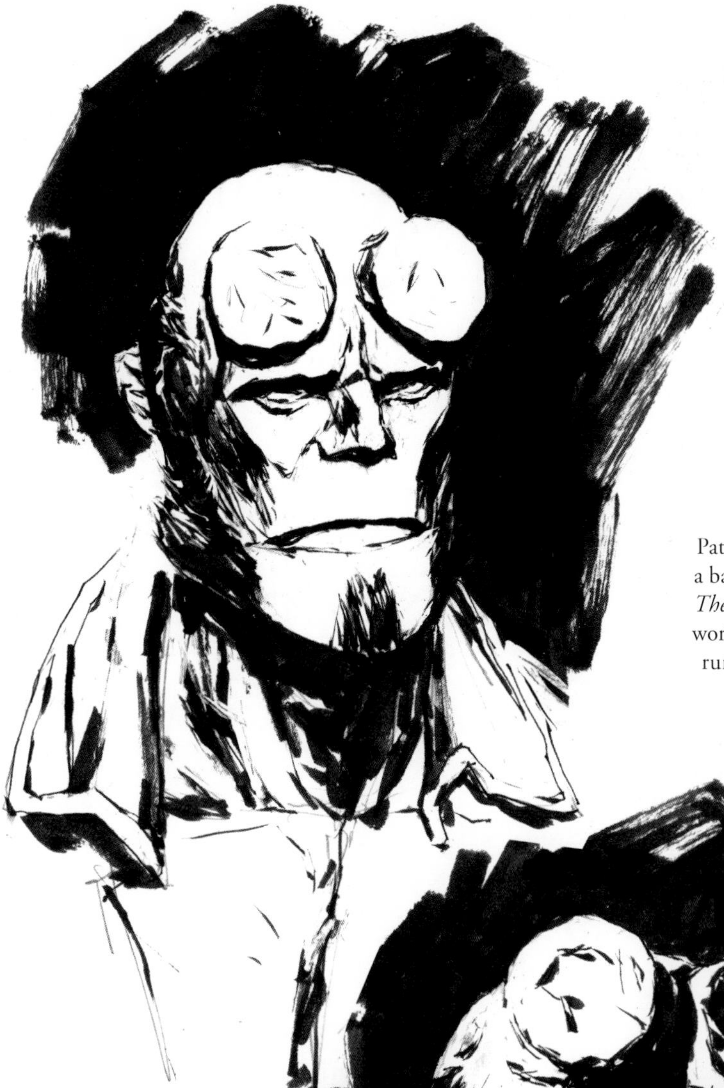

Patric Reynolds's comics debut was a backup in a 2009 issue of *Hellboy: The Wild Hunt*, and he's done other work with Mignola including a long run on *Joe Golem*, but this was his first time drawing Hellboy.

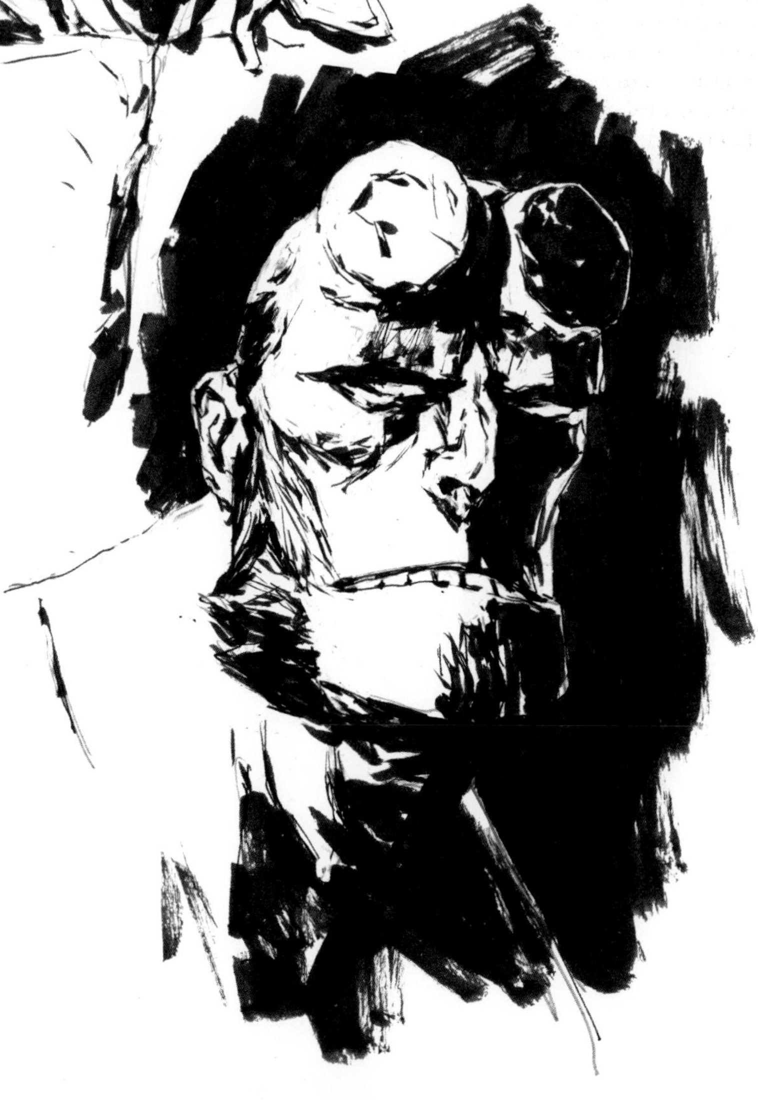

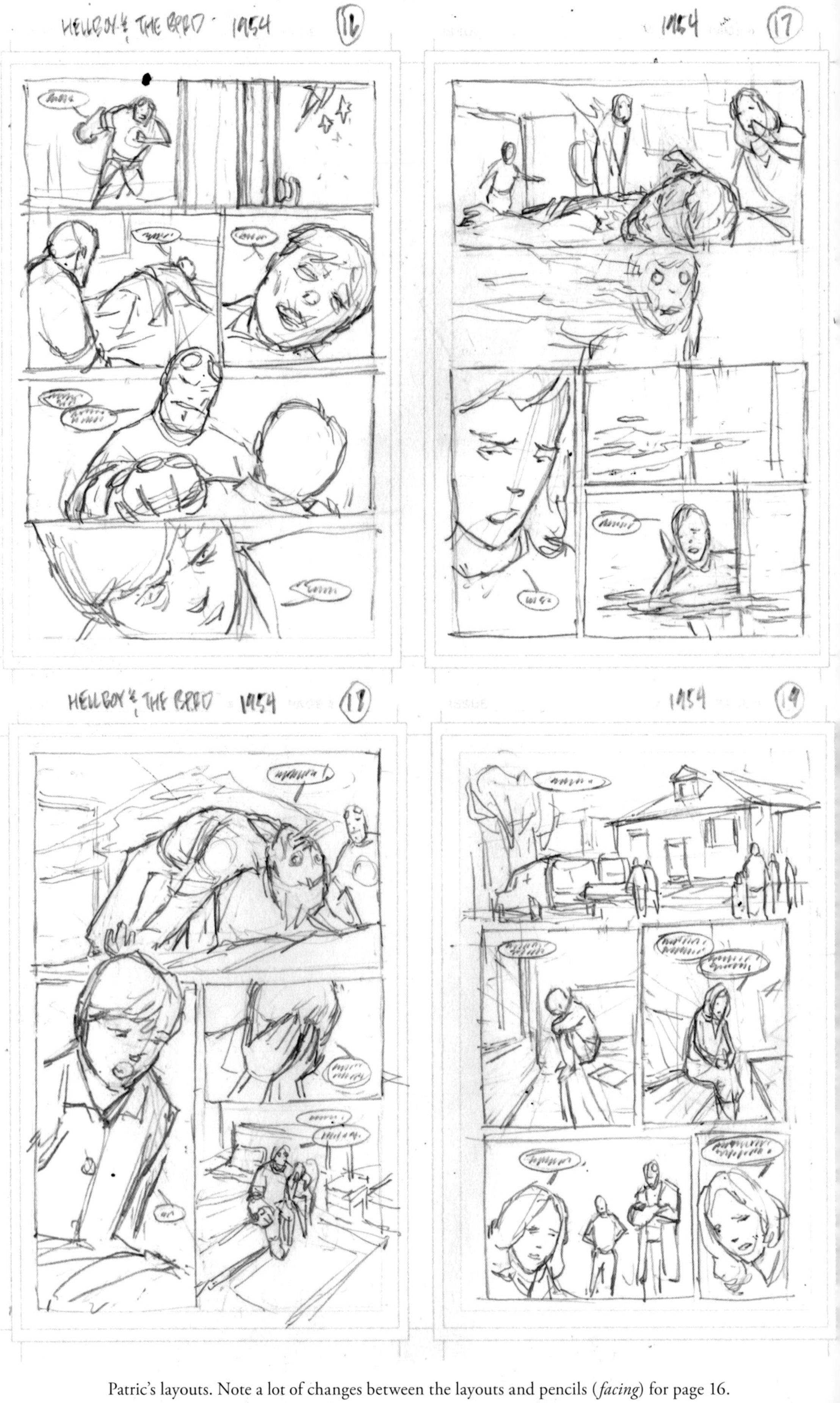
HELLBOY & THE BPRD 1954 16
1954 17
HELLBOY & THE BPRD 1954 18
1954 19

Patric's layouts. Note a lot of changes between the layouts and pencils (*facing*) for page 16.

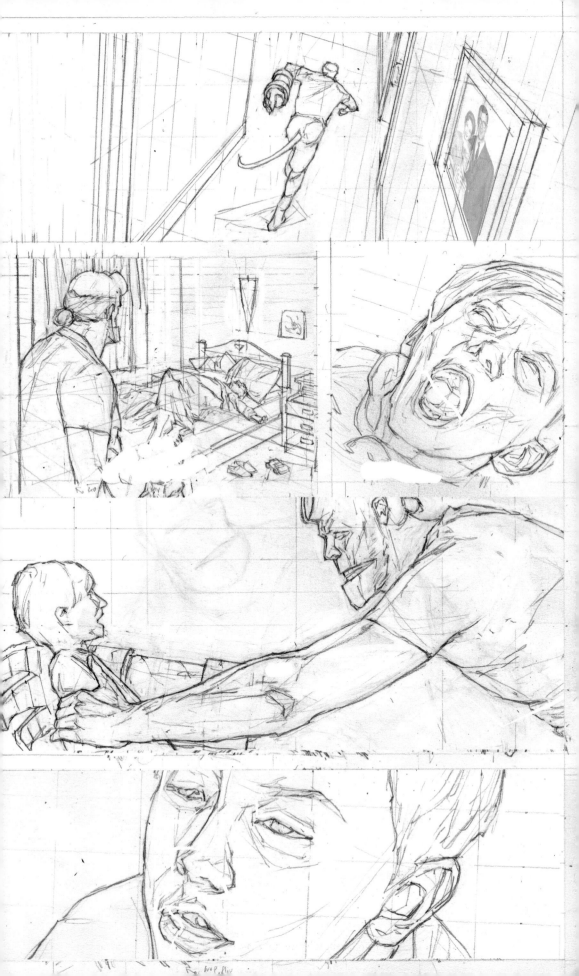

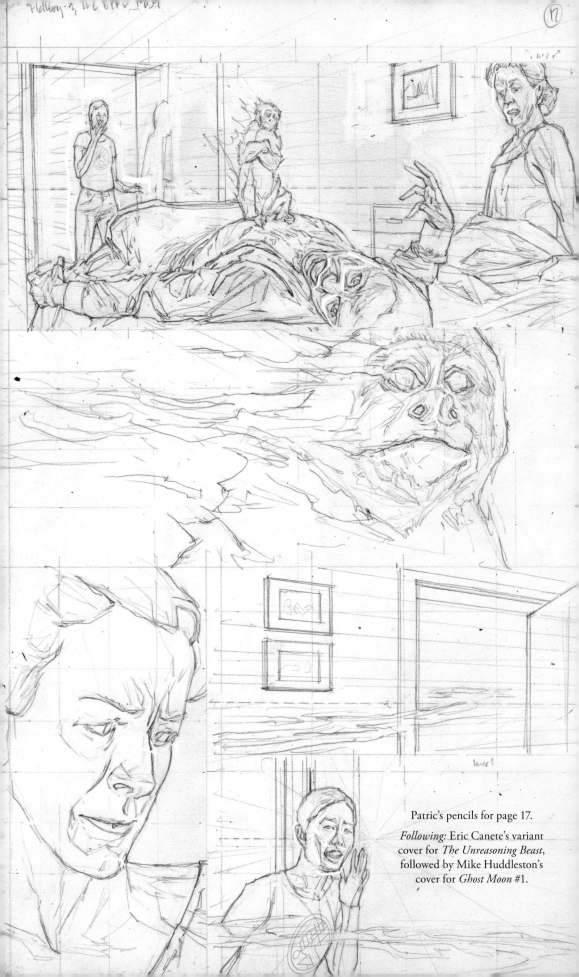

Patric's pencils for page 17.

Following: Eric Canete's variant cover for *The Unreasoning Beast*, followed by Mike Huddleston's cover for *Ghost Moon* #1.

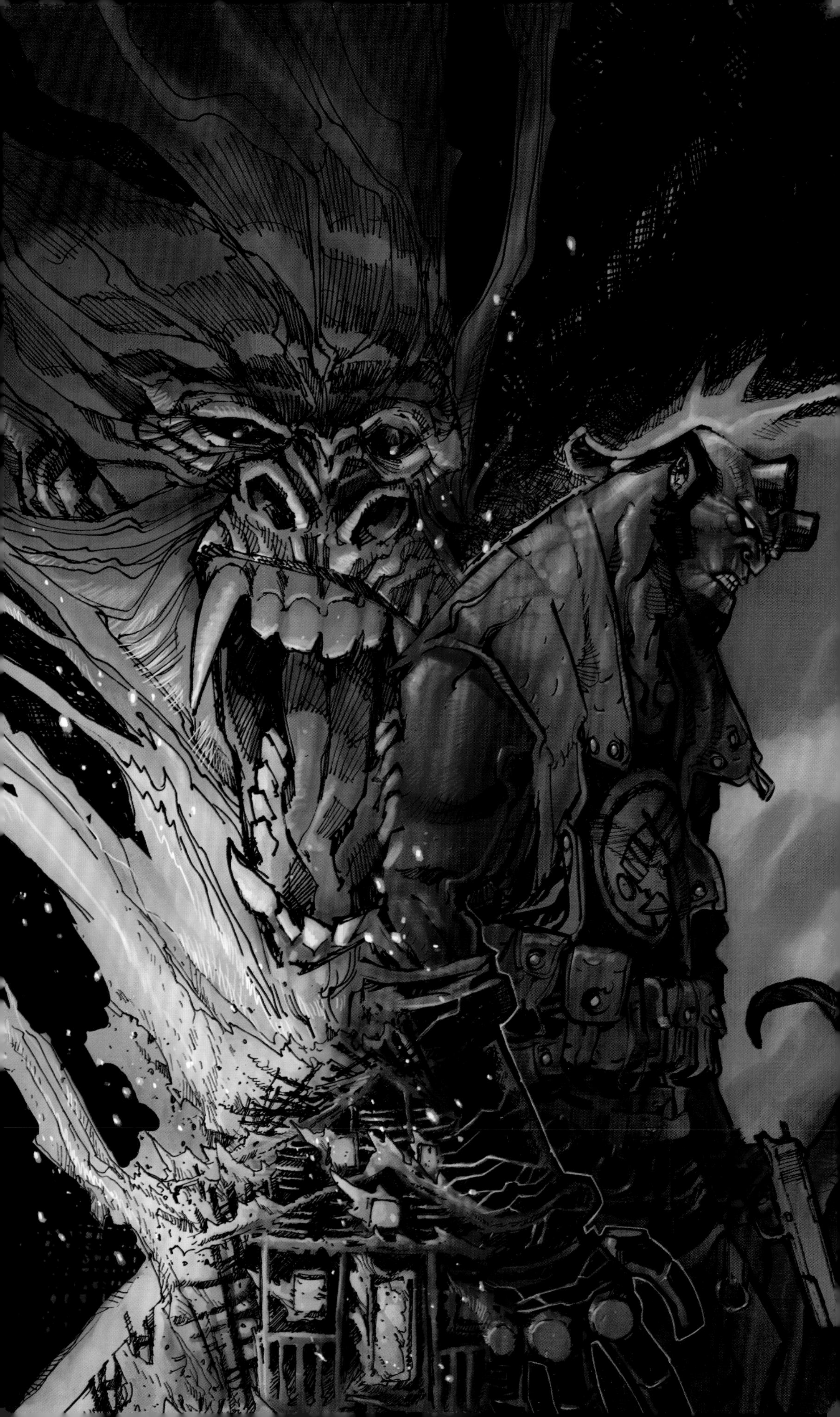

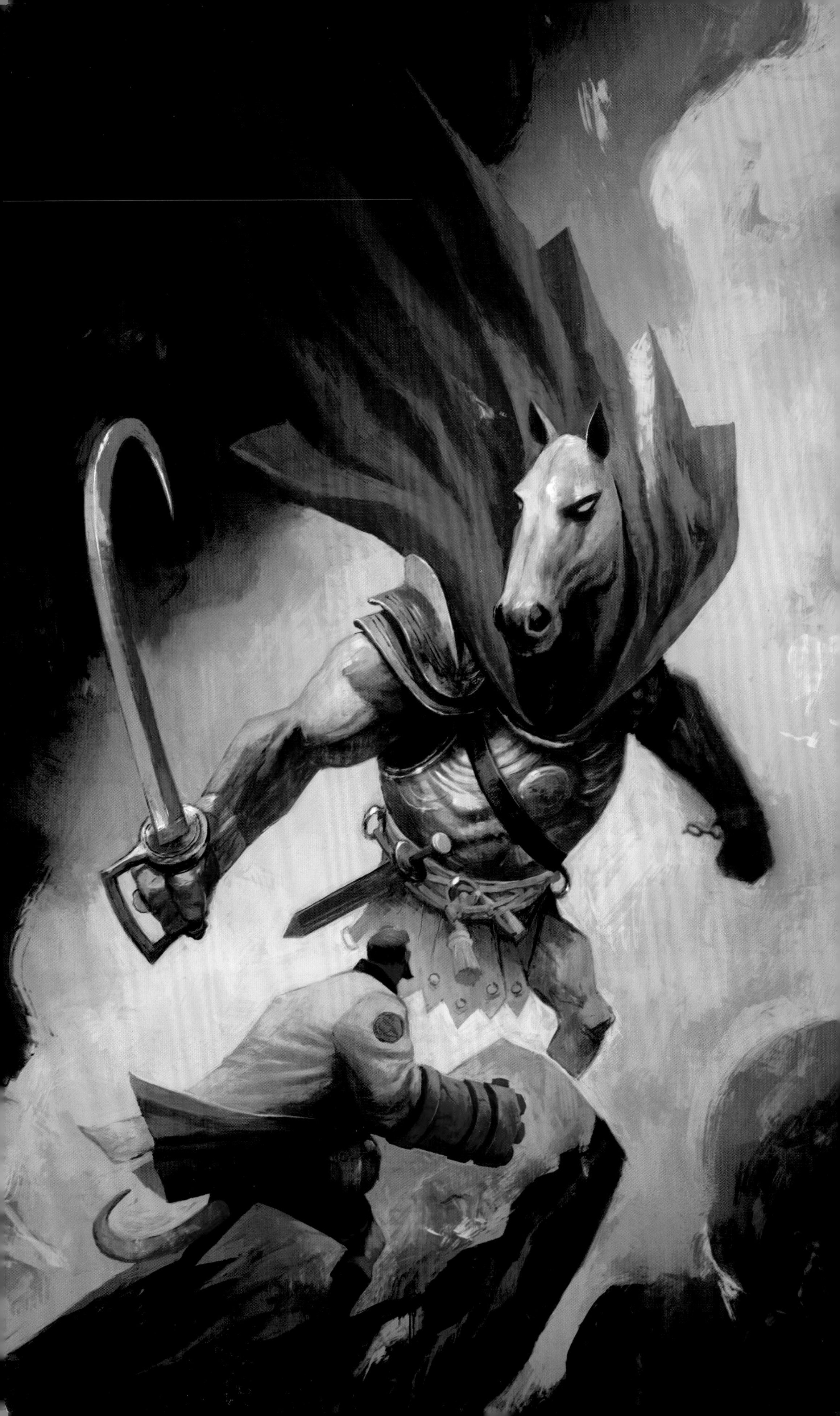

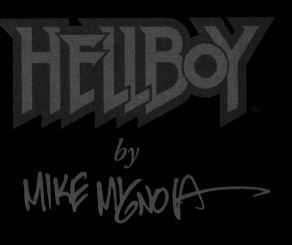

HELLBOY

by MIKE MIGNOLA

**HELLBOY LIBRARY
EDITION VOLUME 1:**
Seed of Destruction
and Wake the Devil
ISBN 978-1-59307-910-9 | $49.99

**HELLBOY LIBRARY
EDITION VOLUME 2:**
The Chained Coffin
and The Right Hand of Doom
ISBN 978-1-59307-989-5 | $49.99

**HELLBOY LIBRARY
EDITION VOLUME 3:**
Conqueror Worm and Strange Places
ISBN 978-1-59582-352-6 | $49.99

**HELLBOY LIBRARY
EDITION VOLUME 4:**
The Crooked Man and
the Troll Witch
with Richard Corben and others
ISBN 978-1-59582-658-9 | $49.99

**HELLBOY LIBRARY
EDITION VOLUME 5:**
Darkness Calls and the Wild Hunt
with Duncan Fegredo
ISBN 978-1-59582-886-6 | $49.99

**HELLBOY LIBRARY
EDITION VOLUME 6:**
The Storm and the Fury
and The Bride of Hell
with Duncan Fegredo, Richard Corben, Kevin
Nowlan, and Scott Hampton
ISBN 978-1-61655-133-9 | $49.99

SEED OF DESTRUCTION
with John Byrne
ISBN 978-1-59307-094-6 | $17.99

WAKE THE DEVIL
ISBN 978-1-59307-095-3 | $17.99

**THE CHAINED COFFIN
AND OTHERS**
ISBN 978-1-59307-091-5 | $17.99

**THE RIGHT HAND
OF DOOM**
ISBN 978-1-59307-093-9 | $17.99

CONQUEROR WORM
ISBN 978-1-59307-092-2 | $17.99

STRANGE PLACES
ISBN 978-1-59307-475-3 | $17.99

**THE TROLL WITCH
AND OTHERS**
with Richard Corben and others
ISBN 978-1-59307-860-7 | $17.99

DARKNESS CALLS
with Duncan Fegredo
ISBN 978-1-59307-896-6 | $19.99

THE WILD HUNT
with Duncan Fegredo
ISBN 978-1-59582-431-8 | $19.99

THE CROOKED MAN AND OTHERS
with Richard Corben
ISBN 978-1-59582-477-6 | $17.99

THE BRIDE OF HELL AND OTHERS
with Richard Corben, Kevin Nowlan, and
Scott Hampton
ISBN 978-1-59582-740-1 | $19.99

THE STORM AND THE FURY
with Duncan Fegredo
ISBN 978-1-59582-827-9 | $19.99

HOUSE OF THE LIVING DEAD
with Richard Corben
ISBN 978-1-59582-757-9 | $14.99

THE MIDNIGHT CIRCUS
with Duncan Fegredo
ISBN 978-1-61655-238-1 | $14.99

INTO THE SILENT SEA
with Gary Gianni
ISBN 978-1-50670-143-1 | $14.99

HELLBOY IN MEXICO
with Richard Corben, Fábio Moon,
Gabriel Bá, and others
ISBN 978-1-61655-897-0 | $19.99

**HELLBOY IN HELL
VOLUME 1: THE DESCENT**
ISBN 978-1-61655-444-6 | $17.99

**HELLBOY IN HELL
VOLUME 2: THE
DEATH CARD**
ISBN 978-1-50670-113-4 | $17.99

**HELLBOY: THE FIRST
20 YEARS**
ISBN 978-1-61655-353-1 | $19.99

THE ART OF HELLBOY
ISBN 978-1-59307-089-2 | $29.99

**HELLBOY II:
THE ART OF THE MOVIE**
ISBN 978-1-59307-964-2 | $24.99

HELLBOY: THE COMPANION
ISBN 978-1-59307-655-9 | $14.99

HELLBOY: WEIRD TALES
ISBN 978-1-61655-510-8 | $24.99

HELLBOY: MASKS AND MONSTERS
with James Robinson and Scott Benefiel
ISBN 978-1-59582-567-4 | $17.99

HELLBOY AND THE B.P.R.D: 1952
with John Arcudi and Alex Maleev
ISBN 978-1-61655-660-0 | $19.99

HELLBOY AND THE B.P.R.D: 1953
with Chris Roberson, Ben Stenbeck,
Paolo Rivera, and Joe Rivera
ISBN 978-1-61655-967-0 | $19.99

THE HELLBOY 100 PROJECT
TPB: ISBN 978-1-61655-932-8 | $12.99
HC: ISBN 978-1-61655-933-5 | $24.99

NOVELS

HELLBOY: EMERALD HELL
By Tom Piccirilli
ISBN 978-1-59582-141-6 | $12.99

HELLBOY: THE ALL-SEEING EYE
By Mark Morris
ISBN 978-1-59582-142-3 | $12.99

HELLBOY: THE FIRE WOLVES
By Tim Lebbon
ISBN 978-1-59582-204-8 | $12.99

HELLBOY: THE ICE WOLVES
By Mark Chadbourn
ISBN 978-1-59582-205-5 | $12.99

SHORT STORIES
Illustrated by Mike Mignola

HELLBOY: ODDER JOBS
By Frank Darabont, Charles de Lint, Guillermo
del Toro, and others
ISBN 978-1-59307-226-1 | $14.99

HELLBOY: ODDEST JOBS
By Joe R. Lansdale, China Miéville,
and others
ISBN 978-1-59307-944-4 | $14.99

Also by Mike Mignola

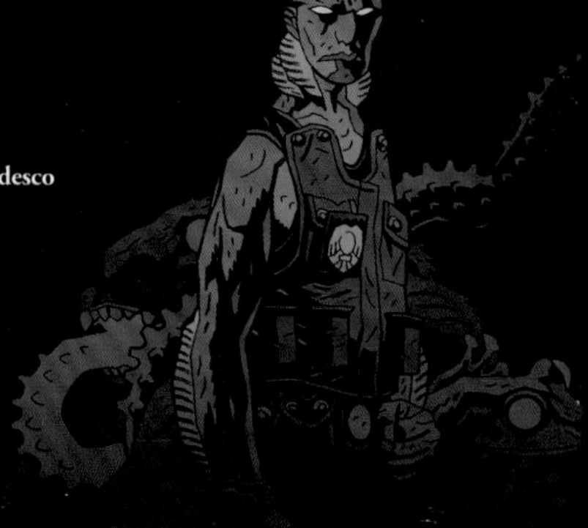

B.P.R.D.

PLAGUE OF FROGS
Volume 1
with John Arcudi, Guy Davis, and others
TPB: ISBN 978-1-59582-675-6 | $19.99

Volume 2
ISBN 978-1-59582-676-3 | $24.99

Volume 3
ISBN 978-1-61655-622-8 | $24.99

Volume 4
ISBN 978-1-61655-641-9 | $24.99

1946–1948
with Joshua Dysart, Paul Azaceta, Fábio Moon, Gabriel Bá, Max Fiumara, and Arcudi
ISBN 978-1-61655-646-4 | $34.99

BEING HUMAN
with Scott Allie, Arcudi, Davis, and others
ISBN 978-1-59582-756-2 | $17.99

VAMPIRE
with Moon and Bá
ISBN 978-1-61655-196-4 | $19.99

B.P.R.D. HELL ON EARTH

NEW WORLD
with Arcudi and Davis
ISBN 978-1-59582-707-4 | $19.99

GODS AND MONSTERS
with Arcudi, Davis, and Tyler Crook
ISBN 978-1-59582-822-4 | $19.99

RUSSIA
with Arcudi, Crook, and Duncan Fegredo
ISBN 978-1-59582-946-7 | $19.99

THE DEVIL'S ENGINE AND THE LONG DEATH
with Arcudi, Crook, and James Harren
ISBN 978-1-59582-981-8 | $19.99

THE PICKENS COUNTY HORROR AND OTHERS
with Allie, Jason Latour, Harren, and Max Fiumara
ISBN 978-1-61655-140-7 | $19.99

THE RETURN OF THE MASTER
with Arcudi and Crook
ISBN 978-1-61655-193-3 | $19.99

A COLD DAY IN HELL
with Arcudi, Peter Snejbjerg, and Laurence Campbell
ISBN 978-1-61655-199-5 | $19.99

THE REIGN OF THE BLACK FLAME
with Arcudi and Harren
ISBN 978-1-61655-471-2 | $19.99

THE DEVIL'S WINGS
with Arcudi, Campbell, Joe Querio, and Crook
ISBN 978-1-61655-617-4 | $19.99

LAKE OF FIRE
with Arcudi and Crook
ISBN 978-1-61655-402-6 | $19.99

FLESH AND STONE
with Arcudi and Harren
ISBN 978-1-61655-762-1 | $19.99

METAMORPHOSIS
with Arcudi, Snejbjerg, and Julián Totino Tedesco
ISBN 978-1-61655-794-2 | $19.99

END OF DAYS
with Arcudi and Campbell
ISBN 978-1-61655-910-6 | $19.99

THE EXORCIST
with Cameron Stewart, Chris Roberson, and Mike Norton
ISBN 978-1-50670-011-3 | $19.99

COMETH THE HOUR
with Arcudi and Campbell
ISBN 978-1-50670-131-8 | $19.99

ABE SAPIEN

THE DROWNING
with Jason Shawn Alexander
ISBN 978-1-59582-185-0 | $17.99

THE DEVIL DOES NOT JEST AND OTHER STORIES
with Arcudi, Harren, and others
ISBN 978-1-59582-925-2 | $17.99

DARK AND TERRIBLE AND THE NEW RACE OF MAN
with Allie, Arcudi, Sebastián Fiumara, and Max Fiumara
ISBN 978-1-61655-284-8 | $19.99

THE SHAPE OF THINGS TO COME
with Allie, S. Fiumara, and M. Fiumara
ISBN 978-1-61655-443-9 | $19.99

SACRED PLACES
with Allie, S. Fiumara, and M. Fiumara
ISBN 978-1-61655-515-3 | $19.99

A DARKNESS SO GREAT
with Allie, S. Fiumara, and M. Fiumara
ISBN 978-1-61655-656-3 | $19.99

THE SECRET FIRE
with Allie, S. Fiumara, and M. Fiumara
ISBN 978-1-61655-891-8 | $19.99

THE DESOLATE SHORE
with Allie, S. Fiumara, and M. Fiumara
ISBN 978-1-50670-031-1 | $19.99

LOST LIVES AND OTHER STORIES
with Allie, Arcudi, Michael Avon Oeming, and others
ISBN 978-1-50670-220-9 | $19.99

LOBSTER JOHNSON

THE IRON PROMETHEUS
with Arcudi, Tonci Zonjic, and others
ISBN 978-1-59307-975-8 | $17.99

THE BURNING HAND
ISBN 978-1-61655-031-8 | $17.99

SATAN SMELLS A RAT
ISBN 978-1-61655-203-9 | $18.99

GET THE LOBSTER
ISBN 978-1-61655-505-4 | $19.99

WITCHFINDER

IN THE SERVICE OF ANGELS
with Ben Stenbeck
ISBN 978-1-59582-483-7 | $17.99

LOST AND GONE FOREVER
with Arcudi and John Severin
ISBN 978-1-59582-794-4 | $17.99

THE MYSTERIES OF UNLAND
with Kim Newman, Maura McHugh, and Croo
ISBN 978-1-61655-630-3 | $19.99

CITY OF THE DEAD
with Roberson and Stenbeck
ISBN 978-1-50670-166-0 | $19.99

RISE OF THE BLACK FLAME

with Roberson and Christopher Mitten
ISBN 978-1-50670-155-4 | $19.99

FRANKENSTEIN UNDERGROUND

with Stenbeck
ISBN 978-1-61655-782-9 | $19.99

JOE GOLEM: OCCULT DETECTIVE—

THE RAT CATCHER & THE SUNKEN DEAI
with Christopher Golden and Patric Reynolds
ISBN 978-1-61655-964-9 | $24.99

BALTIMORE

THE PLAGUE SHIPS
with Golden, Stenbeck, and Peter Bergting
ISBN 978-1-59582-677-0 | $24.99

THE CURSE BELLS
ISBN 978-1-59582-674-9 | $24.99

A PASSING STRANGER AND OTHER STORIES
ISBN 978-1-61655-182-7 | $24.99

CHAPEL OF BONES
ISBN 978-1-61655-328-9 | $24.99

THE APOSTLE AND THE WITCH OF HARJU
ISBN 978-1-61655-618-1 | $24.99

EMPTY GRAVES
ISBN 978-1-50670-042-7 | $24.99

THE CULT OF THE RED KING
ISBN 978-1-61655-821-5 | $24.99

NOVELS

LOBSTER JOHNSON: THE SATAN FACTOR
with Thomas E. Sniegoski
ISBN 978-1-59582-203-1 | $12.95

JOE GOLEM AND THE DROWNING CITY
with Golden
ISBN 978-1-59582-971-9 | $99.99

BALTIMORE; OR, THE STEADFAST TIN SOLDIER & THE VAMPIRE
with Golden
ISBN 978-1-61655-803-1 | $12.99

AVAILABLE AT YOUR LOCAL COMICS SHOP OR BOOKSTORE! • To find a comics shop in your area, visit comicshoplocator.com.
For more information or to order direct visit DarkHorse.com or call 1-800-862-0052 Mon.–Fri. 9 AM to 5 PM Pacific Time.
Prices and availability subject to change without notice.

DarkHorse.com